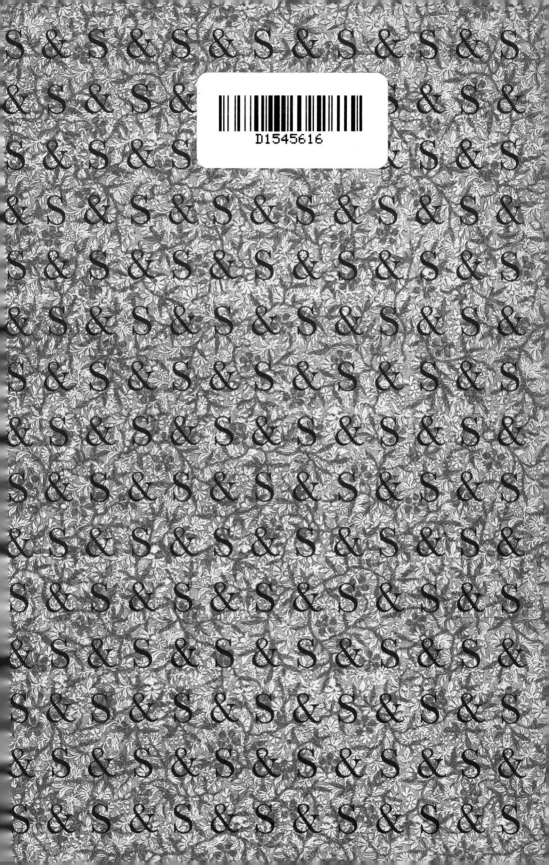

THE
FICTION FACTORY

OR

FROM PULP ROW TO QUALITY STREET

A cover of *Tip Top Magazine* which first featured
Frank Merriwell in 1896

THE STORY OF

100 YEARS OF PUBLISHING AT STREET & SMITH

THE

FICTION FACTORY

OR

FROM PULP ROW TO QUALITY STREET

BY QUENTIN REYNOLDS

RANDOM HOUSE

NEW YORK

On March 16, 1941, an interview with Theodore Dreiser appeared in *The New York Times* Book Review. He told Robert van Gelder of the *Times* staff of his early struggles to survive.

"I worked for a railroad as a laborer for nine months," Dreiser said. "And then with a few pennies in my pocket went hunting for a job. I finally got one at Street & Smith's. They paid me fifteen dollars a week and later made me an editor of *Smith's Magazine* at sixty dollars a week. Boy, is there a story in that Street & Smith outfit. Men writing forty to sixty thousand words a week for fifty or sixty dollars. I'm not kidding you. Yes, the story of that firm would make a book. . . . I tell you it would. . . . "

This is the book which Theodore Dreiser asked for in 1941.

Q.R.

ACKNOWLEDGMENTS

Presenting one hundred years of history of a sort is much like working out a jigsaw puzzle, except that you don't have all the pieces in front of you. Hundreds of the missing pieces came from source books which are listed in the back of this book. But many others came from former or present members of the Street & Smith family. I want to register my thanks to them for filling in so many of the missing pieces.

There were great Street & Smith editors—Archibald Lowry Sessions, Charles Agnew MacLean, Henry Wilton Thomas, Richard Duffy, Edward Stratemeyer, Robert Rudd Whiting and Frank Blackwell—who though dead left legacies in the form of editorials and letters which were an invaluable clue to the reading habits of the American people in their day. Literary agent Carl Brandt and author Samuel Hopkins Adams told me in human terms of the writing giants of the past who fed the voracious jaws of the Fiction Factory week after week. There was Esther Ford, who now presides over the copyright department and also guards the archives which contain every issue of every publication ever to spew forth from the Street & Smith presses these past hundred years. There was Belle Becker, understanding and skillful Random House editor, who did such fine surgery on the huge mass of manuscript I gave her and who worked so tirelessly with Esther Ford to find the old photographs and magazine covers reproduced in the following pages.

And then there was Henry William Ralston, who gave fifty-two years of service to the Fiction Factory. He shared his fabulous warehouse of memories with me, and through his eyes I learned to know Ormond Smith, the genius who made Street & Smith the largest publishing firm in the world; I learned to know the young Theodore Dreiser, who wrote for the firm in the early days of the century, and Upton Sinclair, who at twenty-two was one of the most prolific writers of adventure tales for boys. I learned to know Horatio Alger, and Frederic Dey, who wrote the Nick Carter books, and dozens of others who marched in the pulp parade. In a very real sense, this jigsaw could never have been completed without the generous and friendly co-operation of Henry William Ralston. My special thanks to Arthur P. Lawler, vice-president of Street & Smith, for his invaluable aid and suggestions, to Bradbury Thompson, art director of *Mademoiselle,* for designing this book, Ray Freiman of Random House, Inc. and Matthew T. Birmingham Jr. of Street & Smith for overcoming all of the production problems.

Q.R.

CHAPTER

ONE

THE NEW YORK

WEEKLY.

STREET & SMITH

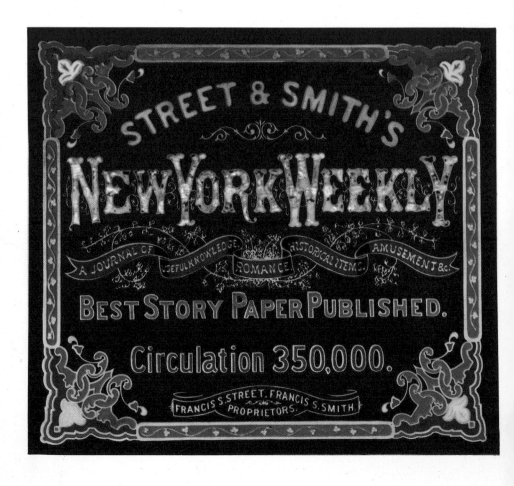

A window advertisement for Street & Smith's *New York Weekly*

CHAPTER

ONE

New York, during the 1850's, was an awakening giant just beginning to be conscious of its strength. Five hundred thousand people lived on the thirteen-mile island which constituted the city, and a few thousand more lived in Brooklyn and across the harbor in far-off Staten Island. There was great wealth in the little strip and there was great poverty; and if preachers like Henry Ward Beecher attracted great crowds of the pious and curious, there was also more crime to the square inch than any place else in the world. It was a transition period for the city. Its personality was beginning to take shape and no one knew whether it would eventually grow into another effete Boston, or whether it would model itself after distant San Francisco which, some said, was even more wicked than Marseilles or Port Said. The mold was not yet set.

To the visitor, New York was a restless, bawdy, vigorous and vulgar place, and people were already saying that it was a nice place to visit but as for living there—never. But visit New York they did. Women came from as far as Newark, Philadelphia and New Haven to shop at the country's largest department store, Stewart's Marble Palace, on Broadway near Chambers Street. Only here could the feminine taste in Lyons silks, Brussels carpets, Paris-inspired clothes, Irish linen, English woolens and cashmere shawls be satisfied. Alexander Stewart, one of the first men in the city to become a millionaire out of retail trade, employed more than two hundred clerks, and he did an annual gross business of six million dollars. People came to New York to stay at least for one night at the new Fifth Avenue Hotel, which not only had private bathrooms, but which advertised a revolutionary "perpendicular railway intersecting each storey"—the elevator. It was probably the world's finest hotel. Visitors decried the luxury and ostentation of the Fifth Avenue, the Saint Nicholas, the Metropolitan and the Astor House, but it gave them something to talk about when they went home to their quiet towns. Delmonico's, the best-known restaurant in America, was a must for the tourists. This restaurant's reputation was built, first, upon the excellence of its food and, equally important, upon the "snob appeal" which its proprietor fostered—you had to "know someone" to get a reservation at Delmonico's. Visitors from the hinterland shuddered at the dynamic tempo of the city, but were awed by its vitality and captivated by the variety of its offerings. The clatter of horses' hooves drawing the hackney coaches, the incessant roar of the crowd, the robust laughter, the clanging of fire-apparatus bells, the shouting of newsboys and the thousand and one noises of a city whose growing pains were never suffered in silence, horrified the visitor, but it was a horror that fascinated.

The feminine visitor could go home with glowing tales of the wonders of Barnum's Museum, of the bloods who exercised their trotters and pacers on Third Avenue, of the World's Fair which had been held uptown close by the huge reservoir at Forty-second Street and Fifth Avenue, of fabulous but pious Jenny Lind, the Swedish Nightingale, who had been brought to Manhattan by P. T. Barnum, of the dramatic feats they had enjoyed at Wallack's Theatre, of Charlotte Cushman who had successfully appeared as Cardinal Wolsey (wearing a full beard), of the music as conducted by Carl Bergmann at the Terrace Garden, and other delights never dreamed of "back home."

Their husbands had other things to report when they reached home. They would talk of the evil Five Points, a section of the city where policemen walked their beats in pairs, and where the gangs met periodically to settle their differences with brass knuckles, knives and clubs. They would brag about the naughty performances they had seen on the stage of Tony Pastor's Theatre, forerunner of the burlesque shows of a decade later. They held enchanted male audiences spellbound as they described the Bowery, which blazed with gaslight until the dawn had sent the last of the revelers home. They'd whisper of the "parlor houses" on Green Street where every other house was a brothel, easily distinguished by its gas lamp tinted red. They'd chuckle with fond remembrance of what they had seen

New York City in 1855

at the Franklin Museum where "female models, the best-formed women in the world" were displayed. They'd caution their listeners about the city slickers who separated the unwary from their bankrolls and expatiate to gasping audiences on the technique of the "panel game," which required the co-operation of a girl of easy or no virtue at all.

Visitors seldom got beyond the doors of the genteel households on Washington Square nor did they often manage to wangle invitations to balls given by Mrs. August Belmont or Commodore Vanderbilt. There were cultured men and women in the city who supported the opera and the Academy of Music, but the stranger would have no way of knowing about them. There were patrons of the arts and students of serious literature, and there were scientists and sincere civic leaders and great philanthropists, but this was all before the day of the gossip column and one heard little about them. New York in the 1850's defied characterization. There was no such thing as a typical New Yorker, and such visitors as Charles Dickens shook their heads in bewilderment when they tried to describe the city in capsule form.

There was no newspaper or magazine which could be called representative of the restless, fast-growing giant. Many claimed to represent the city but succeeded only in representing that portion of the population which patronized their periodicals. There were publications designed to satisfy the appetite of any group, but no one paper or magazine satisfied everyone. The very diversity of outlook and editorial matter of the publications was a reflection of the turbulent, changing mood of the metropolis. No editor had yet evolved the formula which would capture the attention of the masses as well as of the cultured and literate. The two men who came closest to realizing this journalistic ideal were James Gordon Bennett of *The Herald* (a daily) and Robert Bonner, whose *New York Ledger* (a weekly) boasted a million readers.

Bennett was an editorial genius without conscience or scruple. When he died, a journalistic epitaph in *Vanity Fair* read: "As a scurrilist, perhaps James Gordon Bennett was unequaled. His career enriched him at the expense of his character and that of the profession he followed only to degrade." Bennett, handicapped by neither political, religious nor moral convictions, was a merchant of news and sensation, and if the news was degrading or salacious it was, he felt, no concern of his who might be hurt by its publication. He was one of the first to realize that the envy and the jealousy of the masses could be exploited by publishing abuse about the wealthy and the fashionable. It wasn't long before Bennett became the most hated man in New York. His unhappy wife, after finding that the doors of society were firmly closed against her, went to live in Paris. He lost a wife and he hadn't a friend in the world, but he did have a newspaper which virtually everyone read. He had nothing but contempt for his fellow men and for any canons of good taste. His was the only daily newspaper in the city to print advertisements by prostitutes. These were in the "personal columns" of *The Herald* and they were read avidly by wealthy citizens sitting over a late supper at Delmonico's, as well as by the men laboring on the construction of new buildings. If a girl changed from Madam Queen's employment to work for Effie Heath, she would announce her new position in *The Herald*. Marriage, disease and loss of looks were factors which made the life of a brothel keeper a difficult one; she usually recruited new employees by placing advertisements with James Gordon Bennett. *The Herald* certainly mirrored the boisterous, bawdy, devil-may-care aspect of New York, but it hardly considered the thinking or literate public.

The newspapers of the city in the main represented not the city itself, but the character and personality of the publishers. Dignified, austere William Cullen Bryant published *The Evening Post,* and its conservative sober hue and its impeccable literary and moral tone revealed the personality of the respected poet-editor. There was no trivial gossip, no sensational journalism, no shouting on its dignified pages. Bryant took a strong stand against the municipal corruption of the city, but the fact that the corruption continued is evidence that he did not represent a very large portion of the public.

Stout, bald, loquacious, opinionated, white-whiskered Horace Greeley published *The Tribune,* and it was considered to be the most widely read and influential paper in the country. It was a weekly which had a 200,000 circulation. Greeley was a man driven by intellectual curiosity; he felt that the purpose of a paper was to set new ideas in motion. He was the first to hire women journalists and to take an editorial stand on the question of women's ability to perform more than culinary and marital duties. Greeley was a pro-

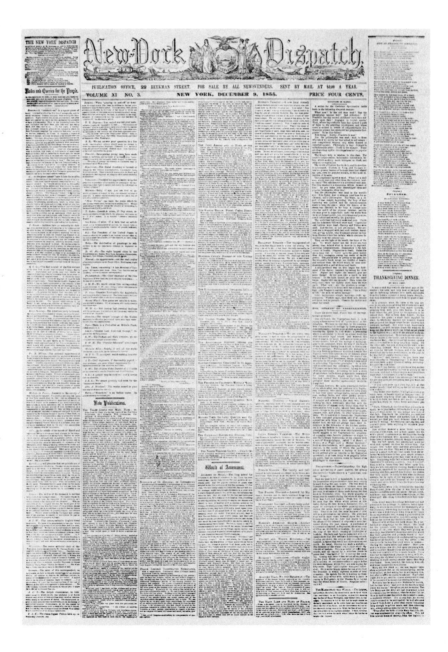

The New York Dispatch as it appeared in 1855

lific writer and lecturer. His outspoken honesty and his hatred of sham made him many enemies. One of them, in writing of him, penned a line that has been used thousands of times since. "Greeley," said Henry Clapp, editor of the *Saturday Press,* "is a self-made man who loves his creator."

There was *The Times,* edited by cultured Henry J. Raymond who had once been an assistant of Greeley's. The literary standard of *The Times* was high; it was one of the few publications which covered foreign affairs intelligently. It was read avidly by Wall Street for its accurate and thorough economic news. Each of these publications had its share of followers, but very few read them all.

Dozens of weeklies and monthlies were born every year during the fifties, chiefly because a kindly national administration had enacted the Post Office Act of 1852. Until then, subscribers had to pay the postage on their magazine or newspaper at the office of delivery; a five-ounce publication cost the subscriber six and a half cents in postage. The new postal law, the greatest boon to mass education ever conceived, reduced the rate to two cents for the same magazine and provided that the publisher could pay the postage at the office of mailing. Publishers found it expedient and profitable to absorb the cost of delivery themselves, and now they could advertise to prospective subscribers, "Delivered Free."

One of the most aggressive and successful publishing figures of the day was Robert Bonner, editor and publisher of *The New York Ledger.* Bonner claimed a million readers for his weekly publication which, like most weeklies, was a combination of newspaper and magazine. Bonner was called the Barnum of the publishing industry. He was immensely talented in feeling the public pulse and giving the public just what it wanted. He was the first to utilize other publications to advertise his own. Bonner would buy an entire page in *The New York Tribune* and fill it with an advertisement of the *Ledger.*

Bonner published what was then the largest advertisement ever to appear in a newspaper when he took seven pages of *The New York Herald* on May 6, 1858, for such an ad. He is said to have spent $1,000,000 with the advertising agency of S. M. Pettengill & Company to spread the gospel of the *Ledger.* He would sometimes print the first three or four chapters of one of his enthralling serials in

Harper's Weekly or in one of the dailies. At the point at which the heroine cried, "Unhand me, villain!" he would suspend publication of the serial and announce: "No more of this interesting story will be printed in this paper. For the succeeding chapters, see *The New York Ledger,* now on sale at all news depots." This "teaser copy" was at first considered excellent "humbuggery," but it eventually provoked considerable resentment.

Fanny Fern (Sara Payson Willis in real life) was the literary darling of the day. She had written a sensational autobiographical novel, *Ruth Hall,* which had captured the imagination of the reading public. Adroit Robert Bonner was never one to turn away opportunity when it had the temerity to knock on his door. He promptly offered the novelist the unprecedented fee of one thousand dollars a story. Her first story came to ten columns in his paper; he double-spaced it so that it came to twenty and then advertised the fact widely that he had paid one hundred dollars a column for the story. He took full-page ads in the *Tribune* and the *Herald.* They consisted of eight words in small agate type. The words were, "Read Fanny Fern's new story in the *Ledger.*" The tiny sentence was entirely surrounded by blank white space. People talked about the ad; they bought the *Ledger.* Barnum said enviously, "Bonner is the best advertiser in America."

The *Ledger* tried to cater to all tastes. Like James Gordon Bennett, Bonner had no editorial viewpoint, but he never stooped to the sale of filth, and character assassination was not a commodity in which he traded. He sought only to entertain his readers. His weekly was a literary miscellany, a hodgepodge of fiction, fact, essay, comment and verse designed to give some weekly spice to the housemaids, the cooks and the nursemaids as well as vicarious escape to the readers who labored at dull, humdrum jobs. No one knew how high his circulation reached, but there was no one to dispute his claim of a million readers.

Bonner sought and obtained the top name writers of his day. Longfellow, Bryant, Phoebe and Alice Cary contributed poems to the *Ledger.* The lady with five initials, Mrs. E. D. E. N. Southworth, Sylvanus Cobb and Mrs. Harriet Beecher Stowe were three of his more prolific and popular serial writers.

A great victory was the capture of Edward Everett for the *Ledger's* columns. Everett had inherited from the dead Webster the mantle of greatness which popular imagination had conferred upon that "Godlike" orator. Able pulpiteer and lecturer, Greek scholar, editor of the *North American Review,* Governor of Massachusetts, President of Harvard, Ambassador to the Court of St. James's, United States Senator, Secretary of State, orator at the Gettysburg dedication—he had run the gamut. He was handsome, cultivated, polished, perfect. Bonner was too shrewd to woo the great man with businesslike offers of remuneration; instead, he looked about for some effective indirect approach. Finally, he found Everett's vulnerable heel in his presidency of the Mount Vernon Association. The restoration of Washington's home as a national shrine was a personal crusade with Everett, and when Bonner offered to donate $10,000 to the cause if Everett would contribute a short article to the *Ledger* every week for a year, the celebrity was captured. Everett took a month to think it over—and yielded. But many good people were shocked by the idea of their paragon's appearing in a story-paper alongside Mrs. Southworth and Sylvanus Cobb. *Vanity Fair* observed, with its wonted sarcasm, that Everett could now be called "Orator, Patriot, Sage, Cicero of America, Laudator of Washington, Apostle of Charity, High Priest of the Union, Friend of Mankind, and Writer for the *Ledger!*"

Henry Ward Beecher, another of the distinguished Americans of the day, was added to Bonner's list of contributors by certain timely financial aid in a personal emergency, and the *Ledger* later paid him $30,000 for his serial novel, *Norwood.* To Longfellow, Bonner paid $3,000 for *The Hanging of the Crane;* and for Dickens' three-part *Hunted Down,* "written especially for *The New York Ledger,*" he paid $5,000. Bonner was an exploiter and something of a sensation-monger, but he performed a great service in the fifties: he proved that good prices could be paid to writers with advantage to the periodical.

Bonner was the first American editor to specialize in regular editorial departments conducted by experts in their respective fields. Paul Morphy, the world's chess champion, ran a column on the game and answered queries. Ministers offered solutions to spiritual problems and fashion experts advised the ladies how to dress. It was a lively magazine, disdaining sophistication and wit but always observing good if conventional taste. Bonner had a sign over his desk to guide his editorial assistants. It read: "Take the most pious old lady in a Presbyterian church, and any word or phrase, innuendo or expression that she would want to skip while reading a *Ledger* story to her grandchild—strike out."

Everyone read the *Ledger*. It could be found in the kitchens of the big brownstone houses which were springing up all over the city as well as in the drawing rooms of the stately Fifth Avenue mansions. Everyone in the publishing business read it hoping to fathom Bonner's secret.

Two young men who worked for a second-rate weekly, *The Sunday Dispatch,* read it as avidly as anyone else. They were Francis Scott Street and Francis Shubael Smith, two good friends brought together originally perhaps by the strange coincidence of the identical "Francis S." which preceded the last name of each. Street, born in 1831, was twelve years younger than his fellow "Francis." He worked for the business department of the *Dispatch* while Smith worked in editorial. Street had a good head for figures; as office manager he handled advertising and circulation problems of the

Amos J. Williamson

Robert Bonner

publication. Smith had worked as a reporter on *The New York Tribune* and had made two attempts at publishing on his own. The first was *The Sporting Rambler,* the second, a boys' publication called *Wide Awake.* Both publications had short, unhappy financial lives and died without causing even the slightest ripple in the publishing world. Francis Smith was a man of talent; he was a writer of verse as well as of fiction, and he became a sort of literary handyman on *The Sunday Dispatch.* He and his friend, Francis Street, would go off to lunch every day talking and dreaming of the time when they would go into the publishing business together.

The Sunday Dispatch was owned and edited by Amos J. Williamson, a Scotsman who had made a fortune out of his principal activity—printing. The offices of his press and the *Dispatch* were at 22 Beekman Street.

Although the circulation of the *Dispatch* was only about twenty-four thousand, it was considered (along with *The Sunday Mercury*) to be one of the leading Sunday publications. The *Dispatch* made no claim to literary distinction; its function was to keep the printing presses of Amos Williamson busy when they weren't otherwise profitably employed. It specialized in crime stories and sensational serials (written for the most part by Francis Smith). It was illustrated with a few badly reproduced woodcuts, and even by 1850 standards, it was a badly printed paper.

Publisher Williamson accepted any advertisements offered to him. In the columns of the *Dispatch* could be found advertisements for contraceptives and other ads lauding the drugs of the day which were guaranteed to produce abortions. This is what New Yorkers read at breakfast before going to church on the Sabbath. Oddly enough, many otherwise respectable publications saw nothing wrong in accepting the same type of advertisements. Francis Smith, a religious man, couldn't have liked the advertisements, but his business-wise friend, Francis Street, probably explained to him the undeniable fact that the publication of an advertisement was in no sense an endorsement of the product by the publisher—and certainly not by an impecunious assistant business manager or an equally impecunious writer of verse.

The two men studied not only the fabulous *New York Ledger* (never dreaming that one day they would put it out of business) but the other publications of the day. There were several weeklies which appeared each Saturday and these they considered direct competitors of the *Dispatch*. There was *The Waverley Magazine,* published by a shrewd Boston printer, Moses A. Dow, one of the first men in American publishing to realize that people would pay to have their stories printed. He threw his columns open to unpaid amateur contributors, but there was, of course, a tacit understanding that contributors would be selected only from the fifty thousand who paid three dollars a year to subscribe to the magazine. Schoolboys and even older swains would write poems to their lady loves and forward same to the editor of the *Waverley*. In the course of time there would appear:

TO ELLEN

I know a maid, a dark-eyed maid,
Who's blithe and debonair.
And on her face, her beaming face
Is pictured beauty rare.

Moses Dow never paid a contributor a single penny. He enjoyed a comfortable income of some $80,000 a year and his policy kept the magazine going for nearly a half century.

The American Miscellany and Holden's *Dollar Magazine* were two weeklies which blossomed for a time, and then there was *Life Illustrated,* a peculiar title in view of the fact that the magazine had no illustrations at all. It purported to devote itself to "entertainment, progress, literature, mechanics, agriculture, phonetic reform and photography." Its memory survives chiefly because one of its frequent contributors was a Brooklynite named Walt Whitman. Whitman also contributed occasionally to the successful weekly called *The Phrenological Journal.*

One of the most interesting and most successful of all weeklies was *Frank Leslie's Illustrated Newspaper* (there was little distinction during the 1850's between "newspaper" and "magazine"). Under one title or another (it achieved its peak under the name *Leslie's Weekly*), it lasted until 1922. There was no Frank Leslie. There was a talented English wood engraver named Henry Carter. As a boy he had sent some of his drawings to *The London Illustrated News,* but fearing the wrath of his father, he signed them "Frank Leslie." They were accepted. He went to London and, in time, became chief of the *Illustrated News* engraving room.

FRANK LESLIE'S
ILLUSTRATED
NEWSPAPER

No. 854—Vol. XXXIII.] · NEW YORK, JANUARY 20, 1872. [Price, 10 Cents. $4 00 Yearly.

NEW YORK CITY.—ASSASSINATION OF COLONEL JAMES FISK, JR., BY EDWARD S. STOKES, AT THE GRAND CENTRAL HOTEL—THE SCENE OF THE TRAGEDY.—See Page 297.

Cover of an issue of *Frank Leslie's Illustrated Newspaper*

The Dispatch, which Francis S. Street and Francis S. Smith bought in 1855

Carter came to this country just in time to sell P. T. Barnum the idea of issuing illustrated programs for Jenny Lind's concerts, a venture so profitable to the ambitious and ingenious Englishman that he was able to finance a publication of his own, *Frank Leslie's Ladies Gazette of Fashion and Fancy Needlework*. Its success enabled him to buy and revamp the *New York Story of Romance*. Finally he founded the immediately successful *Frank Leslie's Illustrated Newspaper* which sold for ten cents a copy.

One feature of the *Illustrated Newspaper* which attracted the public was the coverage of news events through illustrations within two weeks after they occurred. When Jim Fisk was assassinated or when heavyweight champion John Morrissey won an important bout, Leslie's artists were on the spot and lifelike sketches of the events appeared on the cover of the periodical. In addition to the excellent illustrations, readers enjoyed the serials, the voluminous coverage of sports events and articles on the stage, books and music as well as on any conceivable subject of public interest. The young Englishman seemed to know what the public wanted better than did most of his American competitors.

By an act of the legislature, Henry Carter acquired title to the now valuable name of "Frank Leslie," and it is doubtful if anyone ever called him by his real name again. Gleason's *Pictorial Drawing Room Companion*, *The Illustrated American News* and several others competed with *Leslie's Weekly,* but the shrewd artist-publisher always kept ahead of the parade. It was an uncluttered-looking magazine and its illustrations rivaled those of its great European counterpart, *The London Illustrated News*. There is no doubt that the two obscure employees of Amos Williamson studied both the technique of reproducing drawings and the editorial content of this phenomenal publication thoroughly.

It was in 1855 that the now quite well-to-do Amos Williamson decided to leave publishing to younger, more energetic men and to concentrate on his profitable printing ventures. His *Sunday Dispatch* had run its course and he had changed its character and name to *The New York Weekly Dispatch*. He offered to sell this tottering newcomer in the highly competitive field to his two ambitious employees, Francis S. Street and Francis S. Smith. Neither had any real capital, unless one can assess the keen business mind of Street and the brilliant journalistic talent of Smith, as capital. Evidently, Williamson did just that, for the proposition he offered them was obviously based not on what money they had, but on their judgment and editorial acumen. When he told the two young men that they could have his magazine for the modest price of $50,000 they must have blinked in amazement and told him they had less than $100 between them. He did not, he assured them, want the money immediately; he did not, in fact, ask for any down payment at all. Each of the new partners could draw a weekly salary of twenty dollars from the revenue; they could pay all printing and editorial expenses from the revenue, and then they could gradually liquidate the $50,000 debt by paying such sums as seemed reasonable out of the profits. He also made the not unfair stipulation that title to the magazine remain in his name until the debt was liquidated.

"What can we lose?" one can almost hear practical Francis S. Street saying. When it came to matters of business, Smith always deferred to his younger partner, and they closed the deal immediately.

Young Mr. Street (aged twenty-four) shook hands with Mr. Smith (aged thirty-six) and in that moment a partnership that was eventually to provide the industry with the most fabulous publishing firm in history was formed. It is hardly likely that either partner had any inkling that any substantial success would result from publication of *The New York Weekly Dispatch* with its now scant 18,000 circulation. It may well be that the most intriguing part of the deal was the security each would gain as a result of the twenty dollar weekly salary. They realized they would have to sell a lot of weeklies to guarantee the revenue to provide even that modest wage, and both threw all their energies into making the weekly a worthy rival of the giants in the field. Apparently Amos Williamson exercised some supervision over the two new partners at first, for it wasn't until two years later that the *Dispatch* began to assume a distinctive character. The masthead across page one read:

THE NEW YORK
WEEKLY DISPATCH

A journal of useful knowledge, romance, amusement, etc.
two dollars a year
(invariably in advance)

On the editorial page where Amos Williamson was still listed as editor and proprietor, there appeared:

OUR TERMS

The New York Weekly Dispatch is sold by all responsible News Agents in the United States. The price is four cents, but in some cases, where Agents have to pay extra freight or postage, a higher price is necessarily charged. When there is a News Agent in the town, we desire our friends to get the *Dispatch* through him. We do not wish to mail the paper except to places where there is no other means of getting it. When sent by mail, the price will invariably be $2 a year, in advance. Subscriptions taken for six months. Two copies will be sent for a year for $3; four copies for $6; eight copies for $12. Postmasters and others who get up clubs of ten, and send us $15 at one time, will be entitled to an extra copy for their trouble. The bills of all solvent banks taken at par for subscriptions.

The imprint of the personality of Francis S. Smith was first made obvious in the October 10, 1857, issue. It is probable that he had written a great deal of the editorial matter in preceding issues (the two partners had no intention of wasting revenue on outside writers), but now, for the first time, he signed a story with his own name. It was a serial called *The Vestmaker's Apprentice; or, The Vampyres of Society.* It began:

The sun was fast disappearing behind the Hoboken hills at the close of a sultry day in August. A sigh of relief seemed to ascend to Heaven from a half-million weary souls as the Day God rolled his fiery chariot westward and twilight, with her soothing, revivifying influence, approached, to act the part of nature's great nurse in fanning the fevered brows of heat-oppressed and overworked citizens.

The great city lay reeking in its filth. Poisonous exhalations went up from steaming gutters, mud-choked cesspools and decomposed garbage heaps, tainting the air and poisoning the lungs of those who were paying—and dearly too—for the removal of such nuisances.

The first installment was illustrated by a lurid drawing of the spotless heroine, hands clasped piously over her bosom, taking off from the stern of a Hoboken-to-Manhattan ferry boat, while the villain's hand is outstretched in a vain effort to clutch her. Lightning, of course, was playing in the sultry sky mentioned by Author Smith. This story was an immediate and fortuitous success. It is quite possible that if it had not been for the amazing reaction from the public to *The Vestmaker's Apprentice, The New York Weekly Dispatch* would have died in its infancy and the firm of Street & Smith along with it.

Coincident with the publication of the serial came the panic of 1857, a period when hundreds of well-established firms, shops and, of course, periodicals, were wiped out. Numerous bank failures and widespread unemployment resulted in hunger riots and thousands in New York turned to crime as the only possible means of keeping a family alive. One of the most respected and stable publications of the time was *The National Era.* It commented sadly:

> Many of our subscribers are among the intelligent mechanic and industrial classes, and we hear by every mail that some of them, thrown out of employment, cannot find money to renew their subscriptions.

Many of the weeklies founded in the fifties wavered and then fell into oblivion. The casualties among magazines were tremendously heavy. The highly successful *Graham's Magazine,* which had been running for thirty-two proud years, withered and gave up the ghost. *Putnam's* and *Emerson's* perished, and *The Democratic Review,* which had carried stories by the country's most eminent writers, shut its doors. So did *The New York Mirror,* a hardy thirty-year-old publication. There was absolutely no reason for the little *Dispatch* to survive, and the only answer after careful study is an announcement on the editorial page a few weeks after the first installment of Smith's serial had appeared.

MR. SMITH'S NEW STORY
EXTRAS FOR NEWS DEALERS

> We have never before had such a run for anything that appeared in the *Dispatch* as we have had for Mr. Smith's new story. It seems to have taken the country by storm. Notwithstanding the fact that over 60,000 extra copies of the first part of this story was printed, the whole edition was exhausted before the week was out. A second edition has been printed, and from present appearances this will not supply the demand. If the rush continues in the same ratio for this number, we shall be compelled to issue an extra sheet, containing the story complete, as far as it has been printed. In that event we shall supply News Agents with as many copies as they may desire, for gratuitous circulation in their respective towns. News Dealers will, therefore, please indicate their wishes at once, so that we may be able to supply them, in case we decide to print the extra.
>
> P.S.—Since the above was written and in type, we have decided to

get out an extra sheet, containing the portions of the story which appeared in Nos. 45 and 46 of the *Dispatch*. It will be ready on Saturday, October 10. News Agents will, therefore, send in their orders at once, so that we may know how many to print. They can have as many copies as they can use to advantage, free of cost, for gratuitous circulation. They may be had of the Wholesale Dealers, or at the office.

One month later, at the very height of the panic, this note appeared:

OUR PROSPECTS

The success of the *Weekly Dispatch* seems to be a fixed fact. Notwithstanding the hard times, we have the most flattering reports from the News Agents in all parts of the country. It is certainly very gratifying to the pride of the publisher to receive such cheering news at a time when almost every newspaper in the country is falling off in circulation. He can only assure his friends and the public that he shall strive to deserve their good opinion.

Francis Street foresaw that the panic would hurt subscriptions so he decided to concentrate his efforts on newsstand sales. A magazine could not be bought on credit at newsstands. He proceeded to enlist the hitherto despised news agents, and he flattered them into usefulness by this announcement printed in three successive issues:

NEWS AGENTS

We desire to get a list of all the News Agents in the United States. Persons engaged in the business will oblige us by sending in their names, together with the number of circulars they can distribute to advantage; also what number of showbills they require on the commencement of a new story. When we get up circulars, we desire to put the names of the Agents in the different towns on what we print for each locality. Hence the necessity of an understanding with the trade. We have already had letters from a large majority of those engaged in the News business. There are, however, some few from whom we have not yet heard direct. Send in your names, gentlemen. It is as much to your interest as to ours, for you to do so. We design to push the *Dispatch* in earnest, and in doing so, we must benefit you as well as ourselves, as we don't mean to run a tilt against any other paper, but strive to widen the field of newspaper readers and purchasers. To those who have interested themselves in giving the *Dispatch* a start, we beg to return our thanks. We shall try to remember our friends.

It is possible that the most recent arrival in the magazine field was the only weekly in the city which made money during the three years of the panic. *The Vestmaker's Apprentice* had more than doubled the circulation of the publication. Amos Williamson, now satisfied that he had put his magazine into the hands of two extraordinarily gifted men, began to recede into the background. The first radical step taken by the Messrs. Street and Smith was to change the name of the magazine. In March, 1858, an editorial announced that because there were so many newspapers and magazines published under the title of *Dispatch,* this word would be dropped and the publication would henceforth be known as *The New York Weekly.* Williamson's name, however, was still carried on the masthead as "Editor and Proprietor."

The study which Street and Smith had made of the more successful publications of the decade was beginning to prove uncannily accurate. They knew what the masses wanted to read. They wanted to read of girls pursued (but never quite caught) by villains, of poor boys who managed to overcome all obstacles to achieve wealth. Readers wanted to escape, and Smith's serials allowed them to escape into a world they could enter only in their dreams.

The success of his first signed story sent Smith to his desk again. Quickly he turned out *Maggie, the Child of Charity; or, Waifs on the Sea of Humanity.* When it appeared, the editorial page announced that the *Weekly* had been fortunate enough to "secure for our readers the exclusive services of Francis S. Smith."

Readers wanted the saccharine pathos of the incredible Fanny Fern, who could make hearts weep with *The Little Pauper,* which began:

> There seems to be happiness enough in the world, but it never comes to her. Her little basket is quite empty; and now, faint with hunger, she leans wearily against the shop window. There is a lovely lady who has just passed in. She is buying cakes and bon-bons for her little girl, as if she had the purse of Fortunatus. How nice it must be to be warm, and have enough to eat! Poor Meta! She has tasted nothing since she was sent forth with a curse in the morning to beg or steal; and the tears will come. There is happiness and plenty in the world, but none for Meta!
>
> Not so fast, little one! Warm hearts beat sometimes under silk and velvet. That lady has caught sight of your little woe-begone face and shivering form. O, what if it were her child! And, obeying a sweet maternal impulse, she passes out the door, takes those little benumbed fingers in her daintily gloved hands, and leads the child,—wondering, shy and bewildered,—into fairy land.

This period has been called the Sentimental Age by some students of the times and there is reason to believe that the phrase has validity. Religious belief and practice were fundamental precepts observed in every normal household and sin was profoundly deplored. Temperance societies had sprung up all over the nation and a New York temperance journal reported triumphantly (but without any documentation) that more than two thousand distilleries had closed during the preceding three years. The idea of total abstinence had even spread to children, who had been organized into what was horribly called "The Cold Water Army." Each youngster who joined the organization had to memorize the pledge:

> We cold water girls and boys
> Freely renounce the treacherous joys
> Of Brandy, Whiskey, Rum and Gin,
> The serpent's lure to death and sin.

> Wine, Beer and Cider we detest,
> And thus we'll make our parents blest,
> So here we pledge perpetual hate
> To all that can intoxicate.

The New York Weekly conformed in every way to the climate of the times.

The two partners were smart enough to adopt Robert Bonner's technique of the "teaser." Shortly after the story of *Maggie* began to run, the editorial page announced:

A NEW AND EXCITING STORY!

We have now on hand the manuscript of a story which we design to publish in a few weeks, that, we feel assured, will creat a sensation in the reading world. It is from the pen of one of the most popular authors of the day. Like the story of MR. SMITH, it is a Revelation from Real Life. We do not care to deal in fiction and romance when there is so much that is far more exciting than the most fertile imagination can invent to be found in everyday life. In publishing these Revelations, we have a higher motive than the mere production of sensation stories. Their purpose and design is to warn the innocent and suspect of the snares and pitfalls that surround them on every hand. . . . Our aim is to publish a paper that will instruct as well as amuse—one that can with safety and profit be introduced to every fireside in the land. We fear that some of our contemporaries cannot say as much for the contents of their sheets. They will discover, when it is too late, perhaps,

THE NEW YORK WEEKLY.

A JOURNAL OF USEFUL KNOWLEDGE, ROMANCE, AMUSEMENT, etc.

Vol. XIV. By F. S. STREET & F. S. SMITH, No. 22 Beekman Street. NEW YORK, MAY 21, 1859. TWO DOLLARS A YEAR, Invariably in Advance. No. 25.

[WRITTEN FOR THE NEW YORK WEEKLY.]

PASSION.

BY J. MAL ELLION.

We call you—
The burning flashes of the kindling eyes—
The startled flushing of the fair young cheek—
The parted dewy lips—the red sob sigh—
The thrill of hatred joy that makes us weak
And earth is heaven,
When fair round arms twine, woven close with ours,
And crimson fingers light across our face,
And all unheeded moments join in hours,
While Time flies on in his unending chase
And then, anon,
The thrilling of the pleasure-bolted kiss,
Warmer on the fond hearts beating side by side,
The transports of a strange, bewildering bliss
Make a blank waste of all the world beside,
And then the lingering parting—then we cling
As tightly to our idol shrine of clay;
With fear and doubt our hearts are quivering,
Whilfrom we walk the long, long hours away.
We watch anon
But is the love,
Or the hot breath of passion's fierce simoom,
That blinds the eye of true affection, and
Crushes the heart to find they—we seem
Seeking its purity with tired our heart?
How—'tis not love.
Free love is witnessing o'er with innocence,
Subduing passion in a hallowed flame;
Holding unholy dreams and feelings base,
Back in the sinful power from whence they came.
Free love is purer than white virgin snow,
And holy as our churches angels are,
Hearts are but ripened to its lovely glow,
Goodness—not pleasure—is its guiding star.

*** Entered according to Act of Congress in the Clerk's Office of the Southern District of New York

ONE-EYED SAUL;

OR, THE

TORY LEAGUE OF SEVEN.

A TALE OF SOUTH CAROLINA.

BY J. H. ROBINSON,

Author of "NICK WHIFFLES," "BUCK BISON," "HALF-WITTED NAT," "MARION'S BRIGADE," "THE PRISONER OF KENTUCKY," etc.

CHAPTER XVI.

IN WHICH WE RETURN TO JESSIE.

[The remainder of the two main story columns and the illustrated feature consist of dense small-type newspaper prose that continues the narrative of "One-Eyed Saul" and "Chapter XVII — A Night of Horror," together with the adjoining illustration and further columns of text.]

ISHMAEL HAD FASTENED HIS TEETH AND CLAWS INTO THE NEGRO'S BROAD SHOULDERS.

CHAPTER XVII.

A NIGHT OF HORROR.

that the people of the United States will not sustain papers whose editors gather up all the filth from the gutters and dens of infamy to make their columns "spicy." A paper, to obtain a permanent circulation, must inculcate good morals and pay some regard to decency.

The story referred to was *Belle Bingham; or, The Perils of the Poor.*

In addition to serials and occasional short stories which stressed the romance and rags-to-riches theme, the *Weekly* established a department which kept abreast of new inventions. There was the inevitable column of humor, without which no magazine of the time was complete. It was no better or worse than that offered by its competitors. There were "fillers," which in retrospect seem more interesting than do the articles and stories. To fill out a column the reader would find a casual paragraph:

> The price of negroes in some of the southern states has advanced so rapidly, that five young girls were sold near Eutaw, Alabama, a few days since, for $1200 each, calculated to be about their weight in silver.

Obviously the public was interested in the problem of slavery. A "filler" in the following issue read:

> Flight from Canada is the order of the day among the blacks, according to the *Cleveland Plaindealer*. That journal states that scarcely a steamboat arrives at that place which does not contain a number of negroes, fleeing from starvation and misery in the provinces, and going to take their chances in the Western States and Territories. The *Plaindealer* calls this "return trips of the underground railroad."

One of the more important series published during the panic of 1857 was "Evenings with a Retired Physician." Some of the headings of these articles reflect the lurid subject matter. They include "The Opium Eater," "The Victim of Mania-A-Potu," "The Guillotine," "A Death and a Burial," "The Father's Curse" (A Story of Retribution), and "The Blind Boy of the Insane Asylum." They were all by "James A. Maitland," who was not a physician at all but who might well have been Francis S. Smith. There was very little in each issue of the *Weekly* that Smith did not write. He would have one chapter of *Maggie* in an issue, an article signed by himself, "A Visit to the Trenton State Prison," and "A Ghost Story," by Witch Hazel, all showing the unmistakable hand of the prolific Smith. Occasionally he contributed a poem which he signed. Other verses of his in the *Weekly* were signed "Poningoe," "Ichabod Crane, Jr.,"

"Daisey," "Caleb Clootz," "W. A. Devon," or "The Chancellor."
The New York Weekly couldn't be stopped now. It had a runaway circulation approaching the 80,000 mark. And then, on May 21, 1859, a historic announcement appeared on the editorial page. It read:

CHANGE OF PUBLISHER

The management of *The New York Weekly* from and after this date passes into the hands of Street & Smith, gentlemen fully qualified to control its destinies. We need not wish them success, as they have the necessary enterprise and talent to push their own fortunes. The undersigned begs to return his warmest thanks to the public for the liberal manner in which they have sustained the *Weekly,* and to assure them that he takes leave of so large and respectable an audience with feelings of regret.

A. J. Williamson

SALUTATORY

In assuming the proprietorship and management of *The New York Weekly,* the undersigned desire simply to say that they will spare neither pains nor expense in their endeavors to render their pet paper the leading literary journal of the day. Having for years been connected with it in a business capacity, they feel themselves qualified to conduct it, and it remains for the future to show whether they over-rate their abilities or not. It is their intention to add many new features to the *Weekly* which will appear as soon as they get fairly at work. They have also succeeded in securing the services of some of the most brilliant story writers of the day, whose names will be announced in due time. They have no desire, however, to indulge in any extravagant praise of themselves, and they will, therefore, take leave of the subject with the remark that all which can be done to render the *Weekly* perfect shall be done.

After this date, all communications relating to the business of this establishment should be directed to Street & Smith, Proprietors, No. 22 Beekman St., New York.

Francis S. Street
Francis S. Smith

The two young men thus chose Street & Smith as their firm name to celebrate the first milestone in their partnership. But not even the two confident proprietors could foresee that in 1955 the one-hundredth anniversary of their association would be celebrated.

CHAPTER

TWO

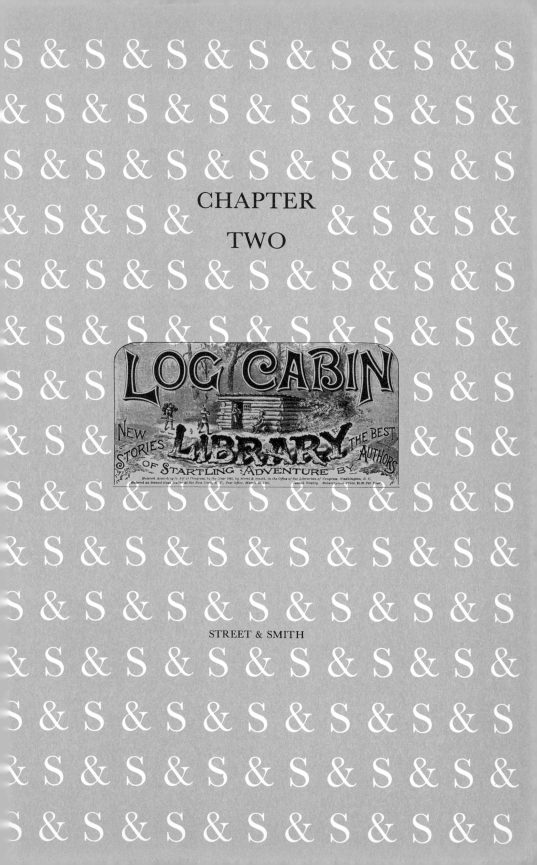

STREET & SMITH

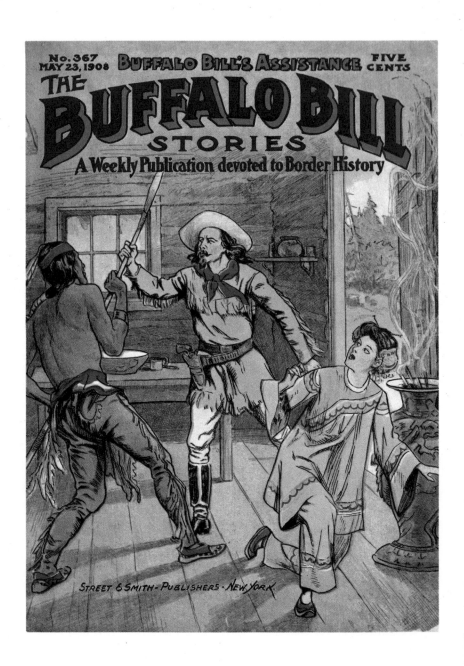

Cover of a *Buffalo Bill Stories,* a series inspired in 1901 by Street & Smith's
1869 introduction of the frontiersman

CHAPTER

TWO

The *New York Weekly* began to rank in importance with the leading weekly publications of the day: *Frank Leslie's Illustrated Weekly, Harper's Weekly, The Weekly Sun* (Shines for All), *The New York Ledger* and a half-dozen others. Compared with most of its rivals it was hardly sensational. Neither Street nor Smith ever tried to edify the public. Instead, they gave their readers what they wanted and they wanted *Bertha, the Sewing Machine Girl* (one of Smith's most successful serials), and the poems, information and gossip which titillated them. *Harper's Weekly,* an offshoot of the well-established and respected *Harper's Monthly,* was born about the time *The New York Weekly* came on the scene. It was published by Fletcher Harper, youngest of three brothers. A devout Methodist (like his brothers) and a fervent Democrat, he leaned strongly on opinionated editorials and placed little emphasis on romance. Fletcher Harper's magazine seemed to have an aversion to paying for material. The owners were honest, pious men, but they felt they were only following current custom in pirating the works of well-known English authors. Dickens, Thackeray, Bulwer-Lytton, George Eliot and Trollope were some of the celebrated who were involuntary contributors to the estimable *Harper's Monthly.*

"The magazine will transfer to its pages as rapidly as they may be issued, all the continuous tales of Dickens, Bulwer, Lever and other distinguished contributors to English periodicals," an announcement read. The word "transfer" was a rather charming euphemism which angry London critics called "stealing." But there were no international copyright agreements in the 1850's, and *Harper's* was merely conforming to the practice of the trade.

It might be noted that when *Uncle Tom's Cabin* appeared in 1852, seventeen English publishers hurried it into print without paying for the privilege. *Harper's Weekly* followed the lead of its eminent sire and immediately began to print short stories and serials by the finest British writers. They were slow, too, in paying their domestic authors, and one of them, Fitz-James O'Brien, caused the respectable brothers Harper considerable embarrassment by parading up and down the street outside of the editorial offices carrying a sign:

ONE OF HARPER'S AUTHORS

I AM STARVING

In those days, most editors were lofty-minded creatures who seemed reluctant to discuss anything as vulgar as money with their authors. The distinguished Brander Matthews wrote to the editor of *International Review* asking for money due for a long-since-printed article. The editor, hurt by the insistence of the critic and essayist, wrote coldly that the contributors to his magazine received a two-fold reward; first, "the signal honor of appearing in its pages; and second, an honorarium in money, the exiguity of the latter being proportioned to the altitude of the former." It is doubtful whether even the scholarly Brander Matthews could unravel such editorial doubletalk, but it boiled down to the fact that Matthews should feel himself honored to be allowed access to the sacrosanct pages of the *International Review*.

Harper's Weekly had a large audience. It did not cater to the shop-girls and nursemaids who devoured the prose of Francis Smith, but there were enough thinking readers in the country in 1860 to boost the circulation to a robust 120,000. *Leslie's* claimed 140,000, while fairly reliable reports placed the circulation of Bonner's *Ledger* at 400,000 (which might have well made good his boast of having a million readers). The brash young *New York Weekly* by now had a substantial 90,000 readers and was gaining more steadily. This was due not only to the editorial content but to the ingenious methods with which the two-man firm caught and held the public's attention.

It was probably the imaginative Francis Smith who conceived the idea of advertising the *Weekly* on billboards erected on private property along the Pennsylvania Railroad, which stretched from Philadelphia to New York. It was a well-traveled route, devoid of any exciting scenery, and thousands saw the virtues of the mag-

"The frail craft cannot live in this sea! Horror! horror! The girl is lost!"

NOW READY IN STREET & SMITH'S

N. Y. WEEKLY

A tale of extraordinary power and thrilling interest, entitled the

Pearl of the Reef

OR THE

DIVERS DAUGHTER

BY EDWARD MINTURN.

This is a story of sea and shore, and is written by the greatest romancist of modern times, who, under another name than Minturn, has delighted the world with his wonderful creations. "THE PEARL OF THE REEF," however, is the very finest of his efforts. The heroine is a noble-souled young creature of high birth and ravishing beauty, who, having been stolen from her parents in infancy and carried to Florida by a bitter enemy to her father, grows to womanhood on that coast in the society of the Divers and is known as "THE PEARL OF THE REEF." While here, a packet from England, commanded by a young nobleman, arrives on the coast, and the latter meets with the heroine with whom he falls desperately in love. From this point the story is truly thrilling, and is worked up with a master hand. Each character introduced is splendidly drawn, and the scenes and incidents are so varied and follow each other so rapidly that the reader has scarcely time to breathe, so thoroughly is his attention enchained. Those who fail to read this great story will miss a treat such as is seldom offered to the public. It reaches a point in interest which is absolutely sublime, and the charm continues from the commencement to the close.

FOR SALE BY ALL NEWS AGENTS.

J. T. PRESTON, Printer, 11 Frankfort Street, New York.

An advertisement for a typical Street & Smith serial

azine extolled prominently on some of the first billboards to be seen in the United States. The owners of the property never even thought of charging a fee for the use of the land. When property changed hands the billboards remained; new owners seemed to have the idea that the billboards were an easement on the property. So successful was this type of promotion that posters were placed wherever a vacant wall appeared in New York. There was now no reason at all for any semi-literate person to deny knowledge of *The New York Weekly*. It became as well, if not better known than its competitors.

Smith conceived another promotion stunt which had an immediate and favorable reaction. He inaugurated the custom of distributing the first installments of serials all over the country. He would send as many as half a million copies to the thousands of news dealers over the nation, and they, in the hope of eventually profiting by the sale of the regular weekly issues, would distribute them to potential customers. It was difficult to read the opening of a serial by Smith or Mary J. Holmes or May Agnes Fleming or Mrs. Georgie Sheldon without wanting to know what was going to happen next. These writers were adroit in the use of the literary device which decades later became known as the "cliffhanger." Each installment ended on a note of unbearable suspense. The heroine might actually be left hanging from a cliff while the villain's heels played an evil tattoo on her poor little fingers. The customer couldn't wait to buy the next installment.

By 1863 the circulation of the magazine had soared to the dizzy height of 150,000 copies a week, and the two owners proudly began to refer to it as the largest weekly magazine in the world. Circulation figures were seldom completely accurate, but rival magazines and writers of the period agree that the 150,000 figure is a fair estimate of the circulation. The $50,000 was now paid off except for $4,423 which Williamson agreed to accept in advertising and the two proprietors for the first time had the means to enjoy the good things of life.

Street liked to boast in the *Weekly* of the many serial writers who wrote "exclusively" for the magazine. It annoyed him when competitors announced the names of their "exclusive" writers. It wasn't often that Street infringed upon the editorial domain presided over

Due Amor J. Williamson Four
Thousand four Hundred and twenty
three Dollars ($4,423) payable in ad-
vertising in Street and Smith's Weekly
at such time as the said Williamson may
elect provided that in no case shall
a larger space than one Column
per week be demanded; the rates
to be charged are to be the same
as charged to other advertisers—that
is to say we ~~agree~~ hereby bind ourselves to put the advertising
done under this agreement on the
most favorable terms extended to
any person advertising in said
paper

Street & Smith.

New York, December 21st, 1865.

Final Street & Smith payment for *The New York Weekly*

by Smith, but now with the money coming in freely, he decided to minimize competition by buying up the work of as many of his rivals' authors as possible. He went on the most amazing buying spree the publishing business had ever seen. He bought and paid good prices for serials, short stories and articles on condition that the writers give the *Weekly* exclusive services. It was an expensive way to meet competition, but he did snare a great many well-known writers who had been laboring under the banners of other weeklies. The word went around that Street & Smith would buy anything, and writers dug to the bottoms of their trunks for forgotten, unsold manuscripts. The office files were soon overflowing with hundreds of manuscripts, most of them so bad as to be unusable.

The partners finally realized that cornering the writers' market was not quite as economically sound as cornering the wheat or grain market. The trouble with buying surplus stories was that they had no resale value; they weren't even worth their weight in the cheap paper on which they were written. But something had to be done about them, and the partners hit upon an idea.

When they acquired rights to the *Weekly,* rights to *The Literary Album* were thrown into the package. This publication had enjoyed a brief, unsuccessful life in the early fifties under Amos Williamson, and it had long since been buried. The partners disinterred it and made it a repository for the vast backlog of fiction which had accumulated in the files. In format, *The Literary Album* was much smaller than the *Weekly* and was set in small, almost illegible type. But it was a clean-looking paper with excellent illustrations. The resurrected *Album* prospered for a time but finally expired as a result of public indifference.

From time to time Francis Smith manifested his concern with the state of the country in an editorial. His sober, thoughtful comments on the election of Abraham Lincoln reflect his views.

THE ELECTION

The election is over, but the waters are still troubled. With the certainty of the election of Mr. Lincoln to the Presidency of the United States, comes the news of ominous movements to carry out the previously expressed determination on the part of the South to secede from the Union in the event of the triumph of the Republican Party. Yet we trust that "the sober second thought" of the Southern mind will prevail, feeling certain, as we do, that the incoming administration will not dare to do aught that would interfere with the Constitutional rights of the South or impair the integrity of the Union—the dissolution of which would be a scandal upon republican institutions throughout the world, and bring serious calamity upon all sections—especially upon the South, which could hope to gain little if any security by such a consummation. Dissolution would seriously weaken our ability to successfully contend with foreign nations, in the event of war, and therefore subject us to additional insult and humiliation abroad; while the South would be deprived of a strong shield against the prejudices of nearly the whole civilized world, which has almost unanimously pronounced against African slavery. It would certainly seem to be the part of wisdom to refrain from taking any extreme measures until something positively encroaching upon the rights of the South has transpired. The mere election of Mr. Lincoln could hardly be considered sufficient cause for dissolution, though it may perhaps justify preparation for any emergency; and we are inclined to the belief—perhaps because we so wish—that the South will pause ere the final, and as it seems to us, fatal step is taken. If so, we are quite certain that it will discover a spirit of moderation and justice in the North that will make continuance in the Union not only tolerable but agreeable and desirable.

The Civil War, strangely enough, impinged hardly at all on the publishing business. For example, there were no industrial controls over such commodities as newsprint. Some publications, however, such as *Harper's Weekly* and *Leslie's* became actively partisan but, for the most part, Street & Smith ignored the tragedy that was virtually tearing the country apart. *The New York Weekly* remained a "journal of useful knowledge, romance, amusement, etc." As private citizens, the partners were undoubtedly vitally interested in the issues which had brought on the conflict. Certainly Francis Smith, with his high sense of moral values, must have felt strongly about the war, but neither he nor his partner ever allowed the editorial content of their magazine to be influenced by their personal enthusiasms or beliefs. They were convinced that more than ever the reading public wanted to escape from reality, and escape fiction is what the *Weekly* presented. They couldn't entirely avoid the terrible conflict, but their periodical didn't feature it.

At the height of the Civil War Francis Smith wrote a wildly exciting serial called *Wild Nell, the Spy,* but Nell was a spy for Washington's army during the Revolutionary War. A Colonel A. J. Duganne submitted a long poem entitled "The Triumph of Sherman," and when the war ended, the *Weekly* acknowledged it with a long editorial headed, "Our Soldiers Are Coming Home." And the publishers of the *Weekly* did consider the assassination of Lincoln important enough to warrant an editorial which was printed framed by a black border.

THE NATION'S MARTYR

President Lincoln is departed!

At last there is but one pulsation of the great heart of loyalty; one throb of popular sympathy; one interchange of national emotion! Alas! that its utterance should be the wail of universal grief; its voice a Requiem; its expression an Elegy!

But what a Requiem! and what an Elegy!

It is the death-song of a Leader—a Ruler—a Liberator; but it is chanted as no death-song was ever before chanted, and undertoned with a feeling deeper than was ever evoked by the demise of monarchs or the immolation of heroes. Great men have perished in all ages! Their funeral processions move from century to century! Their monuments arise in all the corridors of historic Time. But, if we consider the relations which our late President sustained to the most vital interests of humanity; if we reflect upon the tremendous results involved in that mighty drama of Progress, in which Mr. Lincoln was the chief personage; we must acknowledge that no historic tragedy approaches our own in momentous action, and that no victim presents at once so sublime and affecting a spectacle. . . .

Our martyred President needs no labored eulogium. His life was its own panegyric. As a Statesman, clear-seeing, thoughtful, inflexibly honest; as a Ruler, just, discreet, merciful; as a Man, kind-hearted, genial, reliable; as a Citizen, plain, democratic, unassuming; as a Christian, humble, unostentatious, sincere; he walked the ways of private and public station in a single-minded, guileless devotedness to his country's good; climbing, step by step, to greatness, and passing, at last, from martyrdom to immortality. . . .

The firm of Street & Smith had outgrown its office space on the upper two floors of 22 Beekman Street and moved to 11 Frankfort Street. All editorial direction was now in the hands of Francis Smith. In one of the most discerning moves of his whole career, Smith hired Thomas C. Glynn to edit the *Weekly* so he himself could concentrate on writing. The company continued to expand and bought two buildings, 29 and 31 Rose Street. As the *Weekly* increased its circulation to near the 300,000 figure, *The New York Ledger* began to suffer. Even the wily Robert Bonner was no match for the Street & Smith team. The firm was now paying high prices for serials and attracting the type of writer guaranteed to gain even more readers. But very often the magazine introduced new writers.

Smith had met a gentle, kindly young Unitarian minister, the Reverend Horatio Alger, Jr. Alger had written one or two stories for boys which had appeared in *The Student and Schoolmate,* published in Boston. Smith persuaded the minister to try his hand at a serial, and in 1869 the name of Horatio Alger, Jr. appeared in the *Weekly* as author of *Marie Bertrand.* It was not a juvenile, but a novel in the classic *Weekly* tradition. Eventually Alger would become one of the best-known authors of boys' books the world had ever known. Later he wrote seventeen of his famous juveniles for the firm, but at this time he was determined to make his name with more "serious" fiction.

May Agnes Fleming was one of the authors who gave exclusive service to the *Weekly.* She wrote twenty-six romantic serials for the publication and her name became as well known as that of Harold Bell Wright some decades later—and for the same reason. Francis Smith made good friends of most of his writers; when May Agnes Fleming died she named Smith executor of her very sizable estate.

Horatio Alger, Jr.

Charlotte Brame

Edward S. Ellis had achieved fame with his novel, *Seth Jones,* which Beadle's published. It sold more than three hundred thousand copies. A school teacher from New Jersey, this quietly humorous young serial writer became one of the stars in the Street & Smith constellation.

Smith lured the popular English writer, Charlotte M. Brame, away from the *Ledger* by offering her twice as much money as she had been getting. Smith, whose strong religious principles never prevented him from practicing mild deceptions upon his readers, wished to introduce her under a new name and as a brand-new discovery of his magazine. He transformed her initials "C.M.B." to "B.M.C." and then, after trying out a dozen names, settled upon Bertha M. Clay. The name Brame was soon forgotten and the name of Bertha M. Clay became legendary in the publishing world. For years she wrote one fantastically successful novel after another. Her English lords and ladies and the realm of high society in which they moved were especially popular. When she died, her daughter continued writing under her mother's name and later, when Street & Smith branched out, more than a dozen men manufactured stories under the Bertha M. Clay label.

Mary J. Holmes was one of the real favorites with readers of the *Weekly.* Like most writers of the virtue-must-triumph school of the day, she was a sincere believer in the principles on which she founded her success. She wrote twenty-seven serials for the *Weekly,* and at the height of her fame received as much as $5,000 for each one. She held out hope to the overworked, underpaid shopgirls of the time that they, too, might meet a Prince Charming one day. The girls of the nation lapped it up. The temptation to scoff at what she wrote vanishes when one realizes that she received more than a thousand fan letters each week from women readers. Mary Holmes brought color to their drab, dreary lives.

Francis Smith was not a man to be lulled into complacency by success. He believed that the *Ledger* was on the wane only because Bonner obstinately clung to his original formula. Even *Leslie's* had started to lose ground because its founder saw no reason to change his format or editorial policy. Smith had a fine instinct for anticipating a public trend. He began to feel that although the huge shopgirl audience was still there (and always would be), there was a vast potential male audience that would want sterner stuff than was being

Ned Buntline's first Buffalo Bill story, published in 1869

produced by Mary Holmes and Bertha M. Clay—or, for that matter, himself. He began to introduce more detective fiction into the *Weekly*. Harlan P. Halsey, under contract to George P. Munro to write for *The Fireside Companion*, had become celebrated as the creator of Old Sleuth. Smith signed him up, gave him a literary christening, and a brand-new writer, "Judson R. Taylor," made his debut. Under that name he wrote detective stories which gained so much popularity among the *Weekly* readers that they often wrote to say how much better "Judson Taylor's" yarns were than those featuring the Old Sleuth for *The Fireside Companion*.

Then Francis Smith discovered the West. The real beginning of the western story as a tremendous bonanza for Street & Smith began with Francis Smith's friendship with Edward Zane Carroll Judson. The affinity writers had for Smith may have been based on the fact that he was one of them. The mutuality of interests helped him understand their problems. He paid them well, was always available with a sympathetic ear for their troubles and thus gained their devotion and friendship.

Edward Judson had led an incredibly colorful life. He was in many ways the embodiment of the fictional hero of the day. At eleven he had run away to sea. Three years later he dove into the waters of New York Harbor to rescue two children whose sailing craft had capsized. The incident was given such wide publicity in the newspapers that it came to the attention of President Van Buren, who promptly commissioned the youngster as a midshipman. His fellow junior officers resented the upstart and refused to let him dine in their mess. So one by one he took them on in battle.

When Judson was sixteen he deserted the Navy for the Army and took part in the Seminole War in Florida. He emerged as a lieutenant. He went to work for the Northwest Fur Company and learned to know the West as he had once known the sea. His restless feet once took him to Nashville, Tennessee, where he became involved in an argument with one Robert Porterfield. They settled their differences with pistols. Judson, a crack shot since his childhood, put a bullet through his antagonist's head, killing him instantly. He was jailed, and an incensed mob, sympathetic to the cause of the dead man, broke into the jail with lynching in mind. Judson was shot three times and then hung. Neither the bullets nor the rope killed him; they had hung him from an awning and the flimsy rail supporting it broke. The mob left the unconscious duelist for dead, but he was revived and returned to jail. He finally managed to escape and later rejoined the Army to fight in the Mexican War.

When the war ended, he went to New York and started a weekly called *Ned Buntline's Own*. He wrote serials and short stories, mostly about piracy on the high seas. His background lent an authenticity to the stories lacking in most serials. He wrote some tales of western life, and then this stormy spirit became one of the leaders of a secret society called the Know Nothings. He organized a riot during the course of which several men were killed and others badly wounded. Mr. Judson was put into durance vile for one year. He continued to write and edit his paper from Blackwell's Island. From there he wrote stories on hunting, fishing and the Wild West. Apparently, most of his serials were based on either his own experiences or those of men he had known.

He was released in time to join the Union Army, in which he fought with enthusiasm and distinction. Incredible as it may seem, he emerged with twenty bullets in his body—and with the rank of Colonel! He was probably the most wounded man in the whole Union forces. "I've got so much lead in me," he laughingly told Francis Smith, "that if I ever fell into the water I'd sink from the weight of it." When the war ended he went back to the West and roamed the plains with Jack Crawford, the poet, scout Wild Bill Hickok, Texas Jack and a twenty-three-year-old hunter named William Frederick Cody. The Union Pacific Railroad was stretching its rails to the Far West and Cody had been hired to kill enough buffalo to feed the army of men laying the tracks. Judson became enthralled with the loquacious hunter whose career (to hear him tell it) had been as colorful as his own. He wore his golden hair long and he looked and dressed like the prototype of the fictional western hero. When Judson heard Cody's story, he knew that he had struck gold. It has always been quite impossible to separate fact from legend in the life of Cody, for he, himself, had no hesitation in embroidering the details of his adventuresome career. Years later there were critics unkind enough to say that the only Indians Colonel Cody had ever seen were those wooden ones which then stood in front of cigar stores in New York City. But such rumors, others said, had been started by jealous rivals.

He told Judson that he was born in 1846 near LeClaire, Iowa, and that he was helping his father shoot game for the family larder at the age of eight. His father was evidently a turbulent spirit. After making an anti-slavery speech in Kansas, he became involved in an argument more lethal than verbal. He died of a knife wound when his son was eleven. Young Cody soon hired himself out as a helper on an overland wagon train. When the train was attacked, he killed his first Indian. At fifteen he was a Pony Express rider. After several brushes with Indians, he was captured by them and eventually released. He went back to carrying the mails and hunting buffalo. At seventeen he joined the Union Army as dispatch rider, guide and scout.

Judson, after hearing him boast of the hundreds of shaggy bison he had slaughtered, jokingly gave him the name "Buffalo Bill." Cody was delighted with it. He was delighted, too, with Judson's suggestion that he write a few stories about Cody's exploits. The writer returned to New York where, in due time, he presented Francis Smith with a manuscript called *Buffalo Bill, King of the Border Men.* For the first time the public glimpsed the illustrated figure of the scout with the flowing mane and buckskin clothes. A three-column woodcut of the scout appeared on the first page of the December 23, 1869, issue, and Ned Buntline's story began on Page One and was carried over. Not even the perceptive Smith was aware that boys and grown men would be reading about Buffalo Bill for decades to come. The story started with the murder of Buffalo Bill's father. It began:

Ned Buntline's Great Story! !

BUFFALO BILL

The King of the Border Men!
The wildest and truest story
I ever wrote.

By Ned Buntline
[E.Z.C. JUDSON]

Chapter I

An oasis of green wood on a Kansas prairie—a bright stream shining like liquid silver in the moonlight—a log house built under the limbs of great trees—within this humble home a happy group. This is my first picture.

Look well on the leading figure in that group. You will see him but this once, yet on his sad fate hinges all the wild and fearful realities which are to follow, drawn to a very great extent, not from imagination but from life itself.

A noble-looking, white-haired man sits by a rough table, reading the Bible aloud. On stools by his feet sit two beautiful little girls, his twin daughters, not more than ten years of age, while a noble boy of twelve or thirteen, stands by the back of the chair where sits the handsome, yet matronly-looking mother.

It is the hour for family prayer before retiring for the night, and Mr. Cody, the Christian as well as the patriot, always remembers it in the heart of his dear home.

He closes the holy book and is about to kneel and ask Heaven to bless him and protect him and his dear ones.

Hark! The sound of horses galloping with mad speed toward his house falls upon his ear.

"Is it possible there is another Indian alarm?" he says, inquiringly.

Alas, worse than the red savages are riding in hot haste toward that door.

"Hallo—the house!" is shouted loudly, as a large cavalcade of horsemen halt before the door.

"What is wanted, and who are ye?" asked the good man, as he threw open the door and stood upon its threshold.

"You are wanted, you black-hearted nigger worshiper, and I— Colonel M'Kandlas—have come to fetch you! And there's the warrant."

As the ruffian leader of the band shouted these words, the pistol already in his hands was raised, leveled, fired, and the father, husband and Christian, fell dead before his horror-stricken family.

"If them gals was a little older—but never mind, boys, this will be a lesson for the sneaks that come upon the border—let's be off, for there's plenty more work to do before daylight!" continued the wretch, turning the head of his horse to ride away.

"Stop!"

It was but a single word—spoken, too, by a boy whose blue eyes shone wildly in a face as white as new-fallen snow and full as cold— spoken as he stood erect over the body of his dead father, weaponless and alone.

Yet that ruffian, aye, and all of his mad, wreckless crew, stopped as if a mighty spell was laid upon them.

"*You,* Jake M'Kandlas, have murdered my father! You, base cowards, who saw him do this dark deed, spoke no word to restrain him. I am only Little Bill, his son, but as God in Heaven hears me now, I will kill every father's son of you before the beard grows on my face!"

And so little Bill began his incredible literary career. Smith added a note to his readers:

All the friends of Ned Buntline should read of *Buffalo Bill,* who is a living SCOUT, and after enjoying the reading of the daring adventurer, the best horseman, the best-informed guide and the greatest hunter, should go among their friends and tell them what a splendid *true* story we are now publishing in *The New York Weekly*. In the words of Ned, "It is the *wildest, truest story* I ever wrote."

Apparently, Smith wanted to call plenty of attention to his new character. Another blurb read:

> The friends of "Buffalo Bill" are speeding the news all over the country that his *true* life is now being published in our columns, written by his friend, *"Ned Buntline,"* who, while on a recent visit to the Plains, procured the facts from the hero which no other author ever had and which are now first given to the world by us.

Little Bill grew up quickly in the pace of the *Weekly,* and it wasn't long before a typical story would start:

> "Then come on, you red devil, and have it out," shouted Buffalo Bill, and, forgetting General Merritt's orders not to expose himself, he dashed at full speed toward the chief who, likewise, with a wild yell, rode toward him."

The place is somewhere in the region of the Little Big Horn, for Cody has just joined the Fifth Cavalry as chief scout at Fort D. A. Russell. The regiment was driving the Indians before it when news came of Custer's fatal fight with Sitting Bull. The message included a warning that a force of warriors was moving to join the great chief.

Instantly, five hundred picked men of the Fifth set off by forced

Buffalo Bill, French edition

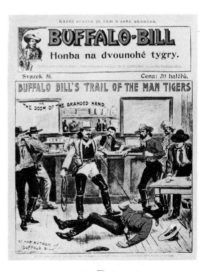

Buffalo Bill, Polish edition

marches to head them off, with Buffalo Bill, of course, a couple of miles in advance. It was the scout, accordingly, who saw the Indians first. At the same moment, he saw two army dispatch bearers riding down the valley in a direction that would bring them straight upon the redskins—assembled in great force—who had already seen them and had sent thirty warriors out to intercept them. Buffalo Bill rode toward the hostile band. At once, and with his matchless rifle, he dropped a couple of redskins and several ponies. Then he wheeled, dashed to the top of the hill, signaled to the dispatch riders and headed at full speed toward the command.

The pursuing Indians were surprised to see the cavalry, but reckoning their own force as twice that of the unexpected enemy, they determined to fight. As two horsemen rode out in front of the warriors to reconnoiter, Buffalo Bill who, at the same time, detached himself from the cavalry, became the object of their attention. They were both full chiefs. Suddenly one of them halted. He called out that he wanted the Great White Hunter to fight him.

At full speed the duelists rode toward each other. There was the crack of rifle and revolver. Two horses writhed upon the ground. There was another shot and still another. A knife flashed in the sun and Cody gave a cry of triumph. Swiftly, at a warning shout, he turned to see the second chief come riding down. He shot again. Another redskin bit the dust. A wave of warriors charged him. Was he lost? The enemy was nearer than his regiment. But there it came, the gallant Fifth. They met the enemy in savage fight, and drove them from the field in wild confusion.

Week after week, more of the same appeared. The appetite of the public was insatiable for stories of the scout. *Buffalo Bill's Best Shot* and *Buffalo Bill's Last Victory* followed, and henceforth, Buffalo Bill, with his inevitable Winchester barking for law and order, became a permanent fixture not only in American fiction but in American folklore. He was undoubtedly the most indestructible character in all fiction. The public couldn't get enough of Buffalo Bill. The stories were translated into every language and were just as popular in foreign countries. No one thought for a moment that Ned Buntline was writing fiction. Buntline wrote a play for his friend Cody, *Scout of the Plains,* and it was a tremendous success. Later, Cody organized his own Wild West show.

Judson was now known as Ned Buntline, not only to the public but to his friends and all six of his wives. Street & Smith had such confidence in his ability to turn out further exploits of Buffalo Bill that they would start printing his serial as soon as he handed them the first installment. Hundreds would stand in line outside of 29 Rose Street, where the paper was printed, eagerly waiting to find out how the famous scout had extricated himself from the cliff-hanging position in which Buntline had left him the previous week. One week disaster struck. Buntline's fourth installment of a Buffalo Bill novel was due on a Monday. The paper went to press on Tuesday. But Buntline never showed up and the partners were frantic with worry. .With press time five hours away, Francis Smith, in desperation, sat down and concocted the essential installment.

Ned Buntline, by now, was living in the Adirondack Mountains in a home he called The Eagle's Nest. A severe snowstorm had made all the roads impassable, and he had not been able to reach New York. He did make it the day the *Weekly* appeared. He read the installment and then turned to Smith in horror.

"You killed off that Indian who was Buffalo Bill's friend," he said. "He was to be my secondary hero all through this story."

"Why not make him a ghost who haunts the villain throughout the rest of the serial?" ingenious Smith suggested.

The ghost became the secondary hero.

At Eagle's Nest, Buntline lived with his wife, Kate, and his children and continued to turn out stories for Street & Smith. One day a discordant chirp was heard at the Nest, issuing from Lovanche Judson, his first wife. It would appear Ned had not bothered to divorce Lovanche before marrying his second wife. The newspapers of the day were thundering at Henry Ward Beecher for alleged indiscretions with one of his parishioners and here was real scandal. Lovanche was met at the railroad station and pacified by a friend of Buntline. She finally agreed to leave him alone for $50 and a draft on Street & Smith for $1900.

Buntline was often the subject of feature stories in the daily newspapers. He once described his method of work to a reporter. He usually worked at night, with a big pot of coffee beside his desk. "I once wrote a book of 610 pages in sixty-two hours," he said. "During that time I never ate or slept. I never lay out plots in advance. I wouldn't know how to do it, for how can I know what my people may take it into their heads to do? First I invent a title. When I hit on a good one, I consider the story about half finished. After I begin I push ahead as fast as I can write, never blotting out anything I have once written and never making a correction or modification. If a book does not suit me when I have finished it, I simply throw it into the fire, forget it and start another."

When the old wounds and a bad heart caught up with him, Buntline died. In those days when a man wrote exclusively for a publication, the publication owned his name and was permitted to perpetuate it after his death. And *The New York Weekly* couldn't afford to let "Ned Buntline" die. Colonel Prentiss Ingraham was immediately assigned to carry on the Buffalo Bill tradition. Ingraham, too, was a fabulous character whose career had not been unlike that of his great friend and predecessor. He had been brought up in Natchez, Mississippi. He was a Southerner in the old tradition—courteous, courtly and kind. He had fought with distinction for the Confederacy and had become a lieutenant at eighteen. He liked fighting, and when Lee surrendered, Ingraham hurried to Mexico where he joined the Army headed by Juarez. A year later, he turned up in the Austrian Army and fought against Prussia. He fought the Turks, he fought in Africa, he fought in Asia, and finally, his sympathy aroused

Col. Prentiss Ingraham

Edward Z.C. Judson (Ned Buntline)

by the fight of the Cubans for independence, he became a captain in the Cuban Navy and then became a colonel of cavalry in its army. He was captured by the Spaniards and condemned to be shot. The American Consul was unable to do anything to help him, so Ingraham appealed to the British Minister on the grounds that he was a descendant of the well-known English family of the same name.

The British Minister, impressed more by the personality of this grave, quiet man than by his rather tenuous claim to British citizenship, interceded for him. The Spanish government refused to do anything officially, but unofficially they allowed him to escape. He then headed for the West, where he met Cody, Hickok, and a great many of the famed scouts of the period. It was at this time that he began to write. His stories of action, peril and bloodshed were woven out of the cloth of his experiences. Ingraham met Pawnee Bill in the West, and his stories about the scout were nearly as popular as Buntline's about Buffalo Bill. Ingraham was in the West when General Custer and his entire command were killed, and he was on the Little Big Horn battlefield within a week after the slaughter. He immediately wrote *Custer's Last Warpath,* the first dramatized and only partly fictionalized account of Custer's stand to be published.

When asked by a reporter how he got his plots, Ingraham answered, "Well, I open up with an action and then just go ahead and write. It's easy. I begin, 'Crack! Crack! Crack! Three more redskins bit the dust.' From there on, it's easy."

Reading the Buffalo Bill stories today, it is impossible to spot where Buntline broke off and Ingraham began. They thought alike and wrote alike. Invariably they would put Buffalo Bill in a situation of great peril, and then extricate him through his own reckless bravery or with the help of a loyal Indian ally. Improbabilities never bothered either of these two facile men. Their own amazing careers had been studded with improbable and even impossible situations and escapades.

CHAPTER

THREE

NICK CARTER IN VARIOUS DISGUISES

STREET & SMITH

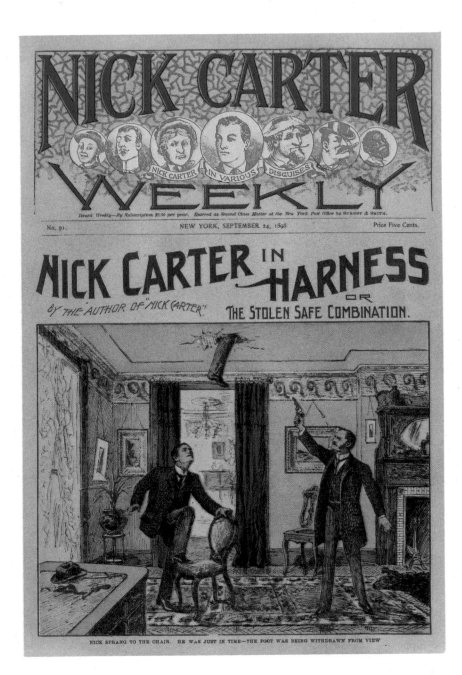

Cover of an issue of the Nick Carter Library,
first published in 1891

CHAPTER

THREE

Francis Smith had never forgotten his first venture, the publication of the boys' magazine, *Wide Awake*. He was firmly convinced that there was an enormous market to be tapped among the youngsters of the country. In his opinion, only lack of capital had prevented *Wide Awake* from achieving a permanent and successful place in the magazine world. Now he felt that he had the necessary capital and editorial experience to launch a juvenile publication profitably.

Boys of the World, A Story Paper for the Rising Generation, made its first appearance on October 21, 1875. It was filled with stories of adventure, and a high moral tone was maintained throughout. Smith established the formula which later made the Horatio Alger books so fabulously successful. Alger and Oliver Optic were among the writers who did their best to sell virtue to American youth.

Two serials were started in the first issue: *Phil, the Fearless;* or, *The Firebrand of the Wabash,* by Hermon Burford, and *The Boy Chief;* or, *The Battles of the Avengers,* by Colonel Prentiss Ingraham. The issue also contained short stories, a puzzles department (riddles, double acrostics and anagrams), and several poems, including:

"To The Boys of the World"

BY FRANCIS S. SMITH

Do not be above your business,
    Let your trade be what it may—
Strive, by industry and patience,
    In the world to make your way.
He who blushes at his calling
    And its title fears to utter,
Shames himself, and, like a ninny,
    Quarrels with his bread and butter.

There were stories for very young readers, "The Two Bears," and "The Little Hero," and, of course, there was an article on a dog. It was "Sport, the Expressman's Dog." The first issue ran nearly two columns of jokes, headed "Fun for the Boys."

But the rising generation apparently wanted tougher stuff and, reluctantly, Smith had to abandon publication of *Boys of the World.*

His disappointment was assuaged by the continuing growth of the parent publication. The *Weekly* did not depend entirely upon writers of escapist tales. Francis Smith was too shrewd to appeal to one class of reader only. Occasionally, a really first-rate writer would manage to creep into the columns of the publication. One of these was Maurice Thompson, and a suit he brought against the publishing firm resulted in a binding legal decision (it still stands) that under some circumstances a man does not own his own name. Under a pseudonym, Thompson wrote a few excellent Indian stories for the *Weekly.* Later, he wrote his famous best-selling novel, *Alice of Old Vincennes.* He put his *New York Weekly* days behind him and continued his career as a serious novelist. At the height of Thompson's popularity Francis Smith dug up one of his old Indian stories and re-printed it, not under the pseudonym, but under the author's real name. Thompson was furious and sued the firm. The opinion rendered by the judge upheld a publisher's right to print an author's work under his true name unless the work had been purchased under a binding contract forbidding the publisher to do so. However, it wasn't often that the firm was sued.

Whether or not Street & Smith were the first to inaugurate the policy of the so-called "due bill" is something that cannot be proved, but hidden in the voluminous files of office correspondence there is a receipted bill which shows that in 1875 the firm did run an advertisement of Glen's Soap and, in return, received not the usual space rates but a diamond ring from Charles S. Sterns, head of the soap company. The acknowledgment from Sterns reads:

Messrs. Street & Smith   April 13, 1875

Bought of Charles S. Sterns, one diamond ring, value—$1,000.
Received payment in advertising Glen's Soap.

Charles S. Sterns

BOYS OF THE WORLD.

A STORY PAPER FOR THE RISING GENERATION.

Entered according to Act of Congress, in the Year 1875, by Street & Smith, in the Office of the Librarian of Congress, Washington, D. C.

Vol. I. 27, 29 and 31 Rose Street, P. O. Box 4896.   **NEW YORK, OCTOBER 21, 1875.** $2.50 Per Annum. Single Copy FIVE CENTS   **No. I.**

THE DYING SOLDIER.

Along the blood-wash'd battle-plain
A warrior heave was lying,
And that was heard his mournful strain,
'Mid cheers of the dying:—

Oh, God of mercy, spare my life!
And I can too earthily,
I have a young and faithful wife,
I have a darling child!

I am their hope, their joy, their all,
That matrch here below—
And shall I thus nutimely fall!
Alas! 'tis often so!

I feel the cold, cold hand of death
Come pressing on my brow;
His word is parted from its sheath,
And I must yield me now

Sot, oh! my baby boy—my wife—
To them no sigh is stealing,
And saved our flattering hoop of life
With more than mortal calmess

God help them now! In this hour
Your sorrows I commend,
Who calls the orphan child its own,
Who is the widow's friend.

Sew farewell all! Death's sable night
Comes stealing o'er mine eye;
My soul hath spread its wings for flight—
Receive it, Lord! I die!

PHIL, THE FEARLESS;
OR,
THE FIREBRAND of the WABASH.
By Harman Burford.

CHAPTER I.
THE ALARM.

PHIL, THE FEARLESS—A SHARP WHISTLE FROM HIS LIPS, AND A HALF SCORE OF SAVAGES ROSE FROM THE BANKS.

THE YOUNG MOTHER.

How fair a picture is a babe at rest,
Its rosce young mother's snow white bosom lying,
In tiny hand in that soft pillow pressed,
In little checra pink red with recent crying,

THE BOY CHIEF;
OR,
THE BATTLES OF THE AVENGERS.
By Col. Prentiss Ingraham.

CHAPTER I.
THE NIGHT ATTACK.

If this was the inauguration of the bizarre custom, hundreds of young reporters over the years owe thanks to the owners of the *Weekly* for vacations at resorts and free theatre tickets offered by advertisers in lieu of paying cash for advertisements. The due bill is a form of paying for advertising frowned upon today by advertising agencies and reputable newspapers and magazines, but at one time it was quite prevalent. Of course, the notation from Sterns does not indicate which of the partners wound up with the diamond ring, a commodity not easily split down the middle and shared equally.

Francis Smith's charm, warmth and generosity became a legend among writers. He was always willing (to the secret dismay of Business Manager Street) to help out writers with advance payments for serials they might never do. Smith was a great friend of Mark Twain and of the popular Josh Billings, whose name was Henry Wheeler Shaw. Josh Billings and Artemus Ward were the country's two best-known cracker-barrel philosophers. Decades later, Will Rogers would become famous as a twentieth-century Josh Billings. Smith paid him one hundred dollars a week for a dozen of his homilies which were featured in the *Weekly*. One issue might have:

> Nobody but a phool gits bit twise by the same dog.

> The man who kan ware a shirt a hole week
> and keep it klean ain't fit for enny thing else.

> Verry few people enjoy munny,
> bekause they kan't git enuff of it.

> To be a suckcessful pollytysian, a man shud be buttered on both sides and then keep away from the fire.

> Yu kan't alwus tell a gentleman by his
> clothes, but yu kan by his finger nails.

> Wimmen are like flowers, a little squeezing makes them the more fragrant.

> Look out galls! the Jack of hartes is alwus a nave.

The dynamic partners did not overlook the fact that women whose husbands earned moderate incomes were becoming fashion conscious. They began a department called "The Ladies Work Box" in association with the New Idea Pattern Company, whose designs were featured. It was the beginning of the do-it-yourself craze which has had such a resurgence in recent years. At the top of the column was the announcement:

> By special arrangement with the manufacturers we are able to supply the readers of *The New York Weekly* with the patterns of all garments described or illustrated in this column at ten cents each. Address the fashion department of *The New York Weekly,* Box 1173, New York City.

The column was edited and written by "Mrs. Helen Wood," but any woman reader who called at the office to see Mrs. Wood in person would have been surprised to find that she wore trousers, sported a mustache and smoked cigars. Running this column, which was highly profitable to the firm, was one of the many chores cheerful, versatile Editor Tom Glynn performed.

The *Weekly* printed many yarns resembling our detective stories of today. This was a type of fiction relatively new in the 1880's. The murder story is as old as Chapter 4 of "Genesis," which told us of the world's first murder in ten words, "Cain rose up against Abel his brother and slew him." This historic fratricide, however, omitted one important element of the classic tale of detection—it lacked a detective. Actually, the detective did not make his appearance on the world stage until 1829, when Sir Robert Peel created the first official police force of London. Literature follows man faithfully; once there were detectives, it was only a matter of time before detective stories followed.

The first detective fiction in short-story form was published in *Graham's* of Philadelphia, April, 1841. It was "The Murders in the Rue Morgue," and the author was Edgar Allan Poe. That one short story sired the Nick Carters, the Charlie Chans, the Sherlock Holmeses, the Sam Spades, and the hundreds of sleuths who followed. It touched off the imagination of many writers for the various weeklies, and Francis Smith, with his genius for anticipating trends, knew immediately that detective fiction was something on which his readers would feed avidly. He gave it to them.

Francis Smith was now in a secure enough financial position to delegate more and more of his editorial chores to Tom Glynn, and the writing of serials to others. He could afford to relax a little and indulge his zest for life. He was a member of the Lotus Club, whose

George C. Smith, Cora Smith Gould, and Ormond G. Smith

membership was restricted to editors and writers. If he had a serious hobby, it was billiards. Often he would hurry from the office to the club to spend hours knocking balls around the green-covered table. His four children, Francis, Jr., Cora, George Campbell, and Ormond were growing up. Francis, the eldest, started working for him when he finished school, but it was Cora who seemed to inherit her father's literary enthusiasms. When Cora was fifteen she used to make the long trip from Brooklyn over the Fulton Street Ferry (the Brooklyn Bridge was still many years away) to watch the presses roll and read the still wet issues as they came off the presses. Cora and her father were very close. She would write parodies of his verses and tell him that one day she, too, would become a writer. Her father would laugh indulgently and her easy-going brother, Francis, would joke with her about it, but she was stubborn about being a writer "when she grew up."

Francis Shubael Smith had eleven brothers and sisters. One of his sisters, Freelove, traveled to far-off California in a covered wagon with her husband. Francis decided to pay his sister a visit in California. He left the *Weekly* in the hands of partner Street and son Francis and took Cora with him.

Cora was entranced with the country as she traveled west. Her inquiring young mind absorbed all the new experiences and, as a result of this trip, she acquired a lifelong love for travel. Her father was the kind of American whose interest in his own country was so great that he thought it slightly unpatriotic to go beyond its borders. He couldn't understand why Americans wanted to go to Europe, but when his daughter pleaded for the chance to see the world he reluctantly allowed his wife to take her on a trip to Ireland. There she met distant relatives of her ancestor, The Reverend John Smith, who had come from Ipswich, England, to settle in Barnstable, Massachusetts in 1630. This trip, the first of many this remarkable young woman would make to Europe, instilled in her a strong enthusiasm for history and family genealogy. In later years she wrote a complete history of the Smith family. She also wrote a great deal of poetry, but the most diligent research cannot find her name ever listed as a contributor to *The New York Weekly*. It is entirely possible that she wrote verse and perhaps stories under a *nom de plume* for the *Weekly*. She published a book of poems, *The Town at the Top of the World,* of which her father was inordinately proud.

By this time in their partnership, Francis Street was completely occupied with the business end of the *Weekly* and with extraneous real-estate ventures which brought him high dividends. Actually, the real-estate activities had become more engrossing to him than the *Weekly;* they were more profitable and, to him, more interesting. Street died in 1883 and young Ormond Smith, just out of Harvard, bought Street's interest in the firm from his estate.

Ormond and his brother, George Campbell, had always been very close and actually remained so until their deaths (eleven days apart) in 1933. Both had worked for their father during school vacations and were familiar with the operation and organization of the company. With Ormond's acquisition of Street's interest, Ormond and George Campbell went to work seriously. Ormond had creative ideas and George had the talent for implementing them. George was three years older, but he apparently recognized that his young brother had an editorial gift which he himself lacked. George concentrated upon the business end of the *Weekly*.

Cora Smith, who might have been a great editor herself, was married to George H. Gould now, and interested only in traveling and in writing her poems and genealogical treatises. Cora was perhaps fifty years ahead of her time. She was an internationalist, a woman of intense intellectual curiosity who eventually became as much at home in London and Paris as she was in Fort Lauderdale, Florida, where she and her husband lived. Her poems, read sixty years after they were written, provoke the speculation that this might well have been the most inherently creative talent produced by Francis S. Smith. But this is sheer speculation.

Francis S. Smith died in 1887, leaving his four children heartbroken and bewildered. Surprisingly enough, it was Ormond, the youngest, who assumed the leadership. He was aware that this was an intensely competitive business which fate had tossed into the hands of four relatively young persons. Apparently, he did not feel that his convivial, easy-going eldest brother, Francis, who had been regarded as the likely heir, could guide the destinies of the firm. Ormond was only twenty-seven, but even at that age, he revealed the traits which would eventually make Street & Smith the largest publishing firm in the world. With his share of his father's legacy he bought out his brother, Francis, an amicable arrangement since Francis wanted to live in Europe anyhow. Ormond Smith became president of the firm and he appointed his brother, George, vice-president. These two men ran the business until 1933.

The death of Francis S. Smith, in 1887, at the age of sixty-eight, elicited wide editorial comment. He was a well-loved man. One newspaper, as a tribute and comment on his life, reproduced a poem he had written in the early days of the *Weekly:*

MY AMBITION

If I can any pleasure give
　To those who daily labor
If I can send one ray of joy
　To any lowly neighbor
'Tis all the recompense I ask—
　I labor for no other;
In any man, however poor,
　I recognize a brother.

If I can cheer an aching heart
　However poor and lowly
Though rude my muse and plain my verse,
　My mission still is holy;
And I care nothing for the sneers
　Of pompous schools and classes
So that I reach the hearts and win
　The plaudits of the masses.

After his graduation from Harvard, young Ormond Smith had spent several months in Europe. He fell in love with France, and for the rest of his life he continued to have a deep interest in and great affection for the people and the traditions of that country. Ormond Smith had the cultural background and tastes of an *Atlantic Monthly* editor. It would seem that the pap printed in *The New York Weekly* would be distasteful to a brilliant young man who devoured the essays on Zola, Dostoevski and Baudelaire which appeared in the erudite *Atlantic*. One would expect him to have a greater affinity for the prose of the brilliant Columbia University professor, Harry Thurston Peck, who was writing so knowledgeably on French writers Rimbaud and Jules Laforgue and Verlaine and Maurice Barrès than he did for the serial writers who appeared in the *Weekly*.

Wealthy, attractive, cultured, Ormond Smith might well have drifted into the pleasantly fatuous world of New York's theatre and society circles, as so many of his Harvard classmates were doing. It was the day of the dandy in New York, where the *bon mot* in the manner of Oscar Wilde or Whistler was accepted as the supreme witticism. It was the day of the Clyde Fitch theatre, trivial and not mentally taxing, and of Edgar Saltus, who could handle such a theme as The Philosophy of Disenchantment with a lucidity and lightness that gave him a reputation for erudition expressed wittily. Saltus once said that the only thing that mattered in writing was style—an oversimplified absurdity that somehow reflected the sartorial smartness and shallow thinking of what passed for New York's intelligentsia. But young Smith liked his work chiefly because Saltus had translated three volumes of stories by Mérimée, Gautier and others from the French. His novels were filled with smart phrases and smart people; although he talked profoundly about style, his own in fiction was purple, and his heroes usually confined their philandering to cerebral affairs with high-born ladies. But Saltus was having a vogue, and fifteen years later Ormond Smith would buy his stories for his first magazine—*Ainslee's*.

People were so sure of themselves and their prevailing standards, that decades later, in writing of the era, Van Wyck Brooks would call them the Confident Years. Ormond Smith might have been pardoned had he mistaken the form for the substance—thousands of his contemporaries were making the mistake—but although he was intellectually curious, he was not socially ambitious. He was, after all, his father's son, and as he grew older he became more like him in his mental and spiritual outlook. It seems apparent, too, that his eminently sensible mother had considerable influence on him (it was she who had taken him to France).

In any case, Ormond made his choice. He would never renounce his love for the best literature of the day, but he would reserve these intellectual enthusiasms for his private life.

Competitors who thought that the relatively inexperienced young Ormond would make enough mistakes to help them put a dent into the circulation of the *Weekly* were startled into uncomfortable attention. It soon became obvious that Ormond was something rare in the publishing business. The original partners had had great courage. If a property wasn't going well, as had been the case with the *Literary Album* and *Boys of the World,* they shrugged their shoulders, said ruefully, "Well, we made a mistake," and immediately closed the publication, taking their not inconsiderable losses in stride. Ormond Smith inherited his father's courage and vision. The death of Francis Street and sale of his interest to Ormond meant that full control of the firm was now in the hands of the Smith family, but Ormond was wise enough to retain the now well-known and valuable firm name. Despite the fact that no "Street" has been connected with the organization for some seventy-five years, the firm is still Street & Smith.

Undoubtedly, Ormond Smith pulled his first great publishing coup when he started the Nick Carter stories as weekly features of the magazine. One of the most prolific writers for the *Weekly* was Ormond's cousin, John Russell Coryell. He wrote detective stories for the publication and, like so many of his contemporaries in the fiction field, his own career rivaled that of many of his heroes. As a young man, he had abandoned college and gone to China to join his family. He nearly lost his life when the small ship he was on was badly battered by a typhoon. The captain told his passengers that the ship could never survive the storm, but young Coryell was apparently more interested in observing the reactions of his fellow passengers than in getting ready for the meeting with his Maker.

Frederick Van Rensselaer Dey

John Russell Coryell

China was the ideal country in which to gather background material and plots. At the time, Coryell never thought of becoming a writer, but he absorbed the colorful, exotic atmosphere of the country and utilized it later when he did turn to writing. He trained Manchurian ponies; he hunted with a bow made from the spliced horns of the Indian buffalo. When he was only twenty, his father wangled a job for him as Vice Consul in Shanghai, and this post automatically made him a magistrate in the civil courts. He listened to stories of murder and robbery and smuggling, and they soaked into the sponge-like recesses of his mind and remained there until he was ready to exhume them. He returned to California, then a boisterous land of adventure, mayhem and larceny. He got a job on a Santa Barbara newspaper and for the first time earned a living by his pen. One of his articles gave grave offense to a local citizen and young Coryell was challenged to a duel. In 1929 his son, Russell Coryell, wrote of that incident in *The Bookman:*

> Father knew nothing about shooting but was afraid, he said, to back out of the encounter lest he be shot anyway. He therefore bought himself a little bulldog pistol which fired one shot, for he said he was sure he would never get a chance to fire more than one. Then he sent word to the gunman, a huge fellow over six feet tall, that he was ready to meet him and set a certain saloon in Santa Barbara as the rendezvous. They were to shoot on sight.
>
> "Tell him," he said to his second, "that my pistol shoots only once —and that once is all I need to shoot." His sense of humor didn't abandon him even then when, as he said of himself, his knees were knocking together with dread of the approaching duel. The curious thing is that when he arrived at the saloon, he forgot all about the pistol in his pocket and jumped at the desperado with his fists. He weighed one hundred and nineteen pounds and the bad man about one hundred and sixty. There you have Nick Carter in action. *The Sacramento Leader's* account is in part as follows:
>
> "Gray, reaching for his pistol pocket, began a tirade of abuse. Before, however, ten words were uttered, Mr. Coryell gave him a sound thrashing, ending by kicking him into the street. Gray afterward threatened to shoot Mr. Coryell, who, arming himself, again sought him and invited him into the vacant store of a building and told him he would fight him a duel with pistols if he (Gray) had the courage. Gray's craven heart forsook him, whereupon Coryell pulled his nose and slapped his face."

The yet unborn Nick Carter could not have handled the situation better. Coryell thought it advisable to go east after that incident, and for the first time he began to engage in the writing of fiction as a paying career. He wrote several juvenile stories for *St. Nicholas, Harper's Young People, Golden Days* and other publications. The stories met with indifferent success and anemic pay checks. Then he walked into the office of Street & Smith and told Ormond Smith quite bluntly that he could write better detective yarns than any of their established writers. His first story was a detective serial. It was well received and Ormond Smith asked, "Do you think you can do the same trick twice?"

"Twice!" Coryell exploded. "I can do it every time I try it."

Ormond Smith was intrigued with his brash cousin's confidence and told him to keep on turning them out. In rapid succession he wrote *The American Marquis* (Nick Carter had not as yet appeared), *The Old Detective's Pupil* (in which young Nick Carter was born as a protégé of "Seth Carter," the "old detective"), *Wall Street Haul* and *Fighting Against Millions.* He had made good his boast and Ormond Smith assigned him to the job of turning out serials under the profitable name of Bertha M. Clay. He did such an excellent job of satisfying the worshippers of the now defunct lady that Ormond kept him at it. But Ormond Smith studied the fan letters which flowed in by the hundreds every week and he knew that the reader interest in Coryell's detective stories was high.

Ormond liked the sound of "Nick Carter," even though the young detective had only been used two or three times by Coryell. Ormond decided that a series of short stories featuring Nick Carter, detective, might prove interesting. One day Ormond, his brother, George, and Frederic Marmaduke Van Rensselaer Dey (to give him his full name) had lunch together. Dey was then, and remained until his death, a man of mystery. He had been born in Watkins Glen, New York, descendant of a distinguished line of Dutch ancestors. He was always rather proud of the fact that Dey Street in lower Manhattan had been named after his family. He was educated at Cornell, practiced law briefly, drifted into newspaper work writing editorials for a Washington daily, and then started sending stories to *The New York Weekly* and other publications of the era. Ormond Smith was very fond of Frederic Dey. He felt that his detective stories were more authentic than most and he knew that Dey was a good friend of Inspector Byrnes, Deputy Police Commissioner Faurot, and other ranking members of the New York City Police.

"I WAS MISTAKEN. I THOUGHT THIS ENVELOPE HAD BEEN TAMPERED WITH."

Nick Carter's first appearance in Street & Smith's *New York Weekly*

At this casual luncheon, literary history of a kind was made. Ormond explained that he wanted a weekly detective story in *The New York Weekly*. Author Dey saw no difficulty about complying with his request. Smith's idea would be to have a central character, a detective, running through all of the stories. Dey thought this a good idea.

"John Coryell could do it easily enough," Smith said, "but he's all tied up with the Bertha M. Clay serials. But I like the name of the character he used in a couple of stories he did for us. He called his young detective Nick Carter."

Dey agreed to try it, and for the next seventeen years he turned out Nick Carter stories as fast as his busy pen could fly. He usually produced a twenty-five-thousand-word story a week. His first was called *Nick Carter, Detective; by a Celebrated Author*. It seems likely that Ormond Smith had a prophetic vision of Nick's future fame and the fact that eventually there would be a dozen men writing the stories. Nick Carter was an immediate success. No character in fiction, not even Buffalo Bill, could match his amazing versatility.

He began, of course, by being the best marksman in the world. He could, and often did, defeat as many as twenty or thirty ruffians single-handed. Nick Carter could imitate the appearance and the speech of a western farmer, a Chicago businessman, a French government official, a Russian spy, a Japanese nobleman or a cowboy. Reading lips in three different languages was just one of his minor parlor tricks. In addition to this, Nick was a good boy. He neither drank, smoked, swore nor lied.

"I never in my life wrote a Nick Carter story that I would be ashamed to read to a Bible class," Dey once told an interviewer.

It was inevitable, of course, that Nick Carter appear in serial form. A typical Nick Carter serial would begin with Nick being asked to solve the mystery of some smuggled diamonds.

> "You should be especially delighted with this matter," says the chief of the United States Treasury agents, "for since I have been connected with the Treasury Department, we have never had a case that has caused one-half the annoyance that I have been put to by this one."

On page nine, after a few swift researches, Nick sails for France with his assistant, Chickering Carter. On page fifteen he meets Princess Olga, the tiger-chief of the Russian Nihilists. "There was a subtlety about her that, even in the shadow where he could not perceive her remarkable beauty, was as manifest as the perfume of an Easter lily." On page nineteen he returns to New York, disguised as a western farmer. He searches the stateroom of the villain, Livingston Carruthers, but cannot discover the diamonds.

On page sixty-nine (second installment), Chick Carter is drugged and tossed into the middle of the Atlantic. Nick Carter, on page seventy-six, is kidnapped in a steel-armored hansom cab, designed for lunatics. On page eighty-six he stuns his two abductors by simultaneous blows to their solar plexi, and takes the next boat to France. He escapes assassination and wins the heart of Princess Olga. Together, they escape from the nest of the Nihilists by a secret passageway. Chick Carter reappears on page 184. A miracle had saved him from the sea, for, "In all those leagues of watery waste there was one spot ten feet square that would support me and I fell upon it. The hand of God placed it there, having read the terrible plot for my undoing in the heart of that oily fiend, Carruthers."

But the end is drawing near. In the third installment, a Nihilist bomb destroys the café where Nick is consulting with his subordinates. He escapes with serious wounds. He takes the steamer for New York; he discovers the smuggled jewels, and on the final page he arrests the villain. Carruthers assaults him, but is shot by Princess Olga, who glides suddenly into the room disguised as a stewardess.

She ran a fearful risk when she fell in love with Nick Carter. Once married, he would cease to appeal to his readers, and therefore his stars and publishers decreed that the great detective should remain single. It was useless for Fred Dey, in his tenderness of heart, to rebel against this ruling. Once he ventured to announce Nick Carter's engagement, but the rash fiancée was done to death at the beginning of the next installment. Once, in a moment of defiance, he described Nick's wedding.

Now it happened that week that the editors did not read his copy. It arrived late, and was sent directly to the linotype room. Suddenly a printer's devil came bounding upstairs with the news that Nick Carter was married. The office seethed like an angry sea. Typewriters, finally beginning to be standard equipment in magazine offices, fell to the floor, the clock stopped, and stenographers paled. Messengers were dispatched to all parts of the city in search of Fred Dey. When he appeared, he was pushed into a chair and compelled to describe the bitter death of the bride, while his own tears blotted the page. For Princess Olga, still other tears would be shed. "I thought that man would kill you, Nicholas," she exclaimed as the smoking revolver dropped from her grasp. She raised her left hand quickly to her mouth. "And now—I die rather than face the consequences of my act."

They tried to prevent her from taking the poison, but of course they were too late.

Ormond Smith thereafter made a strict rule that Nick was never to show anything more than mere courtesy to a lady he encountered in the course of his career. It was quite all right for him to rescue fair damsels from bands of counterfeiters or dynamiters, and it was quite all right for them to toss languishing glances at their hero. But for Nick, alas, he must lead the life of a celibate.

If reader interest is to be the gauge, Nick Carter was undoubtedly the greatest fictional detective of all time. He appealed not only to youngsters but to adults. It is true that John Russell Coryell had brought him into the world and had christened him, but Ormond Smith was certainly his literary godfather. He realized early that in Nick Carter he had a potentially great property, and he worked closely with Fred Dey and his many successors in keeping the character of Nick Carter just as he wished it. The detective was remarkable because he was athletic and sincere, with none of the pretensions and subtleties of Sherlock Holmes, for instance. He was not a poseur, and, of course, he would have had nothing but contempt for a man like Holmes, who was so lacking in character as to smoke tobacco and inject himself with cocaine. No man ever took the terrible beatings undergone by Nick Carter and survived to appear fresh and reasonably debonair a week later. He was drugged hundreds of times, knocked into unconsciousness just as often. He kept walking into traps such as a runaway freight car that was dashing toward a washed-out bridge over a ravine, but he always managed to escape.

He was, of course, a master of disguises. He always carried paints, dyes, wigs and drooping mustaches on his person. He could turn his clothes inside out and transform himself in a moment from a day laborer into a prince of Japan. It goes without saying that he always carried two revolvers and skeleton keys which would open any lock ever devised by man.

Ormond Smith realized that the greatest literary common denominator was the detective story. This amazingly shrewd editor
knew that the Nick Carter stories were being read in the White
House, in prisons, in the mining camps of the West, and even by
the cultivated men of taste in whose homes he was a welcome guest.

Years later, Frederic Dey told a reporter for *The New York World*
how Ormond and George Smith had asked him to lunch that historic
day in 1889. "Who paid for the lunch, Mr. Dey?" the reporter asked
smilingly.

"Ormond Smith did," Dey said solemnly. "As I recall it, our
luncheon check was about four dollars. I don't think that Ormond
Smith ever regretted his investment."

CHAPTER

FOUR

DIAMOND DICK

STREET & SMITH

One of the Alger series books, evolving in 1915 from
earlier publication in the *New York Weekly*

CHAPTER

FOUR

In 1889 Ormond Smith was twenty-eight. The *Weekly* was doing well, but at best, this was the creature of his late father and his partner. Nor did publishing the *Weekly* give enough scope to the talents or the imagination of this ambitious young publisher and his equally ambitious brother. Ormond and George decided to branch out. They would challenge the supremacy of the giant in the field of dime novels, Erastus F. Beadle. This was a little bit like the makers of a Kiddy Kar challenging the supremacy of General Motors, but Ormond had been studying the field of the paper-backed publications for some time, and he thought he had some ideas that might give pause to Beadle & Company and the many others enjoying the bonanza that came from the dime novel. Beadle's *Banner Weekly* was giving *The New York Weekly* some competition, and it may be that Ormond Smith wanted to strike back by competing with Beadle in its own field.

Erastus Beadle had come to New York from Buffalo in 1858 to attempt a daring publishing experiment. In Buffalo he had issued a Dime Song Book, and the tremendous success of that one little pamphlet (it was little more than that) gave him food for thought. He and his brother, Irwin, published a series of dime joke books which sold well.

The first dime novel published by the firm (Albert Johannsen, in his *House of Beadle and Adams*, gives brother Irwin the credit) was *Malaeska* by Mrs. Ann Stephens, a brilliant woman who, in addition to being an assistant editor of *The Ladies' Companion, Graham's Magazine* and *Peterson's,* was a prolific writer of novels. In writing ability and inventiveness, she was several cuts above those who eventually followed her.

On June 7, 1860, the following advertisement appeared in *The New York Tribune:*

BOOKS FOR THE MILLIONS

A dollar book for a dime!
128 pages complete, only ten cents!!!

MALAESKA
the
Indian Wife of the White Hunter
by Mrs. Ann Stephens
Irwin P. Beadle and Co., Publishers

The dime novel had arrived. It would be derided, scorned; sermons would be preached against it and generations of school kids would hide the little paperbacks in their big geography books—but the dime novel would survive and make fortunes for writers and publishers, and give impetus to the growth of the great American News Company. It would be read by presidents and financiers and scholars and workers, and, inevitably, by youngsters. Its detractors could never deny the fact that this was a peculiarly American institution and not a pale replica of English tales of haunted castles and haughty lords and ladies. To say that the dime novel accurately recorded the American scene would be to gild the lily, but it did have its roots in the American scene. For the first time readers who could only afford a dime for a full-length book learned of the western wilderness, of the buffalo-studded plains, of the trapper, the Indian guide and the white scout. They learned of the deadly accuracy of the American-made rifle and they learned of the lusty vitality of a part of their country which, to them, had hitherto been as remote as Tangier or Constantinople. They learned of the battle of men against the sea and of pirates off the Barbary Coast, and they learned of man's search for gold and occasionally they were given a dish of nicely sugar-coated romance. The heroes were courageous, the women characters pure (it would be decades before a dime-novel writer would even admit that girls had legs), the villains cruel and heartless and quite deserving of the fate which was invariably theirs.

To be sure, the West, as drawn by the dime-novel writers, was a highly dramatized version of the true scene, and it is easy to ridicule the absurdities of the more blatant plots, but it did bring the story of the West to the East.

Malaeska was actually a reprint of a serial Mrs. Stephens had writ-

THIRD EDITION.

BEADLE'S Dime New York Library

COPYRIGHTED IN 1883, BY BEADLE & ADAMS.

ENTERED AT THE POST OFFICE AT NEW YORK, N. Y., AT SECOND CLASS MAIL RATES.

Vol. XXI. Published Every Week. Beadle & Adams, Publishers, 98 WILLIAM STREET, N. Y., November 7, 1883. Ten Cents a Copy. $5.00 a Year. No. 263

IRON-ARMED ABE, The Hunchback Destroyer; Or, THE BLACK RIDERS' TERROR.

A TALE OF THE CITY OF THE DESERT.

BY CAPTAIN MARK WILTON,

AUTHOR OF "CACTUS JACK," "DON SOMBRERO," "LADY JAGUAR," "THE SCORPION BROTHERS," "CANYON DAVE," ETC., ETC.

"DOWN!" CRIED IRON ARMED ABE, IN A TERRIBLE VOICE. "DOWN, AND FEED THE VOLCANO FIRES!"

Cover of an issue from Beadle's dime novel library

ten for *The Ladies' Companion* in 1839. It was a highly moral tale (this became a tradition of the dime novel) which dealt with the tribulations of the Indian wife of a white hunter in early colonial days. The scene was not the West but the Catskill Mountains north of New York City, but it pretty well established the traditions of later western stories.

Malaeska was an immediate success. So was the second book hurriedly set into print by Beadle. This was *The Privateers' Cruise* by Harry Cavendish. The third in the series was *Myra, the Child of Adoption, a Romance of Real Life,* by the prolific Ann Stephens. It was actually based on the life of Mrs. Myra Clark Gaines, a wealthy heiress of New Orleans. During the year 1860 thirteen of the paperbacked novels appeared and the House of Beadle was on its way. The appetite of the public was insatiable for stories by Ann Stephens, Edward S. Ellis (a one-man literary assembly line), Clara Augusta, N. C. Iron, Mrs. Metta V. Victor, and others.

By far the most successful of the first year's crop was No. 8 in the series, *Seth Jones; or, The Captives of the Frontier,* by Edward Ellis. Beadle's advertised it, cleverly plastering the East with signs, "Who is Seth Jones?" Newspapers carried only this line as an advertisement. Beadle's sent signs and advertisements to papers all over the country, and finally, a day before the book was to appear, there were posters everywhere depicting a heroic-looking hunter in buckskins and coonskin cap with rifle in hand. The caption said simply, "I am Seth Jones." Beadle himself said later that six hundred thousand copies of the book were sold. It was reviewed favorably by serious critics (they hadn't yet learned to belittle the dime novel).

By 1863 the dime novel was an established success. The firm was now known as Beadle & Adams (brother Irwin had sold out his interest). Erastus Beadle rode herd on his stable of writers. He established strict rules concerning the editorial approach they were to take. Each writer received the following printed directive:

> So much is said, and justly, against a considerable number of papers and libraries now on the market, that we beg leave to repeat the following announcement and long-standing instructions to all contributors:
> Authors who write for our consideration will bear in mind that——
> We prohibit all things offensive to good taste in expression and incident——
> We prohibit subjects of characters that carry an immoral taint——
> We prohibit the repetition of any occurrence which, though true, is yet better untold——

We prohibit what cannot be read with satisfaction by every right-minded person—old and young alike——

We require your best work——

We require unquestioned originality——

We require pronounced strength of plot and high dramatic interest of story——

We require grace and precision of narrative, and correctness in composition.

Authors must be familiar with characters and places which they introduce and not attempt to write in fields of which they have no intimate knowledge.

The success of the dime novels (or of the Beadles, as they were colloquially known) prompted a poet of the day to say:

Despite the critics of the day,
The little Beadles went their way
From home to home; like birds they went
To lonely hut and soldier tent.

The envious critics vainly tried
To stem the Beadles' rushing tide;
This was the Beadles' dreadful crime—
A dollar book sold for a dime!

In all, the firm published six hundred little books, and after the first few issues the covers were printed in orange. It was inevitable that they eventually be called "yellow backs," and the derisive term "yellow journalism" probably had its origin in these covers. Beadle's also published fifteen-cent novels and a fantastically successful English publication series called "The Beadle's American Sixpenny Library." One new series after another spewed off the Beadle presses: "Beadle's New Dime Novels," "Beadle's Pocket Novels," and "Frank Starr's American Novels" (Starr was Beadle's head printer) were some of them.

The tremendous success of Beadle's (the dime novels had sold some seven million copies by 1870) did not pass unnoticed in the trade. In 1875, Donnelly, Lloyd & Company of Chicago issued the first numbers of its ten-cent Lakeside Library with the prim announcement: "The great popular want today is for cheap good literature. Dime novels are issued by the million and good books by the thousand, but to the mass of readers the one is as distasteful as the other is inaccessible." This high moral tone is contradicted to some extent by the fact that most of the Lakeside Library consisted of works pirated from British and French publishers. But it was so successful a challenge that Beadle's had to answer it. The result was the Fireside Library. Frank Leslie saw the gold in the hills and he emerged with his Home Library, and George Munro, never one to let grass grow on his presses, hurried the Seaside Library into print. His first three numbers were *East Lynne, John Halifax, Gentleman,* and *Jane Eyre.* Eventually his presses were turning out a new novel a day for the Library. Harper & Brothers followed with its Franklin Square Library, priced at ten cents each. By 1890 there were about fourteen firms in the field publishing ten-cent books.

This was the well-established field, with Beadle's as its acknowledged leader, which young Ormond Smith decided to enter. In 1889 he began not one, but two series of dime novels, the Log Cabin and the Nugget Libraries. This was a declaration of war against the whole trade, but it appears obvious that the quiet, cultured Ormond Smith was at heart a fighter. The odds never seemed to bother him any more than they had his father.

The Log Cabin Library books were priced at ten cents. The Nugget Library publications were five cents. Smith tried to dress up the

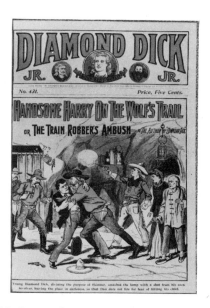

Early Street & Smith dime novels

Log Cabin books so that they would appear more attractive than the publications his rivals were putting out. He dressed them up in four colors. Most of these novels were either westerns or detective stories. Old professionals like Ned Buntline, W. B. Lawson, Harry Temple, Donald J. McKenzie, Marlin Manly, Edward Stratemeyer and Judson R. Taylor produced many of them. Within a year Street & Smith had issued sixty dime novels under the Log Cabin Library name, and it became clear that revenues from this source were potentially greater than *The New York Weekly* could ever produce.

The Nugget Library books were aimed at younger readers. During its first year, thirty-six issues were published under this imprint. Some of the titles were *Billy Mayne, the Sharper*, by Walter Fenton; *His Royal Nibs*, by John F. Cowan; *Billy Bright*, by Aaron DeWitt; *The Brotherhood Detective*, by John Warden.

By now Nick Carter had become so popular and well known that Smith decided to produce the Nick Carter Library as a weekly. Not even the prolific Frederic Dey could produce Nick Carter yarns that fast and the work was farmed out to several other writers. Many years later this would result in a controversy. In 1924, John Russell Coryell died and his obituary was headed, "Creator of Nick Carter Passes Away." That same year Eugene T. Sawyer died, and this time the newspaper story announcing his demise was headed, "Originator of Nick Carter Dies." In 1929, Thomas C. Harbaugh died in the county infirmary at Piqua, Ohio, and again the papers announced that the original writer of Nick Carter stories had passed away. Shortly afterward George Charles Jenks died in Auburn, New York, and the same old headline was revived. When Frederick W. Davis died in New Bedford, Massachusetts, he, too, was credited with being the writer of the Nick Carter stories. Actually, all of them, at one time or another, had written the Nick Carter tales for the library begun in 1890. Most of them died in poverty.

Frederic Dey's death was a particularly tragic one. For some years before his death he had been acting rather strangely. Friends of his said that he often identified himself with the fabulous character he had popularized in more than a thousand stories. One day in 1929, C. A. MacLean, one of the Street & Smith editors, received a letter from Dey stating briefly that he was very tired and that he was about to go to sleep for the last time. He was living in a cheap hotel on New York's East Side. MacLean hurried to the hotel, showed the letter to the manager, and they broke open the door of the writer's room. He lay in bed looking peacefully asleep. He had put a bullet from a .32-calibre automatic into his brain.

But that was all in the unforseeable future. To return to the 1890's —Ormond Smith had inherited his father's dream of creating a successful publication devoted entirely to boys. The elder Smith had failed twice with such projects, but this did not daunt his son. On May 15, 1890, the first issue of *Good News* appeared. It was a five-cent publication.

The lead story was by Oliver Optic, at that time perhaps the most popular writer of boys' stories in the country. Horatio Alger, who, until then, had written *Ragged Dick, Fame and Fortune, Sink or Swim, Tattered Tom, Brave and Bold,* was coming along fast. The full name of his serial was *Only an Irish Boy; or, Andy Burke's Fortunes and Misfortunes.* It began in the style which within a short time would become familiar to almost every literate youngster in the country:

> "John, saddle my horse and bring him around to the door."
> The speaker was a boy of fifteen, handsomely dressed and, to judge from his air and tone, a person of considerable consequence, in his opinion, at least. The person addressed was employed in the stable of his father, Colonel Anthony Preston, and so inferior in social condition that Master Godfrey always addressed him in imperious tones.
> John looked up and answered respectfully, "Master Godfrey, your horse is sick of the disease, and your father left orders that he was not to go out on no account."
> "None of your impudence, John," answered Godfrey angrily. "Am I master or are you, I should like to know."
> "Neither, I'm thinkin'," said John with a twinkle in his eye. "It's your father that's the master."
> A third party was standing just outside the fence. He was about the age of Godfrey, a little shorter and stouter. His coat was ragged as well as his pants. Godfrey looked at the stranger.
> "Who are you?" Godfrey demanded in his usual imperious tone.
> "Only an Irish boy," answered the other with a droll look and a slight brogue.

This, of course, was Andy Burke, and his adventures would continue through the next eight issues of *Good News.*

Good News seemed to have everything to whet the tastes of the young reader. It had Indian stories, stories of the sea, and the indefatigable Horatio Alger followed with *Frank and Fearless* and *Grit,*

A cover of an Alger story from the Medal Library, begun in 1898

but even such sure-fire material could not keep *Good News* alive. The chances are that there just were not enough affluent youngsters who had five cents to pay for a copy, or $2.50 to pay for a year's subscription. It ceased publication in 1892.

Horatio Alger, Jr., was one of those strange phenomena occasionally produced by our country. His writing talent was insignificant and he even lacked the inventiveness of a Frederic Dey, a Ned Buntline, or a Prentiss Ingraham, but he became better known than any of them. His great drawing power was his sincere belief that the poor boy had a very good chance of growing up, marrying the boss's daughter, and eventually becoming president of the First National Bank. Stewart H. Holbrook, who wrote a brilliant essay on Alger in his *Lost Men of American History,* called Alger's philosophy the Upward and Onward theory. Alger, according to his biographer, Herbert R. Mayes, wrote 119 books. Actually, he wrote one book and rewrote it 118 times. Virtue always triumphed in his theme and many variations—something which did not always happen in Alger's own strange life.

Alger, in addition to his professional writing, kept a diary. He began it at Harvard and there was little of interest that he didn't confide to its trusting pages. At Cambridge he was known as Holy Horatio, a name inspired, perhaps, by his announced intention to become a minister like his father. While in college, he roomed at a boarding house and one night the amorous lady who owned the establishment walked into his room stark naked and with acquiescence shining from her eyes. He coldly repulsed her advances and decided to move "where there is more respect for decency." He entered Harvard Divinity School and was licensed to preach.

Accompanied by two friends, Alger made a European tour, and it was in Paris that he temporarily forgot about the ministry and overcame his objection to nudity in a female companion. A singer in a Paris café taught him the facts of life, and never again was he unreceptive to amatory advances. "I was a fool to have waited so long," he told his diary. "It is not nearly so vile as I had thought." He returned home finally to be ordained as a minister of the Unitarian Church. He not only preached for two years but found time to write what amounted to rather sickening sermons for a boys' periodical called *Student and Schoolmate,* edited by William T. Adams who was better known as Oliver Optic, one of the most prolific writers of juvenile fiction in the country. Adams encouraged Alger to write boys' stories, and his first effort was *Ragged Dick* (the story he was to rewrite for the rest of his literary life). The boys of the nation loved it.

There was, at that time, a place at Duane and William Street in New York known as the Newsboys Lodging House. It was run by a kindly man, Charles O'Conner, and he liked *Ragged Dick* so much that he sought out the author. When he told Alger that the lonely, orphaned newsboys who lived at his home were now washing their faces, talking politely and (except in rare cases) giving up most forms of larceny, Alger knew where his future lay; he would continue to write of poor but honest lads. More than that, he made his headquarters at the Newsboys Lodging House. He did much of his writing there, undoubtedly under the inspiration of the little newsboys.

There came a time when he thought that the rural quiet of Peekskill, New York, might be more conducive to his method of bringing sweetness and light to the boys of the land than New York's noisy East Side. Quiet, inoffensive Horatio Alger was never more wrong in his life. Shortly after he went to Peekskill there occurred the brutal murder of a well-known resident of the town. The dead man's hys-

William Gilbert Patten (Burt L. Standish)

A typical Alger scene

107 West 44th St. N.Y.
Aug. 15/79.

Friend Street,

Have just read your biography in the Coney Island News, and need not say with much interest. I can attest the truth of this sentence "He is more fertile in ideas for subject and treatment than the authors themselves." I am indebted to you for the titles of "The Western Boy", "The Cash Boy", "Tony the Tramp", and "The Bully of the Village," all excellent. In all my stories and books I have labored to induce boys to rise in the world by precisely the same means which have helped you to rise. The example of individuals is of more value than the appeals of writers, and you may unconsciously by your success have led to the success of many others.

Yes faithfully,

Horatio Alger

Francis S. Street Esq.

Facsimile of a letter from Horatio Alger to his publishers

terical widow said that she had seen a small, balding, dumpy
stranger leaving the scene of the crime. Local police took one look at
small, balding, dumpy Holy Horatio and tagged him for the crime.
In vain he protested that he was the Reverend Horatio Alger, Jr.,
but they laughed at him for using the name of the celebrated writer.
They threw him into the clink and were painfully embarrassed when
a few hours later, the real murderer confessed and their prisoner did,
in fact, turn out to be Horatio Alger. Everyone in Peekskill tried to
make it up to Horatio. Even the widow of the murdered man asked
Horatio to dinner. She introduced him to her sister, the wife of a
traveling salesman. Horatio seems to have had a fatal attraction for
middle-aged women looking for someone upon whom to lavish affection. In no time at all, Horatio and the lady took up lodging together in New York. The husband finally found them and sent the
lady off to Paris. For a long time Horatio bemoaned the unkindly
fate which had torn the lady from his side (he saved his moralizing
for his books, never bothering to lecture his own immortal soul),
until one day he realized that he was broke.

There was only one thing to do—he would have to start rewrit-
ing *Ragged Dick*. It took him less than a month to write two long
novels. With the proceeds, he hurried to Paris to join the lady in
exile. But the fickle lady had found herself someone else. Horatio
didn't appear as glamorous in Paris as he had in Peekskill and the
unhappy writer returned home. He never knew anything but frus-
tration in his personal life; he never knew anything but success in
his professional career. No one knows exactly how many copies of
his books were sold, but estimates go as high as 250,000,000. It may
well be that his books, most of which appeared in one of the various libraries first, sold more copies than the works of any American
writer before or since. And the influence of this quiet little man
was enormous on the youth of the land.

Alger became a close friend of both Francis Smith and Francis
Street. The latter often helped him with his stories and even suggested some of the titles such as *Terry the Tramp*. All in all he produced eighteen juvenile books for Street & Smith which were published as serials in the *New York Weekly*. In addition the firm put
out 128 Alger stories in the Alger cloth-bound series. Even the
death of Alger did not sever the relationship, for eighteen stories
were posthumously edited by Edward Stratemeyer for the firm.

Horatio's hero is always a prince in disguise, playing the part of a fiddler, a bootblack, a hired boy, but with attractive, cheerful and resolute features under the dirt. His mother, always a widow, is tormented by the village squire. The hero meets a stranger and rescues his child from drowning (or from a mad dog or a runaway horse). The stranger turns out to be a rich merchant, who gives the boy new clothes, then sends him on a mission, a sort of knightly quest. On his triumphant return, the merchant adopts him as a son or ward, discomfits the wicked suitor and settles a little fortune on the hero. Moralists used to complain that this fortune was gained by pure luck. On the contrary, it was gained by the hero's discovery of the place and parentage that were his by right.

Alger, who was never freed from emotional bondage to his own father, must have found compensation in the repetition of this deeply personal theme. In each of his novels he punished his father three times. He killed him before the story opened by making the hero an orphan; he gave Horatio Senior's worst traits to the villainous squire; and finally, he provided the hero with a new father to cherish him.

Struggling Upward is the typical Alger book. It contains his stock characters, settings and incidents, leading to his stock conclusion.

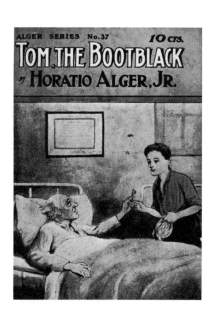

Covers of two early issues from the popular Alger series

"You need be under no anxiety about Luke and his prospects," says the rich merchant to the hero's widowed mother. "I shall make over to him $10,000 at once, constituting myself his guardian, and will see that he is well started in business."

During the late nineties, Smith launched still another weekly publication. This was called *Tip Top*, and it would endure for the next twenty years. It would endure chiefly because of a character named Frank Merriwell, who was created by "Burt L. Standish," who was born William Gilbert Patten.

When a fifteen-year-old boy named Gil Patten read his first dime novel, *Corinna,* the state of Maine lost a potential preacher. It was one of Colonel Prentiss Ingraham's most exciting pirate yarns. The boy was completely entranced by the tale which began:

> A rumbling roar of fury broke from the crew, and they hurled themselves upon their captain while shots resounded through the cabin. They were fired by the youth, and the bullets found the hearts of those they were aimed for, his two pistols spitting red in the dark.
> But it did not check the maddened buccaneers, and rushing forward, a dozen seized the boy and he, too, was crashed bodily to the floor.
> "Freelance is dead!"
> The cry came from the lips of the ringleader, as he rose to his feet, a drawn knife in his hand, the blade crimsoned to the hilt.

Henceforth, young Gil would devour every adventure story he could lay his hands on, and it wasn't long before he felt compelled to write a story of his own. He sent it off to Beadle's. While waiting for the rejection slip, he wrote another and sent that to Beadle's. He enclosed a letter to Orville J. Victor, the editor, telling him of his ambition to be a writer and asking for advice. Apparently Editor Victor saw something in the two short stories. He not only accepted them both, but wrote young Gil a long letter giving him some pointers. He also enclosed a check for six dollars for the two stories. When Gil's father, a carpenter, saw the check, he was dumfounded. He couldn't understand how anyone could be paid just for sitting down at a desk and scribbling anything that came into his head. Gil's mother shook her head sadly; her dream of making her son a preacher was over.

A month later Gil (he was never called anything else) wrote a longer story, and this time he received a check for fifty dollars. It was called *The Diamond Sport; or, The Double Face of Bed Rock.* Gil Patten began to write in earnest.

He went to New York to visit Orville Victor and was entranced by the kindly and sympathetic editor. Victor himself had written a scholarly life of Lincoln and several historical works which had been well received by serious critics. For some thirty years he had been chief editor of all the Beadle publications. The first thing he did for young Patten was to introduce him to Colonel Prentiss Ingraham, who had been Patten's hero ever since he had read that first pirate tale. He also met Edward L. Wheeler, the creator of Deadwood Dick, a picturesque character who, dressed from head to foot in black, face always hidden by a black mask, had galloped furiously through hundreds of stories published by Beadle's.

Orville Victor put Patten to work. He wrote under his own name, William G. Patten, and various pseudonyms. Within four years, Patten had become one of Beadle's most prolific and popular authors. His average pay was $100 a novel. One day in 1894 Patten presented himself to his friend, Victor, and asked for a hundred-dollar advance.

"I know it's the policy of the firm to pay on acceptance," he said, "but I have an unfriendly landlord and I owe him considerable back rent. My new story, *The Thug's Terror,* will be out in ten days. There's a hundred dollars coming to me for that. You would do me a great favor by advancing me the hundred now."

"You'll have to see William Adams about that," the sympathetic editor said. "He's the head of this house now that Mr. Beadle has died. He's inaugurated a new policy. All checks for authors have to come from him."

Patten hurried to see William Adams. Adams listened to his story. Finally he reached for a checkbook and wrote out a check.

"I've broken a rule, Patten," William Adams said sternly, "by advancing you this money. But your story will not be out for another ten days, so I am deducting one dollar for each of those days."

Patten looked at the check and saw that it was for ninety dollars. He immediately resolved to say good-bye to the parsimonious firm. He decided to try Street & Smith. He had considerable trouble reaching either of the partners. A guardian of the Street & Smith portals told him that the firm was not looking for any more stories. "We've got a safe full of them, and we're not buying any more," he told Patten.

Patten hurried to a printer's and had some cards made. They read, "William G. Patten, representing *Boston Globe, American Press Associa-*

THE NUGGET LIBRARY

5 CENTS

Entered According to Act of Congress, in the Year 1891, by Street & Smith, in the Office of the Librarian of Congress. Entered as Second-class Matter at the New York, N. Y., Post Office. August 29, 1889. Issued Weekly. Subscription Price, $2.50 Per Year.   September 10, 1891.

No. 110.   STREET & SMITH, Publishers.   NEW YORK.   31 Rose St., N. Y. P. O. Box 2734.   5 Cents.

TOM EDISON, Jr.'s
PRAIRIE-SKIMMER TEAM.

By PHILIP READE.

IN A MOMENT TOM EDISON AND HIS FRIEND ROSE ABOVE THE AIR-SHIP'S DECK, AND IMMEDIATELY OPENED FIRE UPON BLUE MASK AND HIS VILLAINOUS CREW.

A cover from the Nugget Library, first published in 1889

tion, Golden Hours." Golden Hours was one of the most successful of the Beadle publications. He managed, with the help of the card, to get into the office of Edward Stratemeyer, who doubled in brass as fiction writer and editor for the firm. When Patten told Stratemeyer that he was the William G. Patten who had written so many of the Beadle & Adams novels, Stratemeyer looked incredulous.

"But that's impossible," he protested. "You're too young."

He finally convinced Stratemeyer that he was telling the truth and was given an assignment. Stratemeyer gave him a title, *The Boy from the West,* and told him to take it away from there. Two weeks later he brought in a finished sixty-thousand-word story.

"This is pretty good, Patten," Stratemeyer told him. "We'll give you a hundred dollars for it."

"Not enough," young Patten said. "The title belongs to you, but the story is mine and I'll sell it somewhere else."

But Stratemeyer didn't let him go. He bargained with Patten and finally agreed to give him $150 for the story. This was just as good an investment for the firm as had been the four dollars Ormond Smith had paid for Frederic Dey's lunch a few short years before. During the following years Patten would write twenty million words for Street & Smith.

A year or so after he had begun writing for the firm, Ormond Smith suggested that in view of the fact that he was to be a Street & Smith author, he would appreciate it if Patten would find a pseudonym. The name William G. Patten had been too closely associated with the Beadle publications to please Ormond Smith. They agreed on the name "Burt L. Standish." Shortly after Patten went back to Maine to visit his parents. While there, he received a letter from Ormond Smith. It read:

December 16, 1895

Gilbert Patten, Esq.,
    Camden, Maine.
Dear Sir:

Replying to your favor of December 13, at hand today, we beg to state that the material of which we wrote you in our last letter is intended for a library which we purpose issuing every week; something in the line of the Jack Harkaway stories, Gay Dashleigh series which we are running in *Good News* and the Island School Series, all of which are expressed to you under separate cover, the idea being to issue a library containing a series of stories covering this class of incident, in all of which will appear one prominent character surrounded by suitable satellites. It would be an advantage to the series to have introduced the Dutchman, the Negro, the Irishman, and any other dialect that you are familiar with. From what we know of your work, we believe you can give us what we require, and would be pleased to have you write us one of these stories at once. Upon receipt of it, if satisfactory, we will be prepared to make a contract with you to cover twenty thousand words weekly for this library and a sufficient number of *Good News* stories to keep them running in the columns of *Good News,* if you believe you can turn out this amount of work.

It is important that the main character in the series should have a catchy name, such as Dick Lightheart, Jack Harkaway, Gay Dashleigh, Don Kirk (a character in two previous stories by Patten) as upon this name will depend the title for the library.

The essential idea of this series is to interest young readers in the career of a young man at a boarding school, preferably a military or a naval academy. The stories should differ from the Jack Harkaways in being American and thoroughly up to date. Our idea is to issue, say, twelve stories, each complete in itself, but like the links in a chain, all dealing with life at the academy. By this time the readers will have become sufficiently well acquainted with the hero, and the author will also no doubt have exhausted most of the pranks and escapades that might naturally occur.

After the first twelve numbers, the hero is obliged to leave the academy, or takes it upon himself to leave. It is essential that he should come into a considerable amount of money at this period. When he leaves the academy he takes with him one of the professor's servants, a chum. In fact any of the characters you have introduced and made prominent in the story. A little love element would also not be amiss, though this is not particularly important.

When the hero is once projected on his travels there is an infinite variety of incident to choose from. In the Island School Series, published by one of our London connections, you will find scenes of foreign travel, with color. This material you are at liberty to use freely, with our hero as the central character, of course, and up-to-date dialogue.

After we run through twenty or thirty numbers of this, we would bring the hero back and have him go to college—say, Yale University; thence we could take him on his travels again to the South Seas or anywhere.

If you can do the opening stories of school life, you will be able to do them all, as we shall assist you in the matter of local color for the stories of travel.

This letter will, of course, be held as confidential. After you have fully examined the Island School material, kindly return to us.

Yours truly,
Ormond Smith

January 3, 1896

Gilbert Patton, Esq.,

Camden, Maine.

Dear Sir:

We have just finished reading your manuscript
story "Frank Merriwell; or, First Days at Fardale",
which you submitted in accordance with ours of the 16th
ult., to fill the want spoken of in that letter. We are
entirely satisfied with this story, and satisfied that
you can do the work we require. As previously stated,
it is our idea to issue a library of school adventure,
and we fully expect that this library will be successful.
We are willing to make a contract with you for the entire
work, assured that you will be able to please us. It
must, however, be borne in mind that each story should be
complete in itself.

We shall not care to start the library until we
have at least ten numbers in hand, so that we shall be
in no danger of running bare of material.

You have selected a good name for the hero of the
story. It is understood that this name is to be one of
the firm copyrights and trade marks, just as Nick Carter is.

Hoping that everything will be satisfactory and
that this will be the beginning of a long and favorable
connection, we remain

Yours truly,

Street & Smith

Dict. O. G. S.

Street & Smith contracted with Patten for the Frank Merriwell stories

Patten liked the idea enormously. He had tremendous faith in the editorial acumen of Ormond Smith, and if Smith thought that the time was ripe for such a series, he would go along with him. He was glad, too, to be able to get away from the absurdities of the western fiction which he had been writing. He gave considerable thought to naming his character, and finally came up with the name, Frank Merriwell. He always described his character by saying, "His face was frank, open and winning, and a merry light usually dwelt in his eyes."

Within two weeks he had sent the firm a story which completely fulfilled all specifications laid down by Ormond Smith.

The first Frank Merriwell story which appeared in *Tip Top Weekly* discussed his school days at Fardale. It began:

FRANK MAKES A FOE

"Get out."

Thump! A shrill howl of pain.

"Stop it—that's my dog!"

"Oh, is it? Then you ought to be kicked too. Take that for your impudence!"

Cuff! A blow from an open hand sent the boyish owner of the whimpering poodle staggering to the ground, while paper bags of popcorn flew from his basket and scattered their contents around.

"That was a cowardly blow."

The haughty, overdressed lad who had knocked the little popcorn vendor down, after kicking the bare-footed boy's dog, turned sharply as he heard these words, and he found himself face to face with a youth of an age not far from his own.

This was Frank Merriwell, who had just stepped from the train at Fardale.

This was Frank Merriwell's introduction to juvenile America. It was love at first sight. Fardale was a military academy where the discipline was strict. But young Frank didn't mind it a bit.

Within three months circulation of the *Tip Top Weekly* had climbed to seventy-five thousand. Burt L. Standish continued to turn out twenty-thousand-word stories about Frank Merriwell every week. He never had any trouble with his plots, but finally his hands became tired from pounding the heavy, cumbersome typewriters of the 1890's, and he learned to dictate to a relay of secretaries. All of the Frank Merriwell stories were built on the formula originally concocted by Ormond Smith. Invariably, Frank Merriwell was tested in some crucial way so that certain aspects of his character were thrown into high relief. Frank was brave, honest, intelligent and, unlike most juvenile fiction heroes of the day, he had a sense of humor. Almost overnight he became the American Boy.

Burt L. Standish was shrewd enough to realize that millions of American youngsters were beginning to identify themselves with Frank Merriwell. He cleverly endowed Frank with a few boyish weaknesses, such as a liking for gambling, but needless to say, his strength of character always overcame these weaknesses. The popular story based on character was a novelty during the 1890's.

At one point, Ormond Smith and his brother wondered if Patten wasn't over-emphasizing Frank Merriwell's character and not giving enough play to his physical courage. They discussed this with the author one day at lunch. Long afterward Patten wrote of the conversation in his memoirs.

"Here's what I mean," Ormond Smith said. "In your current story Merriwell does nothing for two pages but take care of his horse —feeds him, waters him, rests him, and so on. I don't believe that appeals to boys."

"I think you're wrong," Patten said. "Merriwell has been repeatedly identified as a humane character. Being kind to animals is part of his nature. In the second place, most of the boys who read these stories are crazy about horses, and when they read how Merriwell takes care of his horse, that brings the story closer to them. Get your mind off action. Pure action is going to eventually kill the dime novel. Action can get pretty dreary unless there is some character in it that you can get interested in."

Smith nodded thoughtfully. "Perhaps you're right."

"Let me ask you one thing," Patten said. "Are these stories selling?"

Smith laughed and turned to his brother. "He has us there, all right. The stories do sell. They may lack excitement, but they've got something that youngsters love. I guess we'd better let Patten alone to do his stories his own way."

After four years at Fardale, Patten sent Frank to Yale. He made the football team immediately, and every year won the game against Harvard single-handed in the last minute of play. Old Eli never had a student or an athlete like Frank Merriwell. During Merriwell's junior year, Patten went to see Ormond and George Smith with a troublesome problem.

TIP TOP QUARTERLY

Issued Quarterly. By subscription, $2.00 per year. Entered as second-class matter at the New York post-office by Street & Smith.

VOL I. No. 1.   SEPTEMBER, 1896.   PRICE FIFTY CENTS.

FRANK MERRIWELL ON HIS METTLE
or FIELD DAY AT FARDALE
By the Author of FRANK MERRIWELL

LAUGHING AND BLUSHING, FRANK WAS LIFTED TO THE TOP OF A BOX.

An early Frank Merriwell story

"A year from now Merriwell will graduate from Yale," he said seriously. "What then? I can't keep him in college more than four years, but when he graduates he'll be a man, and young readers are apt to lose interest in him."

They concocted the idea of having Frank's parents lose all of their money, which necessitated his leaving college at the end of his junior year. So he set Frank Merriwell to working on the railroad. He did pretty well for a college junior. He settled a strike, recovered the fortune his parents had lost, and then finally went back to finish his college career. He, of course, had a fabulous final year at Yale, just as fabulous as the circulation of *Tip Top*.

Because his academic standing was so high, Frank was able to take a few days off whenever he felt like it, which was a great boon to Author Patten. He could invent all sorts of adventures for his hero on New York week ends. Occasionally, he had to lead Merriwell into a bar where (to protect a friend) he had to simulate drinking. The first time this happened his friend, Jack Diamond (in the clutches of two gamblers), was horrified. Merriwell had calmly ordered a straight gin with a water chaser. Diamond, a little the worse for alcoholic wear, pleaded with him not to take the drink.

> "We are old friends, Merriwell," said Diamond, still with the same air of polite intoxication, "and I'd do anything for you. You know it. You're the best all-around man in Yale—the best man that ever entered the college. You have no vices. You are clean from your toes to the tip-ends of your hair. You've never poisoned yourself with tobacco or drink or high living of any sort. You've always taken the very best of care of your body and your mind. Now, don't tell me you are going to spoil it all by making a fool of yourself and drinking gin!"

Diamond did not know, of course, that the canny Frank Merriwell switched the two glasses; he drank the water and pushed the straight gin back to the bartender. It is hardly necessary to add that Frank never allowed liquor of any kind to pass his lips. The bartender had heard Diamond and the two confidence men mention Merriwell's name.

> "Are you Frank Merriwell of Yale, the great athlete I've read so much about in the papers?" the bartender asked in awed tone.
> "I presume I am the same," Merry answered modestly.

The two men who were out to fleece the affluent Mr. Diamond led the little party to Canfield's Gambling Casino. Here, Author Patten did a rather surprising thing. He described the de-luxe gambling establishment minutely, and then introduced Canfield himself as one of the characters. Patten often did this; it added verisimilitude to his stories and convinced millions of youngsters that this was not fiction at all—it was all true.

Patten's knowledge of Yale was derived from attending four or five football games and walking around the New Haven campus, and if his picture of the University lacked a certain authenticity, it was a pleasant picture accepted by the boys of America, and it is a fact that hundreds of them in later life entered Yale because their interest in the institution had been aroused by early reading of Merriwell stories.

The Merriwell series just about sunk Beadle & Adams, and it made Street & Smith the biggest firm in its field. Ormond Smith (he was now referred to as "O.G." by the trade) had a wonderful knack for realizing the full potential of any literary property. When the success of the Merriwell yarns in *Tip Top Weekly* was assured, he exploited the character further by gathering three or four of the tales, giving them a loose continuity, and publishing them as fifteen-cent paper-backed books under the title, *The Frank Merriwell Series*. This, of course, met with phenomenal success and more than two hundred of them were published. He did this with Nick Carter, Diamond Dick, Buffalo Bill and a dozen others.

Numerous newspaper and magazine articles have been written to explain the astounding popularity of Frank Merriwell (and to a far lesser degree, that of his younger brother, Dick Merriwell). James Cain wrote a long analysis for the *Saturday Evening Post* in 1927. George Jean Nathan, writing for *The American Mercury,* then edited by Mencken and himself, wrote an article in 1925 in which he discussed the impact the All-American Boy had on the youth of the nation.

> A book I should like to read—and doubtless there are thousands of ex-youngsters of the 1880's and early 90's who have the same feeling about it as I have—would be a biography, or better still, an autobiography, if he is still living, of the man known as Burt Standish, author of the famous Frank Merriwell literature . . . I doubt, in all seriousness, if there was an American writer of twenty-five and thirty years ago who was so widely known and so widely read by the boys of the time. His readers numbered millions, and included all sorts of young men,

rich and poor. For one who read Mark Twain's *Huckleberry Finn,* or *Tom Sawyer,* there were ten thousand who read Standish's *Frank Merriwell's Dilemma,* or *The Rescue of Inza* and *Frank Merriwell at Yale,* or *The Winning Last Quarter-Mile.* The little candy and cigar stores of that day, the chief distributing centers of the Standish *opera,* had longer lines of small boys with nickels in their hands every Friday than Barnum's or Forepaugh's circus could ever boast. . . .

Merriwell was one of the most profitable publishing ventures, I am told, that the country has ever known, and Street & Smith, his impresarios, made a fortune out of him. . . .

Deadwood Dick had always been one of Beadle & Adams' greatest successes. The character had originated with Edward L. Wheeler of Titusville, Pennsylvania, and if it be true—as his critics claimed— that he never set foot west of that city, he certainly gave many millions the flavor of the gun-totin' frontier folk. His personal stationery read, "Edward L. Wheeler. Sensational Novelist," and he was just that. Deadwood Dick was adventure, glamor, romance; he was called prince of the road as he roamed the Black Hills straight into the hearts of American boys.

Legend has it that Wheeler used Richard W. Clark, a Nebraska prospector, as the prototype of his hero. Clark was quite a man in his own right. As a young man, he wasn't exactly a bandit—he was just mischievous (this, at least, is the story widely printed in afteryears, and if there is little truth in it, apologies to the shade of Richard Clark are humbly made). Clark, who liked to look upon the grog when it was red, would often stagger from a gambling hall, ride a few miles out of town and wait for the stagecoach. He had found a black branch from a tree that closely resembled a gun; he would point this at the stagecoach driver and utter the classic formula, "Your money or your life." The driver would not spend too much time deciding as to which alternative was the more attractive. He would toss the gold he was transporting to the masked figure and hurry away. Clark, after a decent interval of hiding out, would hurry back to the town, buy drinks for everyone in the joint and proceed to do his best to lose the rest of it gambling. He would tell with lusty laughter how he had held up the gold-laden stagecoach with a harmless stick, and no one ever prosecuted him. By the bizarre standards of the day, he was a harmless prankster. He was then in his early twenties. He became an Indian fighter in the 21st Cavalry, a Pony Express rider, and then a scout for Custer.

Very sincerely Yours,
W. B. Lawson.

Well, Boys ! the publishers wanted my picture in the first number of GOOD NEWS, so here I am.

Messrs. STREET & SMITH instructed me to get up the best paper that money can produce, and a glance at the material in this week's GOOD NEWS will show that we have begun well.

Those of you who have read my "DIAMOND DICK" stories cannot doubt that it is a congenial task for me to work for your pleasure, whether with my pen, or through the acquisition for our paper of the choicest stories by your favorite authors.

Your patronage will indicate how well I shall succeed, and if you want the best weekly out, I am certain to win you all over to GOOD NEWS.

William Wallace Cook (W.B. Lawson)

Somehow Wheeler heard about him and based Deadwood Dick on this colorful character of the Black Hills. Wheeler added something that hitherto had been lacking in stories of the Wild West—a feminine character, Calamity Jane. She was quite a gal with a six-shooter, but although she was fond of her friend, Deadwood Dick, she would never marry him.

Ormond Smith obviously had to find a rival for this popular Beadle character, and he found it in Diamond Dick. The similarity of the names was hardly a coincidence. Smith seldom did anything editorially that wasn't carefully calculated. William Wallace Cook began this series under the name of W. B. Lawson and it continued for many years, with various writers doing the actual scribbling. But in the beginning (we lean on legend and newspapers of forty years ago here) it was Richard Tanner, an old frontier fighter, who inspired Cook and his successors. After his hard-riding, quick-shooting days on the plains with Custer, Tanner joined a Wild West show and gave exhibitions of his marvelous shooting skill to open-mouthed eastern audiences. In the late 1890's no one heard much of Richard Tanner, but they heard a great deal about Diamond Dick. It wasn't long before he rivaled Beadle & Adams' Deadwood Dick. He and his friend, "Handsome Harry" (who believed that his mission in life was to protect his hero from harm), galloped through millions of words and into America's affection in the Diamond Dick Library.

CHAPTER

FIVE

NEW YORK
FIVE CENT LIBRARY

STREET & SMITH

A cover of *Popular Magazine* by N. C. Wyeth; the magazine
was first published in 1903

CHAPTER

FIVE

The Mauve Decade, as Thomas Beer called the ten years embracing the 1890's, was a period when sophistication, realism and satire had not yet come into fashion. The middle class surveyed life and found it good. Politicians and financial giants talked glowingly of new frontiers, of opportunity, and pointed out that a man, no matter how humble his birth and circumstances, could, by diligence, rise above them.

The people had confidence in the future. The experiment called democracy, borrowed from the philosophy of Jean Jacques Rousseau, was working well, and this was by far the best of all possible worlds. Ostrichlike, people ignored the sordid stains on the shining escutcheon; ruthless, unprincipled, uneducated men were ruling the nation with a cynicism and dishonesty which had become congenital in public life, but the people looked on apathetically. Individuals of unparalleled energy were killing individualism for the benefit of their private purses, but people were so dazzled by the possibility that their sons might eventually join the ranks of the giants that they closed their eyes to the cynicism and dishonesty.

There was an educated class of men and women who were aware that this was not the best of all possible worlds, but their feeble voices were drowned out by happy choruses of "Only a Bird in a Gilded Cage" or "My Gal Sal" (written by Theodore Dreiser's brother, Paul). This small minority was reading Stephen Crane's *The Red Badge of Courage,* the first unsentimental war story to appear in American literature. They were reading *Harper's Magazine,* which had published Walter Pater's *Apollo in Picardy,* and *Lippincott's Magazine* which had published Oscar Wilde's *The Picture of Dorian Gray.* They

Universitas
SCHOLA
BIBLIO ⁀RUM

read *The Century, The Nation, The Arena* and *The Atlantic,* all of which published "serious" articles and "serious" fiction. But Ormond Smith (who, for his own enjoyment, read Voltaire in French and studied and rejected the philosophy of Friedrich Nietzsche) felt that the public was not ready for anything that didn't appeal to the mass mind. The others could publish stories for the "Four Hundred"; he would continue to publish for the four million. It was not cynicism on his part; he was simply being realistic. Highly cultured himself, already in the process of collecting what would eventually be one of the finest private libraries in New York, he still understood the quality of the mass mind in the nineties. He knew exactly what it would assimilate and he gave it to them.

Whether or not Smith ever read Bacon's line: "Creative literature is nothing but feigned history," it was a precept Smith took to his editorial heart. What were the Buffalo Bill stories but feigned history? The Nick Carter stories and the tracts of Holy Horatio were nothing but sugar-coated imitations of contemporary history. He gave the public more of the same, and in the process made Street & Smith the largest publishing firm in the world.

It was the many libraries for adolescent readers which really catapulted the firm into its great success. There was the New York Five-Cent Library, which had a strong sports flavor. There were stories about "John L., Jr." patterned after the great John L. Sullivan. Frank Merriwell, Nick Carter and Diamond Dick had libraries of their own, of course, and then there was the Red, White and Blue Library designed to cater to the spirit of patriotism presumably inherent in the breast of every red-blooded American boy. The stories were alternately about two boys, Ralph in the Navy and Phil in the Army. These two youngsters performed military and naval feats never dreamed of by the experts, and they were at all times ready to cry, "Hurray for the Red, White and Blue." But this one lasted only a year.

It was followed by *The Army and Navy Weekly,* which also appealed to the patriotic instinct.

Each week it presented a story about Mark Mallory of West Point or Clif (with one "f") Faraday of Annapolis. Just about everything was tossed into this publication (printed in such small type that only lads with perfect twenty-twenty vision could read it). There would be a page illustrating in drawing and text the setting-up exercises which made West Point cadets such marvels of posture, endurance and health, and this might be followed by *Tom Fenwick's Fortune; or, The Gold of Flat Top,* a story involving territory two thousand miles from either of our academies and presenting traditional western characters.

It survived for nearly three years. Meanwhile, still another little five-cent number was launched. It was called *The Starry Flag Weekly.* By now, the Spanish-American War had broken out and the first shots had hardly been fired before this publication dedicated to our brave boys fighting for Cuban independence hit the newsstands. Henry Harrison Lewis was the editor of this one, which featured a character named Hal Maynard of the U. S. Army. Lewis wrote a few of the Hal Maynard stories and then turned them over to a young man of considerable writing promise. He was unknown but articulate, and he could manufacture stories fast. His name was Upton Sinclair.

He was working on his first novel, *King Midas,* at that time, but he never allowed the left hand which wrote the novel to interfere

Pawnee Bill

The *New York Five Cent Weekly,* 1892

with the right hand which told how Hal Maynard was making out in Cuba. The Upton Sinclair whose fierce advocacy of socialism, diatribes against corruption and economic injustice would make him a controversial figure for half a century, had not yet emerged. The twenty-year-old Upton Sinclair was happy to lounge in Editor Lewis' office and discuss the plots which Lewis gave him to embellish.

Forty years later, when Upton Sinclair was running for Governor of California, a reporter dug up the fact that he had once labored in the Street & Smith vineyard. He confronted the candidate with the awful truth, and the candidate nodded and smiled happily.

"Yes, I wrote many of the Hal Maynard stories," he said. "And I wrote a lot of other stories for Street & Smith. You want to know something? I'm not ashamed of one of them. I was very young, but they were pretty good stories and they never did the boys who read them any harm."

True Blue was another weekly, "Devoted to the Stirring Adventures of Our Boys in Blue."

The ubiquitous Clif (still with one "f") Faraday was begun again. On the back cover was the admonition that "In these stirring times of war every American boy should wear a patriotic emblem to show where his sympathies lay. Any boy who sends us three coupons, one from each of any three of our weeklies, will be sent a Dewey medal." Thousands and thousands of requests for the medals poured into the office; thousands and thousands of extra copies of the various weeklies were sold.

Some of the advertisements in *True Blue* and *Starry Flag Weekly* are, in retrospect, rather puzzling. These two, for instance, seem hardly the type to make boys rush to buy the products.

TORMONS TABLETS

cure all disorders of the Liver, Stomach, and Bowels, Headache, Dyspepsia, Constipation, Biliousness, Dizziness; Clears the Complexion, Increases the Appetite, Tones the System, and is a Sure Remedy for Depression of Spirits, General Debility, Kidney Complaints, Nervousness, Sour Stomach, Disturbed Sleep, etc.

Mention *Army and Navy*

CONSUMPTION CURED

An old physician, retired from practice, had placed in his hands by an East India missionary, the formula of a simple vegetable remedy for

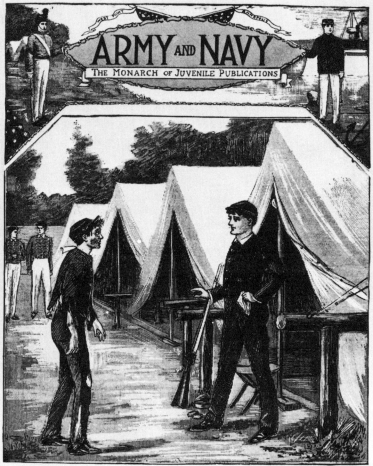

Cover of *Army and Navy Weekly,* first published in 1897

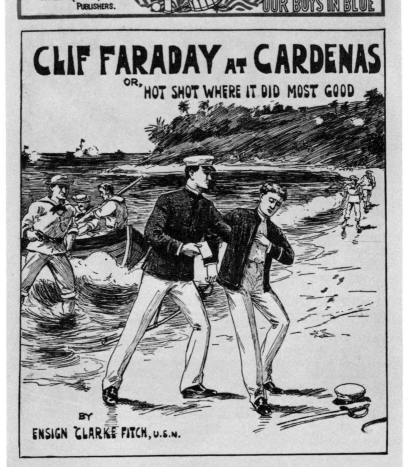

Upton Sinclair takes his hero to Cuba in 1898

the speedy and permanent cure of Consumption, Bronchitis, Catarrh, Asthma, and all Throat and Lung Affections, also a positive and radical cure for Nervous Debility and all Nervous Complaints. Having tested its wonderful curative powers in thousands of cases, and desiring to relieve human suffering, I will send free of charge to all who wish it, this recipe, in German, French, or English with full directions for preparing and using. Sent by mail by addressing, with stamp, naming this paper. W. A. Noyes, 320 Power's Block, Rochester, N. Y.

Unfortunately for the firm, the Spanish-American War didn't last long enough to develop into a lasting economic asset. When it ended, the patriotic weeklies soon died of inattention. But the firm was always ready to replace a fallen library with a new recruit. Klondike Kit was such a draftee. Klondike Kit was an intrepid young man who went off to Alaska to hunt for gold. He had to be constantly on guard against the bad men who had deserted the western camps to prey upon fine young men in Alaska, but Kit was lucky enough to find a brave and beautiful ally—Nugget Nell was her name. William Wallace Cook, experienced and able, wrote this series, and thousands of boys fell in love with the brave, resourceful and sweet Nugget Nell.

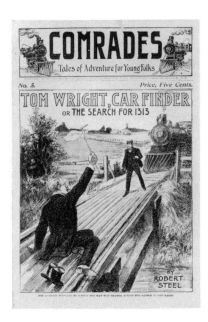 

Comrades and *Do and Dare* were two weeklies first published in 1900

Other publishers, envious of the success of Street & Smith weeklies, began to turn out imitations. There were several attempts to capture the Frank Merriwell public, and Ormond Smith, dazzled by his own success, conceived the brilliant idea of becoming his own imitator. The firm issued the *Do and Dare* series, a pallid copy of its own product. These were written by Ernest A. Young and were based on the adventures of a new fictional character, Phil Rushington. Phil first went to Springvale Academy (just as Merriwell had gone to Fardale). Phil joined a circus, went on the stage, became a miner, in fact, he did everything and more than Merry had ever done. Phil lasted two years. No one could really compete with Frank Merriwell.

To thousands of youngsters in the 1890's, the railroad engineer had become almost a godlike creature. Not many of these youngsters could ever become engineers, but Ormond Smith saw to it that they could read about a boy who did. *Comrades* was a five-cent weekly which highlighted the adventures of Tom Wright, a youthful railroader who became an expert locomotive engineer. The stories were turned out by Weldon J. Cobb, Frederick R. Burton, and John H. Whitson, all writing under the name of Robert Steel. The first issue announced:

> Tom Wright, the hero of *Comrades,* is a bright boy who has decided to devote his life to the service of "King Steam" in one of the great railroads of our land. Rest assured he will reach fame and fortune on the lightning express. The life of an ambitious railroad man is full of exciting incident, and Tom has his full share of adventures. Through all of these, he will be found Wright by name, right in word, right in deed, and always right . . .

Now Ormond Smith decided to do something really radical in the way of a weekly. He would give the girls of America a publication of their very own. It was called *My Queen, a Weekly Journal for Young Women.* Lurana W. Sheldon wrote these stories, which concern themselves with a farmer's daughter named Marion Marlowe. She was not subjected to the usual peril of the conventional farmer's daughter pursued by traveling salesmen, but her life was brimful of excitement. In succeeding issues she was presented as a hospital nurse, an actress and a detective. When Marion Marlowe walked into a department store,

George C. Smith, Ormond V. Gould, George C. Smith, Jr., and Ormond G. Smith

MY QUEEN
A WEEKLY JOURNAL FOR YOUNG WOMEN

No. 5.

PRICE, FIVE CENTS.

MARION MARLOWE ENTRAPPED
OR
THE VICTIM OF PROFESSIONAL JEALOUSY

BY GRACE SHIRLEY

PUBLISHED WEEKLY BY STREET & SMITH, 238 William Street, New York City.
Copyright, 1900, by Street & Smith. All rights reserved. Entered at New York Post-Office as Second-Class Matter.

My Queen was first published in 1900

. . . every person in the store stopped work to stare at her. Such a vision of loveliness was seldom seen in this atmosphere of business life. . . . Marion Marlowe was a little over seventeen but tall for her age, and her lithe, slender form was beautifully molded. Her skin was perfect, and her lips like cherries, while the wealth of chestnut hair that adorned her queenly head was as soft and rippled as daintily as an infant's.

Marion's diverse activities can perhaps be best summed up by listing a few of the titles which appeared in *My Queen*.

1 - FROM FARM TO FORTUNE;
OR, ONLY A FARMER'S DAUGHTER

2 - MARION MARLOWE'S COURAGE;
OR, A BRAVE GIRL'S STRUGGLE FOR LIFE AND HONOR;

3 - MARION MARLOWE'S TRUE HEART;
OR, HOW A DAUGHTER FORGAVE

4 - MARION MARLOWE'S NOBLE WORK;
OR, THE TRAGEDY AT THE HOSPITAL

5 - MARION MARLOWE ENTRAPPED;
OR, THE VICTIM OF PROFESSIONAL JEALOUSY

6 - MARION MARLOWE'S PERIL;
OR, A MYSTERY UNVEILED

Covers from the Bertha M. Clay Library, begun in 1900

A feature of the publication was the department called "Questions and Answers," which announced:

> Note—This department . . . will be conducted by Miss Grace Shirley, whose remarkable ability to answer all questions, no matter how delicate the import, will be much appreciated, we feel sure, by all our readers, who need not hesitate to write her on any subject. Miss Shirley will have their interests at heart and never refuse her assistance or sympathy.

This became a tremendously successful column, a forerunner of the Advice to the Lovelorn soon to be nationally syndicated in newspapers. Grace Shirley (the pen name of Lurana W. Sheldon) advised the hundreds of young girls who wrote to her never to argue politics with a man, never to accept the attentions of young men they had just met and to forget hopeless infatuations for married men (nearly every issue presented this problem to the helpful Grace Shirley). Each week, letters such as the following would elicit saccharine advice from Grace Shirley:

> Will you kindly answer the following question? Can two people live comfortably on twelve dollars a week? I am engaged to be married to a young man who earns eight dollars a week while I earn four. By putting our salaries together, do you think we could live in comfort?
>
> M. C.
>
> We do not approve of marriage on a financial basis. You do not mention in your letter whether you love the young man or not. We shall have to hear your sentiments and his, also, on this subject before advising you. If you really wish Grace Shirley's advice, you must tell me your age, your expectations and ambitions.

One ad which always appeared in *My Queen* was the popular one advertising a cure for drunkards, by Dr. J. W. Haines. It read:

THE JESSE JAMES STORIES

A WEEKLY DEALING WITH THE DETECTION OF CRIME

Issued Weekly. By Subscription $2.50 per year. Entered as Second Class Matter at New York Post Office by STREET & SMITH, 238 William St., N. Y.

No. 90.   **Price, Five Cents.**

JESSE JAMES ALARMED

OR TRAILED BY OLD ZEKE THE DETECTIVE

W. B. LAWSON

JESSE JAMES RAISED HIS REVOLVER, TOOK AIM AT THE SWAYING FIGURE OF THE HANGING DETECTIVE, AND FIRED

A cover from *Jesse James Stories,* first published in 1901

DRUNKARDS

We Want All Our Readers to Know How Mrs. Chas. W. Harry Cured Her Husband

Costs Nothing To Try

It takes a woman to overcome obstacles. Mrs. Chas. W. Harry, 522 E. 4th St., Newport, Ky., had for years patiently borne the disgrace, suffering, misery and privation due to her husband's drinking habits. Learning there was a cure for drunkenness which she could give her husband secretly, she decided to try it. She mixed it in his food and coffee, and, as the remedy is odorless and tasteless, he never knew what it was that so quickly relieved the craving for liquor. He soon began to pick up in flesh, his appetite for solid food returned, he stuck to his work regularly, and they now have a happy home . . .

Dr. Haines, the discoverer, will send a trial package of this grand remedy free . . . securely sealed in a plain wrapper, also full directions how to use it, books and testimonials from hundreds who have been cured, and everything needed to aid you in saving those near and dear to you from a life of degradation and ultimate poverty and disgrace.

Marion Marlowe's life was not long, editorially, but it was amazingly profitable. Actually, the young women of America had more enthusiasm for the New Bertha M. Clay Library. Bertha Clay herself had long since died, but a half dozen of the most prolific men in the Fiction Factory were turning out the Bertha M. Clay stories rapidly and efficiently. These continued to make money for years. Ormond Smith might have summed up his editorial policy in the 1890's in one word—"diversity."

If George C. Smith seems neglected in these pages, it is not because he wasn't an immensely valuable partner in the enterprise. Ormond seldom launched a new venture without long consultation with his vice-president brother whom he liked and admired tremendously. When they agreed on a project (and they seldom disagreed), George C. busied himself with the task of physically launching the new publication. It was up to him to purchase the newsprint, to oversee the actual printing of the publication and to handle the hundreds of details involved in its distribution and advertising. The brothers formed a felicitous team. O. G. was the Boss, G. C. was second-in-command and the various editors worked under their joint direction. Few editors (except a veteran like Tom Glynn, still running *The New York Weekly*) were given free rein to direct their publications. Any new ideas or above-budget expenditures had to be approved by one of the owners. Editors never objected to the set-up; it was pointless to quarrel with success, and O. G. and G. C. had proven themselves to be masters of the trade.

A company practice had been to work a vein until it ran dry and then try to revive it with a new treatment. *Shield Weekly* was one such experiment. Frederick W. Davis, of Onset, Massachusetts, had been writing successful detective serials for the *Boston Globe* for years under the name of Scott Campbell. Ormond Smith lured him away, and for some time he had been a handy literary jack-of-all-trades, filling in wherever needed. O. G. suggested to Davis that if he could create a satisfactory character Smith would give him a weekly in whose pages the character could roam. The result was "Sheridan Keene," a master detective who became very popular with readers of the *Shield Weekly*. Later, these stories were lengthened by Davis and published by the firm as paper-backed books.

The Jesse James stories began to appear in the form of a weekly. They were signed by W. B. Lawson (who was either Prentiss Ingra-

A complaint killed the *Jesse James Series*

ham or L. W. Sheldon). This five-cent weekly was tremendously popular. Jesse James was one of the first outlaws to be made a hero in Street & Smith publications. Of course, Jesse (in fiction) was rather a humane type of outlaw. After 121 Jesse James titles appeared (at considerable profit to the firm), Ormond Smith took notice of the attacks on the publication because it glorified crime—which indeed it did. Smith, convinced that for once the critics were right, dropped it overnight.

Teddy Roosevelt had hardly dismounted from his horse after charging up San Juan Hill when the firm of Street & Smith emerged with *The Young Rough Riders Weekly*. Each issue consisted of a five-thousand-word short story describing the adventures of Ted Strong who, needless to say, had been one of the volunteers with Teddy Roosevelt and who had fought in the Philippines. All of these were written by Ned Taylor.

Later, a column, "A Chat with You," was added. Many of the letters of extravagant praise sound as though they had been written in the office of the firm, but actually, the old files show that hundreds of letters did, in fact, come in from young readers every week.

These five-cent weeklies followed each other in bewildering succession. As soon as one of them started to slip by way of newsstand returns, it was scrapped and a new one begun. They had different titles, but each had the same appeal. The Bowery Boy Library enjoyed great popularity for a time. Its appeal was articulated in an editor's note which introduced the first issue:

> American lads have always eagerly read stories of life among the street Arabs of our great cities. There appears to be some peculiar charm connected with these scenes among the lowly, even to boys who have never seen New York. To them the Bowery stands for all that is adventurous and mysterious, while its jostling crowds are the various actors in the exciting drama of real life. Believing that an up-to-date weekly would be gladly welcomed, if devoted *exclusively* to stories based upon the exciting adventures experienced by wide-awake street boys, we have launched the Bowery Boy Library. It speaks for itself.

Edward Stratemeyer, a nervous, kindly, near-sighted, stocky man who had begun by editing *Good News,* was now doing everything but set type. He was writing dime novels under the names of Jim Bowie, Nat Woods and Jim Daly, and writing serials aimed at women for the *Weekly* under the name of Julie Edwards. He was also acting as a sort of editor-in-chief without title for the firm. When Horatio Alger died in 1899, he left a few unfinished manuscripts. Stratemeyer picked up where Alger left off and finished them to everyone's satisfaction. Stratemeyer was one of the few writers of his day who was also a good business man. He eventually left Street & Smith to start a little series called *The Rover Boys*. He wrote thirty of them in the form of novels (published by Grosset & Dunlap) which sold for fifty cents, and he lived to see five million copies of them bought. He did these under the name of Arthur M. Winfield. His *Motor Boys,* by Clarence Young, and his *Tom Swift* books, by Victor Appleton, were just as popular. Stratemeyer trained a whole stable of writers to manufacture these stories, and he died a wealthy man. But during the late 1890's he was just one of Ormond Smith's hired hands—and one of his best.

Meanwhile, what dish was Street & Smith serving to adults? What else but the old *New York Weekly,* still going strong as it approached the half-century mark. It had grown up a bit (but not too much).

There were still Bertha M. Clay stories, Nick Carter adventures

Edward Stratemeyer

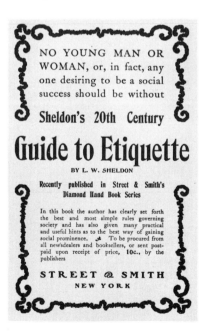

First "how-to" handbook

and serials by Mrs. Georgie Sheldon. There was still a column of homespun philosophy by Josh Billings, and the "Ladies' Work Box" was as popular as ever. The editorials were on such sparkling and provocative subjects as "The Practice of Reading Aloud" or "Economies in the Home." *The New York Weekly* had changed very little since 1855.

Ormond Smith, who was always more interested in books than in his weeklies, was going in for book publishing in a big way, and during the nineties this activity brought in huge profits. Smith was the first publisher to use four-color covers on his books. He bought the plates of more than a hundred novels which had first appeared in Robert Bonner's *Ledger*. He also acquired plates from M. J. Ives and Company, Norman L. Munro and from any other publishers who were in a selling mood. He published sixteen books by Laura Jean Libbey, thirty by May Agnes Fleming, and then established the Arrow Library to publish reprints by foreign authors. Rudyard Kipling, Hall Caine, Conan Doyle, Robert Louis Stevenson, Marie Corelli, Victor Hugo, Jules Verne, H. Rider Haggard and many others were included among the 325 authors published in the Arrow Library. Another enterprise was the Magnet Library, which published only detective fiction. Needless to say, Nicholas Carter was well represented in this library.

In 1898, Ormond Smith published the Diamond Handbooks, fabulously successful guides to more or less useful knowledge. These books would give instructions on how to write a letter, cook a steak, photograph animals, interpret dreams, tell fortunes, and how to make everything that could conceivably be of use in the home. During that same year, Street & Smith published a series of religious books under the title of The Alliance Library. Included in this was *In His Steps,* by the Reverend Charles M. Sheldon, which may well be the greatest best seller of all time (always excluding the Bible). The book was translated into twenty languages, and Sheldon himself said that it sold thirty million copies—probably an optimistic estimate. *What Is Christ to Me?* by the Reverend W. C. Stiles was another book which had an enormous sale in this fifty-cent edition.

These are just a few of the book ventures the firm launched during the nineties; all of them were an unqualified success.

CHAPTER

SIX

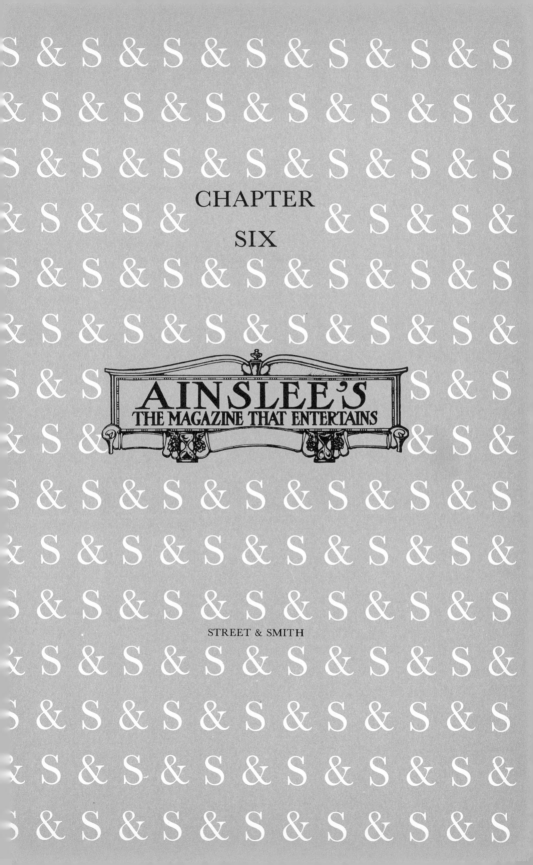

AINSLEE'S
THE MAGAZINE THAT ENTERTAINS

STREET & SMITH

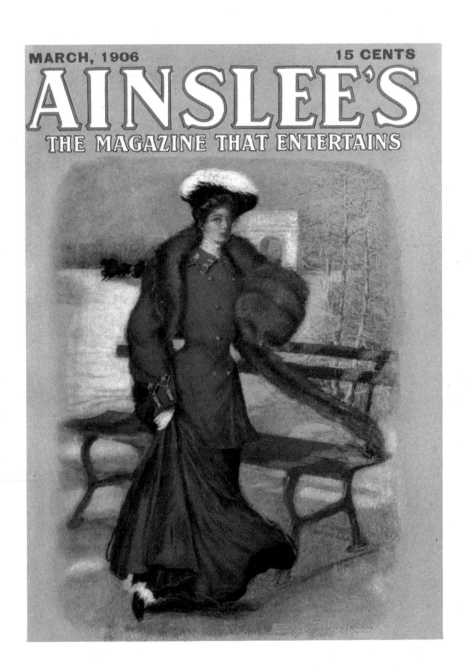

Cover of an *Ainslee's* magazine, first published in 1898

CHAPTER

SIX

In 1898, two important events occurred in the affairs of Street & Smith. A seventeen-year-old boy named Henry William Ralston joined the firm, and Ormond Smith decided to enter the magazine field with *Ainslee's*. (The *Weekly* had never been referred to as a "magazine"; neither had any of the Tip Top publications.) We'll consider the advent of young Ralston first, because successful as *Ainslee's* turned out to be, Henry Ralston outlasted it.

It was not Ormond Smith's policy to award titles, but a man by the name of Charles Bunce held a rather important job in the company as a combination circulation-promotion manager. One of his tasks was to arrange for advance blurbs of serials to be sent to strategic circulation points around the country. Bunce lived in Brooklyn, just a few doors down the street from the Ralston family. Henry Ralston, at seventeen, was concluding his second year at Adelphi College. He told his father's friend, Charles Bunce, that he wanted to work during the summer vacation. Bunce was glad to give the youngster a job in his department. Young Henry Ralston worked hard that summer helping to address and mail out thousands of pieces of promotional matter. He enjoyed the atmosphere at 238 William Street, liked many of his 180 fellow employees and welcomed the five-dollar-a-week salary he received. When fall came, he decided not to return to college. Bunce, pleased with his work, allowed Ralston to stay on. He had been with the concern for two years when Bunce died of pneumonia. One day Ormond Smith called him into his office.

"You think you can handle this job, Will?" he asked. He always called him Will, though he was Henry or Bill to his co-workers.

"I don't know," Ralston said frankly. "But I'd like to try it."

"How long a trial will you need, Will?" Smith asked.

"A year," the nineteen-year-old youngster blurted out. "Give me a year, and if you think I can handle it, let me have it. If not, fire me."

Smith nodded. "That sounds reasonable," he said. "Try it."

It was exactly a year later that he was again summoned to the august presence. Smith pointed to a desk calendar. "You know what day this is, Will?"

Ralston, puzzled, shook his head.

"You've been handling Charlie Bunce's job for exactly a year today. Do you think you've handled it well?" Smith asked.

Ralston gulped. "I—I—just don't know. That's up to you."

"I think you've taken over very well," Smith reassured him. "The job is yours. Starting tomorrow, your salary is eighteen dollars a week. That is, if you want the job."

Ralston took it. He remained for fifty-two years, eventually became Ormond Smith's right-hand man, vice-president of Street & Smith and a tower of editorial and administrative strength. He retired in 1950, and today raises the finest roses in Elmsford, New York. His neighbors, who think of this deceptively young-looking man as being in his early sixties, may well disbelieve the records which show that he went to work for the firm fifty-seven years ago.

During the late 1890's a furious newspaper war broke out between Joseph Pulitzer, owner of *The New York World,* and William Randolph Hearst, who had bought a defunct daily called *The Journal.* Until the advent of Hearst, the *World* had a monopoly on New York's mass circulation; Hearst set out to capture this circulation. Pulitzer was a crusader, and although he insisted upon accuracy, he saw no reason why facts should not be presented in a sensational manner. Hearst began to give Pulitzer lessons in the sensational presentation of news. The *Journal* specialized in lurid stories, juicy scandals, provocative, strident headlines, and if there was no news on any given day, Hearst created it.

He published all kinds of features and fostered the talents of the greatest cartoonists, humorists and writers in the land. He wooed the naïve with a column by the first of the "sob sisters"; he attracted the literate with articles and stories by Mark Twain, Rudyard Kipling and Jack London. From Pulitzer, he borrowed the idea that vigorous intervention in public affairs would increase circulation. Readers of the *Journal* felt that he was their champion against the forces of entrenched privilege. Thousands who scorned his astonishingly flexible political principles bought the paper for its entertainment value. Ormond Smith observed the battle of the titans with his keen editorial eye. It was a battle which, in retrospect, seems to have ended in a draw. Both papers increased their respective circulations enormously.

This, however, was not the significant thing which caught Smith's eye. What undoubtedly disturbed him was the fact that people could buy for a penny reading and visual entertainment that he couldn't furnish them in his five-cent *New York Weekly*. He had a feeling that the time was coming when the *Weekly* would be outpaced by newspapers which printed fiction and feature stories. Its circulation was still tremendous, but Smith could sense the ground swell still far off but nonetheless inevitable.

New York was changing in a great many ways, and Smith studied the effects carefully. New habits, new tastes, new interests were simmering and bubbling over among the citizenry. The acceptance of

Henry William Ralston

An early *Ainslee's* cover

A cover of *The Yellow Kid,* first comic book, 1897

good writing by first-rate authors in both the *Journal* and the *World* was merely one straw in the wind. There were others. Even the face of the city was changing. The embryo giant called New York was beginning to stretch.

The first skyscrapers appeared as the city reached upward. The city started to sprawl in all directions and mass migrations began to the Bronx, Brooklyn and Staten Island. The Sixth and Ninth Avenue elevated railroads had been built and the upper West Side began to lose its rural aspect. Until that time, this neighborhood was the locale for the huge barns which housed the cars and horses of the Eighth Avenue surface trolley line. More than one million people were living on Manhattan Island and another ninety thousand lived in its suburbs.

The stretching giant made a great deal of noise as he flexed his muscles. All day long the rat-tat-tat of the automatic riveting machines, the shrill squeal of winches and the roar of old buildings being wrecked to make room for the new combined to form an ear-splitting symphony. It was evident now that Manhattan was becoming a vertical city. The thirteen-story Tower Building at 50 Broadway, the first of the island's skyscrapers, had weathered several winters of high winds without collapsing, and the more daring architects turned their backs on the traditional and began to plan tall edifices with skeletons of steel. The American Surety Company Building rose opposite Trinity Church on lower Broadway, and even further downtown the towering St. Paul Building climbed twenty-five stories into the startled sky. New hotels were being built uptown, and Times Square was beginning to take shape as the amusement center of the city. No matter where one worked in the city, the noise of construction was deafening. At the end of the day a worker had to fight his way onto one of the crowded "els" or horse-drawn trolleys to reach home. After supper he would be too tired to do anything that required exertion. This may have had a great deal to do with the astonishing fact that New York suddenly became a city of readers.

At this fortuitous moment a man named Clarence Vernam entered the picture. He was connected with an advertising firm that had done a considerable amount of business with Street & Smith. His father, Remington Vernam, was a man of wealth. He had bought a huge tract of swamp and dunes on Long Island, had named it Arverne, and was in the process of chopping it up into small lots and selling it to eager buyers. Vernam, impressed by the possibilities in the magazine business, approached O. G. with a proposition. He would like to invest in a Street & Smith magazine—a "class" magazine bearing no resemblance to the libraries with which the firm was flooding the country. His thinking and the ideas of O. G. coincided. Launching such a venture would entail a big financial risk—Smith wasn't quite ready to gamble all of the profits of his *New York Weekly,* his dime novels and his libraries on a new publication which would inevitably have to compete with the established giants in the trade.

Two years earlier Smith had published *The Yellow Kid,* dedicated to the glorification of a comic-strip character of that name. The Kid was America's first comic-strip character. He had been created for *The New York Journal* by Richard Felton Outcault. Since Smith never had great faith in that venture he did not publish it under the respected imprint of Street & Smith. Instead, he formed a new concern, Howard, Ainslee & Co., with offices at 2 Duane Street, the address of the printing establishment which turned out the Street & Smith products. No one to this day knows whether there actually was a "Howard" or an "Ainslee." Smith's lack of confidence in *The Yellow Kid* was justified, but it was the ancestor of the millions of comic books published today. After two years he changed the name to *The Yellow Book,* but it still continued to languish. Vernam's offer was a fine opportunity to scrap *The Yellow Book* in favor of a worth while magazine. Smith, underneath his proper façade, was a gambler. When a venture began to lose money he would discontinue it, take his loss stoically and immediately look around for some other publishing idea on which to bet. Smith allowed Vernam to buy a half-interest in the new publication, which he decided to call *Ainslee's, the Magazine That Entertains.* It was the only time O. G. would ever permit an outsider to have a financial interest in the firm. The magazine was to be published by the nonexistent Howard, Ainslee & Co., and its first editor was a brilliant man named Richard Duffy.

Duffy had acquired some editorial experience working for newspapers, but at the moment he was a clerk in James McCreery's department store. His wife was a good friend of Mrs. Smith, and it was she who recommended her husband to O. G.

The first issue appeared in February, 1898, on glossy slick paper. For nearly thirty years thereafter it would be one of the most successful magazines in America. People who bought that first issue received their money's worth for their five cents. The ninety-five pages of the first *Ainslee's* were a literary potpourri calculated to satisfy a variety of tastes. The lead story, "The Capture of Lusigny," was a swashbuckling tale by Stanley J. Weyman, author of *Under the Red Robe* and *A Gentleman of France*. This was followed by a poem, in which the author, Theodosia Pickering, took a dim view of Love.

The third feature was one guaranteed to titillate the curiosity of any nineteenth-century reader. It was called "The Household of the Sultan," by Anetta Halliday-Antonna. It began:

> The millions of Abdul Hamid's struggling subjects willingly contribute to the advancement of that time-honored institution of the Moslems, where wifehood is so little esteemed and motherhood so highly honored, the harem, where upon Thursday evening, that sacred night of gallantry in all Turkish homes, the master visits his "rose-leaves" and bestows upon them his imperial favor. . . .

The article described the duties of the court muezzin, the chief doctor, the armorer and the chief chamberlain but only hinted at the rites which went on behind the closed door of the harem.

Bret Harte

Rudyard Kipling

This was followed by two pages of jokes. The humor was broad and the jokes lacked subtlety by today's standards.

But the reader only had to turn the page to be greeted by an excellent short story by Anthony Hope, author of *The Prisoner of Zenda* and *Rupert of Hentzau*. Anthony Hope, in 1898, was one of the most popular and highest-priced writers in the land. Hope's story was followed by several pages of humor and verse.

The next three pages contained a serious appreciation of the French novelist, Alphonse Daudet, who had recently died. This was a penetrating analysis of the novelist and his work by Editor Richard Duffy. Richard Duffy was an exceptional writer and critic as well as a superb editor. Pages of humor separated articles and stories throughout the issue. A really magnificent article, "Submarine Navigation Accomplished," was signed by one E. S. Bisbee. Only seven weeks before this inaugural issue of *Ainslee's* had appeared, Simon Lake had made his first successful descent in the submarine *Argonaut*. He had worked fourteen years on this underseas craft to the accompaniment of derisive yells from the critics. But the strange craft had actually worked, and Reporter Bisbee had witnessed the maiden trip and had drawn some very interesting conclusions. The newspapers regarded it as a toy, but Bisbee (was he also Editor Duffy?) saw the possibilities of the new craft and went on record with his prophecies (all of which have withstood the test of time). After describing the operation of the *Argonaut* in considerable and fascinating detail, he wrote:

> It is no speculative fancy but an established fact; the boat sinks and swims at the whim of the operator. As a destroyer in time of war it must stand pre-eminent. She can leave her dock in the city, sink beneath the water and proceed to sea where she can glide beneath the man-of-war and discharge a torpedo upward from any reasonable depth and annihilate the enemy in a trice.

He ended his article by saying:

> Thus, the generation that produced the electric light and the telephone, the automobile carriage and the phonograph, which has made greater scientific strides than any other age in history, is grandly closing its cycle by solving the greatest riddle of all—unless aerial navigation be excepted—for as a valuable invention the subaqueous boat is paramount.

Ten pages of the issue were devoted to the stage. This department is merely signed "Aristarch," but from the excellence of the writing and the sound judgment on actresses Mary Mannering, May Irwin and Julia Marlowe, one is again tempted to suspect the versatile Duffy.

The only full-page advertisements were taken by Street & Smith. One page shouted the virtues of three books, the lives of General Grant, General Sherman and General Sheridan, each of which could be obtained for twenty-five cents. Another page listed six popular plays which had been put into novel form and were offered to the public for twenty-five cents each.

It wasn't long before Editor Duffy shook the bugs out of the magazine. Each succeeding issue became less diffuse and better looking. Duffy hired a promising young writer from the Midwest to contribute a weekly article. His name was Theodore Dreiser. This was not the Dreiser of the somber *American Tragedy* or *Jennie Gerhardt,* nor was it the Dreiser whose ponderous literary style would be the target of critics a decade later. This was a writer of charm and humor. He was apparently given rather a wide latitude as to choice of subject matter (or perhaps Duffy assigned subjects to him). His first article (always called "sketches" in *Ainslee's*) was called "Historic Tarrytown." It has borne the test of time so well, it would bear reprinting today. Interesting is the fact that even then "increase of population in New York has brought a thriving brood of bankers and brokers into this lovely village." His second article was a perceptive appreciation of Benjamin Eggleston, a popular American artist of the day. Later, he wrote other articles on art and on such odd subjects as "The Making of Small Arms."

Rudyard Kipling contributed a poem, "Mulvaney Regrets," in an early issue, and it wasn't long before Bret Harte, Opie Read and A. Conan Doyle were writing regularly for the magazine. In May, 1901, O. Henry sold his first story, "Money Maze," to *Ainslee's* for fifty dollars. It began in the style which was afterward to become his identification:

> They will tell you, in Anchuria, that President Miraflores of that volatile republic died by his own hand in the coast town of Cibolo. That he had reached thus far in flight from the inconveniences of an imminent revolution, and that a quarter of a million *pesos*, government funds, which he carried with him in an American leather valise as a souvenir of his tempestuous administration, were never afterward found.

O. Henry was always grateful to Ormond Smith, who had given him his first chance in the magazine big league.

During the decades that followed, the question of who discovered O. Henry was often debated. In 1934, Franklin P. Adams, who ran "The Conning Tower" in *The New York Herald Tribune,* opened his column to a discussion of the question. A letter from Richard Duffy seemed to make it quite clear that the honor of encouraging the impecunious writer belonged to *Ainslee's* and Ormond Smith.

> One day we received a letter from O. Henry in which he hinted humorously that the City of Pittsburgh had become intolerable to him, and that he believed if he could get to New York he would be able to produce more stories and enjoy more sunshine. The advance amount of money O. Henry asked was not large, but it was something to expect of Ormond G. Smith—or of any publisher—willingness to "stake" a writer whom none of us had ever seen.
>
> Our argument was that the O. Henry stories that had been published in the magazine had received a notice quite unusual, and we felt that he was certain to "carry on." So the firm sent O. Henry the sum he had requested, and with it he came to New York and began his general fame as a distinctive master of his art. Incidentally, he paid that money back to the company very promptly by offering everything he wrote first to *Ainslee's Magazine.* In one number of the magazine there were three stories, under various pen names, which had been written by him.
>
> Richard Duffy

In 1902 he sold six stories to *Ainslee's* and received $75 apiece. O. Henry was a fast man with a dollar and frequently found himself in

O. Henry   Sir Arthur Conan Doyle

financial straits. The pay sheets of Street & Smith headed "O. Henry (Sydney Porter), 2419 Milan Street, New Orleans," are studded with the notation: "Advance on account of story—$200." He never received more than $200 for a short story.

O. Henry's popularity was probably due to the fact that his writing had such a universal appeal. He wrote about businessmen and clerks and chorus girls and doctors and policemen. He had an unfortunate enthusiasm for Kipling at his worst, and the few exotic tales he wrote in the manner of Kipling have little to redeem them. But "The Four Million" and other stories of New York did catch the tumultuous spirit of the city. In many of his stories he had the courage to tell the honest and sometimes devastating truth, but more often than not he indulged in romantic handsprings. He was a master of the trick ending and unfortunately leaned on it heavily. He was only granted ten brief years of productive writing, but his imitators have been at it ever since.

None, however, has ever been able to picture the trivial or the flashy side of New York as he did. O. Henry discovered the hall bedroom and the free-lunch barroom, and he had the knack of capturing an amusing moment and holding it fast. The image he drew of New York imprinted itself upon the minds of men and maids all over the country and probably had a considerable influence on the migrations and rebellions which later led to Greenwich Village. He was not only popular in his day but in time became an example of the perfect short-story writer in university courses.

The men and women who wrote for *Ainslee's* were good craftsmen. With their highly developed skill and superior writing ability, they helped to create a taste for the short story as a form of expression. They still specialized in happy endings, however. The public expected of art not reality but a fantasy world to which it could escape. Readers were not yet ready for the realism of a Stephen Crane or a Frank Norris.

National advertisers were quick to spot public interest in *Ainslee's*. In some ways, the advertisements in early issues reflect the tempo, the mood and the problems of the day to an even greater degree than do the articles and fiction. In 1898, a German chemist, Gerhardt Dressen, had discovered a drug called heroin. This derivative of opium was hailed by the medical world as the greatest boon to mankind since the discovery of morphine back in 1803. Both heroin and morphine were pain killers, and the best thing about them, experts said solemnly, was the fact that neither was habit forming. There were no laws against importing either of the drugs (it wasn't until 1906 that Federal legislation outlawed the importation of opium and its derivatives). Heroin was just beginning to trickle into the country, but you could buy morphine almost anywhere, and doctors prescribed it often for what, in those days, were known as "women's complaints." Gradually the medical profession realized its frightful mistake about the habit-forming qualities of the drug. So did such organizations as the St. James Society, which advertised in *Ainslee's*.

MORPHINE

Laudanum, Cocaine and all other

DRUG HABITS

FREE TRIAL TREATMENT AT HOME

Painless, Harmless, Sure, Permanent,
Entirely New

We will send any one addicted to Morphine, or other drug habits, a trial treatment sufficient for ten days, *free of charge,* of the most remarkable remedy for this purpose ever discovered, containing the great vital principle, lacking in all other remedies. Send name and address, and prove the truth or falsity of our claims, at our expense. Correspondence invited from all, especially with Physicians. From the time of taking first dose of our remedy, all desire for drugs disappears. You begin at once to sleep well, eat well, and gain weight and strength. The only remedy that cures without causing patient any suffering whatever. Refractory cases solicited. Indorsed by Physicians, and dissimilar in every respect from any other known treatment. Our remedy is sure and permanent, and at the end of treatment, leaves patient with health entirely recovered, and free from all desires formerly possessing them. Correspondence strictly confidential.

St. James Society,
1183 Broadway, N. Y. City

Mrs. Lydia Pinkham, whose vegetable compound would later become famed in legend and song, was now enshrined in the hearts of American women. She began a campaign against the use of morphine, and a typical advertisement of hers read:

BEWARE OF MORPHINE

Mrs. Pinkham Asks Women
to Seek Permanent Cures and Not Mere
Temporary Relief from Pain

Special forms of suffering lead many a woman to acquire the morphine habit.

. . . She has [symptoms] she cannot bear to confide to her physician, for fear of an examination, the terror of all sensitive, modest women.

The physician, meantime, knows her condition, but cannot combat her shrinking terror. He yields to her supplication for something to relieve the pain. He gives her a few morphine tablets, with the very grave caution as to their use. Foolish woman! She thinks morphine will help her right along; she becomes its slave!

A wise and a generous physician had such a case; he told his patient he could do nothing for her, as she was too nervous to undergo an examination. In despair, she went to visit a friend. She said to her, "Don't give up; just go to the nearest druggist's and buy a bottle of Mrs. Lydia E. Pinkham's Vegetable Compound. It will build you up. You will begin to feel better with the first bottle." She did so, and after the fifth bottle her health was re-established . . .

There were advertisements guaranteed to make you stop smoking, and even ads telling you how you could rid yourself of the pernicious habit of chewing tobacco.

Albert Payson Terhune

E. Phillips Oppenheim

133

Dr. John H. Woodbury took full-page advertisements to extol the virtues of his facial soap. He headed the Woodbury Dermatological Institute with offices in Boston, Philadelphia, Chicago and New York. His intriguing ad read, "If Beauty is only skin deep, we can make you beautiful." He guaranteed to cure oily skin, itching, falling hair; to remove moles, warts, liver spots, wrinkles; to correct projecting ears and to "set them back close to the head—no pain—no failure."

Male readers were not ignored by advertisers early in the century. "Buckingham's Dye for the Whiskers" was extolled and readers were solemnly warned:

BEFORE YOU DYE

See that you have the dye
that colors a perfect brown or black.

Tobacco (for chewing and smoking) was extensively advertised, as were bicycles, Dewars Whiskey, cameras and Diamond Crystal Eye Glasses which George Mayerle, expert optician, said, could "be fitted by mail."

Richard Duffy departed the scene a few years later. He was a fine editor, but he didn't quite see eye to eye with Ormond Smith. Once the success of *Ainslee's* was assured, Duffy went to Smith with a proposition which was, in a way, an ultimatum.

Smith was paying him well and liked him well enough to become godfather of Duffy's son, Gerald. But although Smith was fond of Duffy and his wife, he also preferred to run the firm himself.

"I don't want to work for a salary all my life," Duffy told O. G. "I want a percentage of the profits of *Ainslee's*. I want to be a partner in the magazine."

"A partnership is the worst ship in the world," Smith said coldly. One word led to another. Duffy refused to retreat from his stand, and a stormy conference ended with Duffy's leaving the organization. (He became an editor of Funk & Wagnalls' *Literary Digest*.)

Duffy was succeeded by Gilman Hall. Hall ran things for awhile, but then an unfortunate postscript to a letter lost him his job. Ormond was interested in a writer named Charles Garvice. He had submitted a story to Smith and Smith became very enthusiastic about it. He sent it to Hall with a dictated letter attached. In it he extolled the virtues of this "fine, powerful story" and directed Hall to schedule it as soon as possible. Smith dictated this note to his secretary. She typed it and then added a postscript of her own addressed to her friend, Gilman Hall. She said she thought the story was terrible, that O. G.'s judgment was bad, and she added, "After all, you can't make a silk purse out of a sow's ear." It was forwarded to Hall's office, but the editor wasn't in that day. One of his assistants read the letter with its damning postscript, and then (perhaps satisfying a grudge against Hall) sent it to Smith. Smith was not amused. He demanded implicit loyalty from his employees, and it was evident from the postscript that he wasn't getting it. He immediately fired the secretary and Gilman Hall.

His eye fell upon the nearly bald pate of an old friend, Archibald Lowry Sessions. Sessions was a lawyer who had an innate editorial feeling for writing and criticism. Smith appointed this lovable and sensitive man editor of *Ainslee's* and it was one of the smartest moves he ever made. "At least I know he's incapable of disloyalty," he told his brother. Smith had an intuitive sense which seemed to guide him in picking men. Occasionally, but not often, this sixth sense betrayed him, but usually the men he plucked from newspapers or other professions had potentials which, once realized, transformed them into fine editors. Sessions was such a man. He was one of the greatest. His hearty humor, his long drooping mustache, his knack for friendship, attracted O. Henry and other writers who swore by him, accepted his criticism and became better craftsmen for it. It was under Sessions that *Ainslee's* reached its peak.

Within a few years *Ainslee's* was publishing such writers as Mrs. Baillie Reynolds, Samuel Hopkins Adams, I. A. R. Wylie, Justin Huntly McCarthy, Albert Payson Terhune, Carolyn Wells, E. Phillips Oppenheim, John Fleming Wilson, Frank Leon Smith and Channing Pollock. Albert Payson Terhune, later famous as a writer of dog stories, did a very popular series for *Ainslee's* in 1916 called "Stories of the Super-Women."

In that same year, eighteen years after the first issue of the magazine appeared, Street & Smith took inventory of the history of *Ainslee's* to date. In a column called "Talks with *Ainslee's* Readers" the publishers stated with pride:

With this issue *Ainslee's* starts upon its nineteenth year. Birthdays and anniversaries are the times at which men, institutions, and nations check off past disappointments against past hopes and take stock of the achievements which they have to build upon for the future. Let us look back.

Ainslee's, designed to afford entertainment for cultured American readers, first appeared in February, 1898, as a five-cent illustrated monthly. Only ninety pages, and, according to present standards, crude in make-up, the very first issue indicated the future quality of its fiction with stories by Stanley J. Weyman, Anthony Hope, and Harold MacGrath. Before the year was out, the magazine had added to its list of contributors, Bret Harte, A. Conan Doyle, Ian MacLaren, Robert Barr, Rudyard Kipling, Albert Bigelow Paine, Opie Read, Morgan Robertson, and Lincoln Steffens. It was soon seen that this high standard could not be profitably maintained at five cents, and in September, 1898, the price of the magazine was raised to ten cents.

In the second year we note among the names on our contents page such notable additions as Sir Walter Besant, I. Zangwill, Lloyd Osbourne, Charles G. D. Roberts, W. W. Jacobs, F. Hopkinson Smith, F. Marion Crawford, Robert W. Chambers, Grant Allen, A. T. Quiller-Couch, General Charles King, Jerome K. Jerome, and E. W. Hornung.

It is interesting to note that a frequent contributor of short stories to *Ainslee's* in those days was Brand Whitlock, whose distinguished services in Belgium have given him world fame.

Up to 1900, *Ainslee's* had for the most part been printing the work of well-established writers. It was about that year . . . that we began to have such success in unearthing new writers whose brilliant contributions were to bring them later fame. In 1900 came a stirring group of tales of the new mining camps in the Northwest, by the then little-known Jack London. The fine homely humor of Joseph C. Lincoln's Cape Cod stories was given to the world through *Ainslee's.* And about this time came the greatest of modern American short-story writers [O. Henry] . . .

English writers of note whose work was first made known to American readers through *Ainslee's* are William J. Locke, Jeffery Farnol, E. Temple Thurston, and Leonard Merrick.

. . . We were constantly adding to our list of contributors such people as Stephen Crane, S. R. Crockett, Justus Miles Forman, Caroline Duer, Elizabeth Duer, Edgar Saltus, Alice Duer Miller, Herman Knickerbocker Viele, Carolyn Wells, Ethel Watts Mumford, Holman Day, Robert Hichens, and Anatole France.

It was in 1902 that the increased cost of manufacture brought a new problem to the magazine world. Hitherto publications had been either ten cents or twenty-five cents. The former price could no longer permit a publisher to give his readers the best there was, and twenty-five cents necessarily limited the circulation.

People's magazine, first published in 1906

"Why not fifteen cents?" asked one of the proprietors of *Ainslee's* . . . so *Ainslee's,* increased to its present size, became the pioneer of fifteen-cent magazines. Its immediate success established the popular price for high-class magazines.

Ainslee's in the past ten years is too well known to you to need review. The list of contributors reads like a *Who's Who* of the literary world: Joel Chandler Harris, May Sinclair, John Oliver Hobbs, Katherine Cecil Thurston, Marten Maartens, Baroness Von Hutton, Gouverneur Morris, Richard Le Gallienne, E. F. Benson, Edith MacVane, David Graham Phillips, Edith Wharton, Alice MacGowan, Grace MacGowan Cooke, Emerson Hough, Will Irwin, Henry C. Rowland, E. Phillips Oppenheim, George Barr McCutcheon, Harry Leon Wilson, George Bernard Shaw, and a host of others almost equally well known.

We believe we are also printing each month, just as we did in the days of O. Henry and Joseph C. Lincoln, stories that will bring their authors reputation in the future.

"Rather pleased with themselves," an outsider might think after reading the foregoing. But we are not writing for outsiders. We are merely talking to ourselves. For *Ainslee's,* by reflecting the tastes of its readers, makes its readers its real editors.

So much for birthday reminiscences. . . .

In 1906, Smith had launched another magazine called *People's,* with Thomas O'Halloran as its first editor. This was a shrewdly calculated effort to sell adventure stories to a more sophisticated audience than that which read the libraries. Wyndham Gittens, Gardner Hunting and John DeRuyter were among the editors who nursed

H. G. Wells

Dorothy Parker

People's along toward success. Smith didn't think that *People's* was making progress fast enough, so he switched Sessions from *Ainslee's* to breathe quick editorial life into *People's*. He did. Sessions was succeeded at *Ainslee's* by Robert Rudd Whiting, a man as homely as Lincoln but with a warm, friendly smile that would light up a room. Under Whiting's guidance, *Ainslee's* continued to enjoy great success. Whiting was stricken by the influenza epidemic during World War I and died at the age of forty-five. Sessions occasionally spent weekends in Maine with his good friend, Gilbert Patten. After one such strenuous trip, he suffered a heart attack, and Ormond Smith lost a great editor and friend. But *Ainslee's* and *People's* kept right on.

Ainslee's discovered a young girl named Dorothy Parker who not only knew a great deal about the theatre but who could write about it gracefully and with wit. Miss Parker was given a department called "In Broadway Playhouses." After reading her reviews three decades later, one wishes that the incomparable Dorothy was still a theatre critic. In a 1920 issue she reviewed *Clair de Lune* by Michael Strange (Mrs. John Barrymore). The stars were John and Ethel Barrymore. Dorothy wrote:

> Well, of course if you have two Barrymores in a play you can't want much more. . . . The play itself always seems as if it were going to burst forth into a great play, but it never quite does. There are moments of beauty, flashes of wit, and then there are a great many words. . . . After you get one look at Ethel Barrymore, as Queen Anne, in the white costume of her entrance scene, you want to rush out to the box office and tell them there must be some mistake; five dollars is an undercharge. John Barrymore has designed several of the scenes: a park, a forest scene, and an enchanting setting for the boudoir of the duchess—red-lacquered furniture standing sharply against the hydrangea blue of the walls, and reflected in the polished floor.
>
> Ethel Barrymore has an allotment of sparkling lines, of which she can make an incredible amount, and her brother has a remarkable dance on the mountebank's platform, the above-mentioned love scene, and a tender moment in the last act. And that is, really, about all that they are given. The impression that one takes away from the theatre is of their few scenes, of a succession of increasingly lovely costumes, and of a flow of long and tortuous words.
>
> But what does it matter what any one says about *Clair de Lune*, anyway? Almost to a man, the critics spoke harshly of the play. And the morning that their reviews appeared in the newspapers, the line in

front of the Empire Theatre was longer than it had been when, before the play opened, people stood for hours, waiting their turn to buy tickets in advance. Many stood, in fact, reading the reviews which condemned the play, to while away the time.

It simply goes to show that two Barrymores will outbalance all the critics in the city. Which is just about as it should be.

Smith followed up the success of *Ainslee's* by establishing *Popular Magazine,* with Henry Harrison Lewis, a veteran editor of juvenile periodicals, in charge.

The purpose of the magazine, as stated in its inaugural issue, was to publish a monthly magazine that "will be read by every boy in the United States and one that will be welcomed by the fathers and mothers of the boys. . . . We start with the belief that every boy worth having on our list has good red blood in his veins; that he is fond of out-of-door sports and that he likes to read about boys who are fond of athletic sports. . . ."

Within four months the magazine had grown so successful that its size had doubled. It published two complete novels, six installments of two-part novels, and seven short stories. Gradually it became obvious to Ormond Smith that more men than juvenile readers were being attracted to *Popular.* Ormond Smith had a genius for discerning this subtle shift in his audience. In the sixth issue, in a column called "A Chat with Our Readers," an announcement appeared:

> The mission of the *Popular Magazine* is to give pleasant relaxation from the sordid routine of existence. We particularly wish to see it in the hands of the tired man of business and in the hands of those who feel constrained to seek an hour's relief from the cares of their daily life. We will be satisfied when the time comes that our magazine is looked upon in the same spirit as the modern theatre is regarded—as a place of entertainment whence comes amusement and diversion and thorough enjoyment. If we give you entertainment, we will feel repaid.

Smith replaced Henry Lewis with Charles Agnew MacLean, destined to become one of the most distinguished of all Street & Smith editors. Under MacLean the magazine outgrew its juvenile status and became a magazine for adults. MacLean was a man of wisdom and warmth. He was also an excellent judge of writing, whether it be the hurried tale or a serious poem. Zane Grey always said that it was MacLean who had encouraged him to write his westerns. Grey's *Heritage of the Desert,* his first great success, was (the author said) a "discovery of MacLean's." MacLean was acknowledged as the first to recognize the potential greatness of H. G. Wells. This gentle Scotsman was revered by writers for *Popular,* and many of them grew to literary maturity (and were frank in acknowledging their debt to him) under his guiding hand. Under his editorship the department, "A Chat with You," became widely read and highly commended even by critics who had little taste for the action-type story featured by *Popular.* But these chats, which were often serious and always intelligent essays, reflected the personality of the man better, perhaps, than did the fiction he printed. He felt that the storyteller, as opposed to the delineator of character or the commentator on the times, had a real and important place in literature. In one of his "Chats" he wrote an essay which could be read today with profit by any students of writing. It read, in part:

> Every now and then we run across a book which attempts to teach its readers the way to write stories. Some are worthless. Some have a great deal of sound sense and careful analysis in them; but from all of them we turn back to a single sentence in a novel by George Moore. It tells in the briefest and yet most explicit form what can and cannot be done in the way of teaching people how to write fiction. Here it is:
>
> "Style and presentation of character and a fine taste in the selection of words are secondary gifts, and secondary gifts may be acquired, may

Charles Agnew MacLean

Zane Grey

be developed, at least; but the story-teller comes into the world fully equipped almost from the first, finding stories wherever he goes as instinctively as the reaper in the corn field discovers melodies that the professor of counterpoint and harmony strives after vainly in his university."

This explains why the true writer frequently comes into his own so early in life, and why experience, which is so necessary in other callings, seems to count less in this.

After all, although style and character and other things aid and strengthen and embellish, the one essential without which all the others are useless is the story itself. They talk about building up or constructing a story, but does that give the right idea? We think that George Moore's expression is a truer and happier one. "Finding stories," as he puts it, "is the calling of the fiction writer." To "find" them in the life about him needs a sort of insight on the author's part. . . . Life, as most of us see it in the raw, is a sort of confusion and disorder. Its rhythm and design are hidden from us. The story-teller catches up the tangled threads of many colors and casts them into a pattern of beauty and coherency; he discards the useless rubbish, and builds out of the broken fragments of experience the palace of our heart's desire . . .

A good author is a man who sees something interesting, romantic, noble and glamorous in the human drama that he fears others may miss. He wants them to see it too. He cannot be content to keep the vision to himself. That is what starts him writing. It is easy to understand how imperative must have been the need of expression for the young Kipling, for instance, his mind filled with the strangest, most dramatic,

Jack London   Mary Roberts Rinehart

and vivid pictures of a strange life, and it is hard to believe that any amount of discouragement could have prevented him from communicating his earlier Indian tales to others. Thackeray wrote to his mother about *Vanity Fair:* "These thoughts pursue me plentifully. Will they ever come to a good end? I should doubt God, who gave them, if I doubted them." To say that Thackeray was trying to write a book is not a fair description. To say that a book was imprisoned in Thackeray and clamoring to be written, comes nearer the truth. Any one who has ever felt this sort of inspiration will recognize it at once.

. . . A magazine, if it is worth anything, acquires a personality, too. This is not the personality of any one man. It is made up of the publisher's personality, the editor's personality, its readers' personalities as well as that of the authors'. The magazine has a spirit just as real as that of a human being. It comes to have its own way of looking at things. . . .

MacLean hated pretension, whether it be in a man or in a manuscript. He urged his authors to write simply. One of his finest essays was on literary style.

We have all had hammered into us, at school or elsewhere, a certain admiration for the great books of the past. Marlowe and Chaucer, Ben Jonson and Shakespeare, Spenser and all the rest—we can look up and see their names, in gilt against morocco, on the higher shelves of any proper library. We cheerfully admit that they are great—but how often do we reach up for a book and spend a quiet hour with any one of them? We are, most of us, more familiar with the names of these worthies than with the books they wrote. We are qualified to write an essay on "Great Books I Have Never Read but Often Heard About." We are going to read them, of course, "when we get time." But any honest person knows that we almost always find time, somehow, for the things we really want to do.

It is too bad. They are all worth reading. They all carry some message of wisdom or hope or laughter for each one of us. No one will ever get to the real core of English literature without knowing Shakespeare, and no one can fully understand the spirit of modern thought and inquiry without making the acquaintance of Francis Bacon. The trouble with all the old-timers is that they are hard to read. The English language was once a more ponderous machine. It was more or less indirect. It took longer to say a thing three hundred years ago than it does today. The tendency through the years has been toward brevity and simplification. Just as old machinery is heavier than modern, so is old English more cumbersome than the clipped, brisk speech we use today. It is not the fault of the great masters that their style is ornate and diffuse. They wrote, not for the mass, but for a choice few, educated aristocrats. They suited the style to the audience. It was the fashion once to be refined, exotic, and precious in speech. Only a few could read or write, and those few made the most of their distinction by putting on verbal airs and showing off. Shakespeare, who was the most gifted and instinctive of all writers, bowed to the fashion, and gave us pages of rounded periods and sounding rhetoric, but he broke the bonds of fashion now and then and spoke in terms of simple brevity.

A man who has ambitions to write, and has a natural love for the great literature of the past, is too likely to forget this and to copy the more leisurely style of an age with more time on its hands. To write well today is not to display one's scholarship, but to say the things simply and effectively. The stilted phrases, the formal oratory, belong now to cheap melodrama which still lives in the dead husks of a dead past.

The best writing is the most unpretentious, the most sincere, the most readily understandable. The best writer is not the man who is trying to show how much he knows, but the man who is trying to convey his feeling to the reader in the straightest possible line. Some writers—indeed, all great writers—are endowed with a sense of the music of speech, and with command of an imagery and metaphor that can sometimes turn plain prose to exalted poetry.

Literature is changing as the time passes by and we, among others, are helping it change. It moves toward the chaster, simpler, more energetic style, further and further away from the ornate and artificial. You can try, if you write, to approximate the written word to the spoken. Try reading your stories aloud, if you are ambitious to become a writer. It may teach you something.

MacLean had the ability to spot potentially fine writers. He discovered John Buchan, the author of *Thirty-Nine Steps,* and Richard Washburn Child (later Ambassador to Italy). Early in their careers he recognized the storytelling talents of Rex Beach, Jack London, Octavus Roy Cohen, Mary Roberts Rinehart, Courtney Riley Cooper, and a host of others. George Horace Lorimer, the great editor of *The Saturday Evening Post,* frankly admitted that he used *Popular* as an incubator for *Post* writers. Dozens of them who began writing for MacLean ended up getting the big prices paid by Lorimer, but without exception, they retained their friendship and admiration for MacLean. When MacLean took over the magazine it had less than 70,000 circulation. Within two years it had climbed to 250,000. At its peak in 1911 it reached 417,500. For twenty-four years this remarkable man edited *Popular Magazine.*

CHAPTER

SEVEN

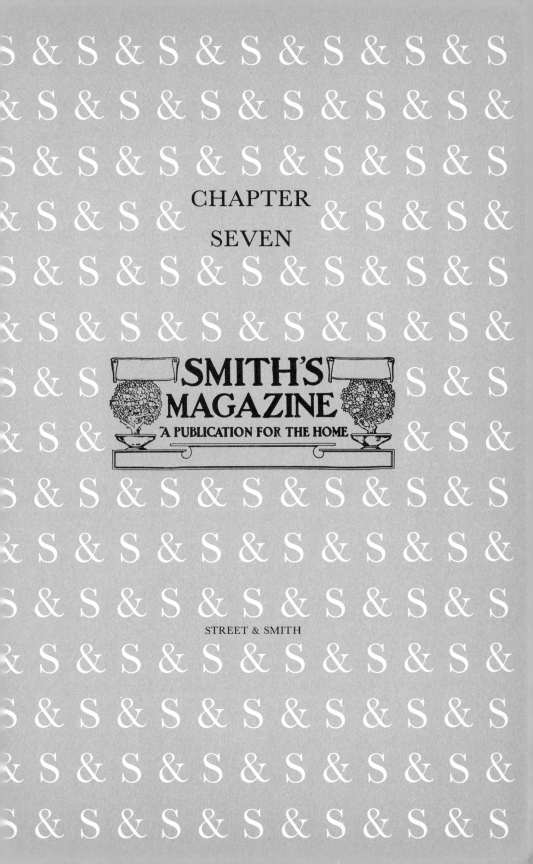

SMITH'S
MAGAZINE

A PUBLICATION FOR THE HOME

STREET & SMITH

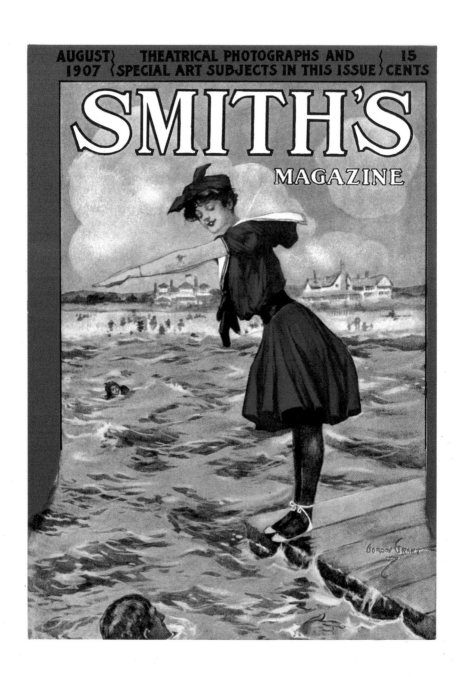

A *Smith's* cover by Gordon Grant; the magazine was
first published in 1905

CHAPTER
SEVEN

I want a magazine," Ormond said one day to his brother, George, and to Editor MacLean, "that will appeal to the John Smiths of America. There are an awful lot of them."

"Why not call it *Smith's?*" MacLean said.

His suggestion was adopted. When it first appeared (April 1, 1905) the trade thought that the title derived from the ownership, but Ormond Smith was not a vain man. The thought of naming a magazine after himself would have been repugnant to him.

Smith had come to depend more and more on the sound judgment and editorial wisdom of MacLean. He asked "Mac" to suggest an editor.

"Theodore Dreiser," MacLean replied promptly. "He's a moody man, but he's intelligent and his work for *Ainslee's* has been first-rate."

"Good idea," Smith said, and Theodore Dreiser, the most unlikely choice in the world for editor of a magazine created to attract the interest of the John Smiths of the country, became editor of *Smith's.*

In 1898, the twenty-seven-year-old Dreiser had walked into the Street & Smith office looking for a job. Richard Duffy was in the process of making up the first issue of *Ainslee's*. Dreiser brought with him a couple of articles he had written. Duffy took a liking at once to the young man who was obviously down on his luck. He listened to his story. Dreiser told Duffy of his childhood in Terre Haute, Indiana. He spoke with bitterness of his sternly religious, German-born, very Catholic father and with great tenderness of his gentle mother. He told Duffy of his brother, Paul Dresser. Paul had dropped the family name and had become a successful actor and writer of popular songs. The two, Dreiser said, had collaborated on a song called "On the Banks of the Wabash Far Away." People were singing it, but they hadn't made much money out of it. He said that he had worked on newspapers in the Middle West and in Pittsburgh but hadn't been able to get a writing job in New York.

"There's a fellow named Chauncey Depew, president of the New York Central Railroad," he told the listening Duffy. "I knew a newspaperman down on his luck who went to him for help, and damned if Depew didn't make him a conductor on the New York Central. I wrote a letter to Depew telling him I wanted a job—any job—so I could support myself and write on the side. Well, he didn't give me a job as a conductor but he gave me a card to one of the foremen and for the past nine months I've been working on the railroad. Now I've saved a little money and can take a chance on writing."

"Where are you living?" Duffy asked.

"In Williamsburg, over in Brooklyn. I got a room for one dollar and fifty cents a week."

"Can you write feature articles?" Duffy asked.

"I can write anything you want," Dreiser said intensely.

"I'll give you fifteen dollars a week to write for a new magazine we're starting," Duffy said.

Dreiser accepted it. He was a capable newspaper-trained feature writer and he allowed none of the bitterness of his rebellious nature and tortured soul to creep into the excellent articles he did for *Ainslee's*. When MacLean started *Popular*, he and Dreiser became friends. MacLean recognized that this was an exceptional, if unwieldy, talent. Unwieldy because it could not be channeled into the Street & Smith assembly-line tradition, or, for that matter, into the tradition of American literature at all. But as a man of unquestioned ability, Dreiser interested the experienced MacLean. He unburdened himself to MacLean as he did to few other men, for Dreiser was not a man to make friends easily. He told MacLean of the fine men he had met working as a laborer for the railroad. He had a passionate love for people and a mind that was constantly probing their motivations. He had a strong conviction that man—left alone—was a pretty decent human being. It was economic, social and religious pressure that made man into a conforming nonentity.

Dreiser had just finished *Sister Carrie* but was unable to find a publisher for it. *Sister Carrie* was in the tradition of the naturalists. The school of naturalism in writing was based on a resistance to delusion and vain sentimentality. It was a revolt against decorum and propriety, and the great exponents of naturalism were invariably men inspired by moral ardor and a passion for the ultimate truth. In the 1900's sex was something which, in art at least, had to be denied out of existence. Dreiser, frank, sharp and profoundly serious, dealing with sex as a primordial and creative force shocked and horrified publishers and critics. He treated man's generative instinct with dignity, but the critics used the phrase "animal behavior." He wrote of actual relations between man and woman, and the critics shuddered and said that he was obsessed with sex when actually Dreiser was obsessed with truth, and therein lay his greatness. Sometimes the power and truth of his work were obscured by the massive and slovenly style, but the veracity of his moral indignation was too overwhelming not to shine through the pages of *Sister Carrie*. He told MacLean that one publisher had handed *Sister Carrie* back to him with the icy remark, "If you want to write such stuff, I suppose there is no way to prevent it, but never bring it to me again."

Experience had forced upon Dreiser the conclusion that Chicago

Channing Pollock

Joe Weber

and New York were jungles where only those with brute strength could survive. Sister Carrie was a simple-minded girl. The city lured her and she became a kept woman. But instead of meeting with the total tragedy which moral precepts of the day demanded be the lot of the fallen woman, she went on to become a successful musical-comedy star. This was a violation of the pious principles of Horatio Alger and of the great American public. Dreiser wanted to compel middle-class America to face the actual, if tawdry, stuff of existence in the raw. The country was not yet ready to examine its conscience.

Mrs. Edith Wharton in her later years told of her first literary lesson. She wrote a story at the age of eleven (when she was Edith Jones) and showed it to her mother. Her story began, "If only I had known you were going to call, I would have tidied up the drawing room." Her mother read no farther. She glared sternly at her daughter and said, "Edith, drawing rooms are always tidy." The mass mind of the country believed that life, as portrayed by fiction, should always be tidy; it should be as neat as the parlor, with every chair in place. Dreiser, and those who believed with him, wanted to invade the tidy parlor with some harsh, unpleasant truths. Life, he wanted to thunder, was a complex problem in social justice, not a simple problem in social tradition. But no one would listen.

It was this bitter man, this powerfully molded man with piercing eyes, shaggy brows, and a mouth that looked like a half-healed wound, who stalked heavily into the office assigned to the editor of *Smith's Magazine.* He approached the task of editing the magazine on a strictly professional level and not as the tortured artist he was. He had a strong mother-fixation and a deep hatred for his father which manifested itself in an unquenchable rage against his father's religious faith. Yet none of this was ever evidenced in either the fiction or the articles he bought and edited for *Smith's.* With the exception of MacLean, Duffy and Ormond Smith, he had few friends in the firm. In Ormond Smith he recognized an intellectual capacity more disciplined and tolerant than his own. But at least the man had read everything. He could discuss the works of William Dean Howells and Henry James with O. G. as easily as he could with MacLean. Through Smith, he discovered many French writers who had only been names to him, and he envied Smith his ability to read them in the original. Dreiser led a split life during his Street & Smith days. Eight hours belonged to the firm and its popular-level literature; the rest of the time belonged to himself and his dreams of great writing. One day young Ralston was sent to Dreiser's office with a batch of proofs. He was surprised to find Dreiser on his knees with a rosary in his hand. Tears were streaming down his face as he mouthed the prayers he had learned as a child. Ralston stood still with shock. Dreiser looked up and said pathetically, "My mother is deathly ill— maybe this will help her." Ralston was sensitive enough not to tell anyone of the incident. Dreiser appreciated Ralston's tact and took a strong fancy to the young man.

The policy of *Smith's Magazine* was announced in a full-page statement undoubtedly written by Editor Dreiser.

THE PUBLISHERS' WORD

This is the first number of *Smith's Magazine*. We do not consider it necessary to go into any extensive description of its contents or to make any detailed prophecy concerning its future. The contents of the present number are yours to read, and the future will take care of itself. What we do wish to say, however, is that we intend to make a magazine that will meet your every wish.

Our policy is simple. We will not tamper with the higher education or attempt to alter the present formation of the universe. If we afford you entertainment, and perhaps render you some assistance in enduring the little sorrows and tragedies of life, we will be satisfied. . . .

In the matter of illustrations we purpose to make *Smith's Magazine* unique of its class. We will have more illustrations and better illustrations, and a greater variety of illustrative effects, than any other publication in the field. We have ideas, plenty of them, and the power to carry them out. This policy will prevail from cover to cover, and on the covers.

Another thing—we would like to start fair with you; we would like to have you understand clearly that *Smith's Magazine* will not be a class magazine, nor will it build for itself a high pedestal of ultra cleverness. It will be kept within the focus of the every-day reader who seeks entertainment.

The first issue (and years of successful succeeding issues) conformed to these basic principles. The magazine furnished entertainment to readers too mature to take the fiction in *The New York Weekly* seriously. The first number had a story by the indefatigable Charles Garvice, a short story by Mary Roberts Rinehart and an article, "The Serious Side of Burlesque," by Joe Weber, half of the famous team of Weber and Fields, then starring in the musical, *Higgledy-*

"The greatest printing house in the world"

Piggledy. There were a dozen "art studies" on fine coated paper showing scenes and stars of the play—Marie Dressler, Bonnie Magin, Anna Held and the two comedy leads. Channing Pollock, just emerging as one of the best of the younger playwrights, headed a department, "The American Dramatist," in which he reviewed new plays and wrote generally about the theatre.

Mr. Pollock also obliged with a bit of verse to accompany a photograph of Everybody's Sweetheart. It read:

TO LILLIAN RUSSELL

A little glint of sunshine
    'Tween the shadows in her hair;
Her eyes, the blue of heaven,
    Prisoned in by lashes fair.
A little red-rose petal
    Cleft in twain to make a mouth,
And a little sigh that might be
    Breath of Spring-time in the South.
A little row of seashells
    'Twixt her lips, as on a beach;
A little flush of color,
    Such as one sees on a peach;
A little hint of noon-day
    In her smile a friend might trace—
The composite of a June-day
    In this portrait of her face.

There was a curious five-page department headed:

The Passing Hour
An Illustrated Chronicle of World Doings

This section was devoted to the activities of European royalty or Long Island and New York society. The first issue contained a eulogy of Queen Alexandra of England and an announcement of the forthcoming marriage of the Crown Prince of Germany to the Duchess Cecilia of Mecklenburg.

> The Crown Prince, who will one day be Kaiser of Germany, is a healthy, sensible youth who bears his honors with becoming dignity. He is a daring horseman, a strong swimmer and a hunter of note. . . .

This is the same Crown Prince who, a brief decade later, would be a symbol of German imperialism and cruelty. This department, read by the same kind of people who today read Cholly Knickerbocker and other society columnists, was heavily biased in favor of royalty.

> The Grand Duke Vladimir of Russia has been vilified in the American press as being responsible for the massacre of workers in St. Petersburg. This is not in accordance with the American spirit of fair play. There is no evidence to support accusations that he was in any way connected with the death of so many workers in St. Petersburg.

The department isn't signed, and one can understand the reluctance of any writer to have his name attached to such trivia as:

> The noble families of England do not spend useless lives of luxury. The Countess of Essex, for instance, has recently opened up an establishment for the purpose of cleaning fine laces and linens. She is the former Adele Grant of New York City.

Month after month "The Passing Hour" passed on more of the same to eager readers.

Within two years *Smith's* reached a circulation close to 200,000. It was the kind of steady circulation dear to the heart of a publisher. The loyalty of readers of *Smith's* never wavered. The magazine grew in size to 160 pages, and there appeared on the cover the proud boast: The Biggest Magazine in the World. At its peak, it sold 300,000 copies a month.

Eventually the Butterick Publications lured Theodore Dreiser away from *Smith's*.

In 1905, Street & Smith celebrated its fiftieth anniversary and its new plant on Seventh Avenue and 17th Street, by issuing a booklet entitled: *The Greatest Publishing House in the World.*

It read in part:

> Fifty years ago, the firm of Street & Smith occupied a small building on Frankfort Street and issued one publication—*The New York Weekly.* Today, besides this publication, the firm publishes three magazines with a combined circulation of 700,000 copies monthly. A growth of this kind furnishes the best proof as to the wisdom of the policy pursued by the firm.
>
> *Ainslee's Magazine,* the *Popular Magazine,* and *Smith's Magazine* each occupy their individual spheres, and are far in the lead of any other magazine of similar purport.
>
> To the advertiser who invests his money in these magazines, the solidity and strength of the house backing them is of tremendous importance. It is a guarantee that the policy of the publication, which induced him to invest his money in advertising space, will be carried out, and that the cumulative value of his advertising will be assured.

An executive office

The shipping department

> The new Street & Smith building, the most complete plant of its kind in the world, is solid and substantial and typical of the firm itself. In outward appearance it is simple in architectural treatment, yet showing how cleverly plain bricks can be put together to form an imposing structure.

The impressive booklet described the magnificent building at great length. It told of the giant rotary presses on the second floor which were kept rolling day and night. It waxed lyrical on the subject of the modern electrotyping, engraving rooms and linotype machines on the seventh floor, and the bindery operation which was confined to the fourth floor. It told of the $70,000 worth of paper always on hand and added that if these rolls of paper were unwound and the flat sheets placed end to end, the ribbon of pulp would reach from New York to Cleveland. In 1905 it would take a complete floor to house $70,000 worth of paper; today you could put that much worth of paper in a freight car. But newsprint in the early days of the century was one of the most inexpensive of all commodities; there were millions of miles of forests in the country just waiting to be denuded and transformed into paper pulp.

The only commodity cheaper than paper was editorial talent. The heads of the firm never believed in paying editors high salaries and they paid writers well only when they were in such demand that high pay was essential to keep them laboring in the Street & Smith vineyard. But neither of the partners ever skimped when it came to buying the most up-to-date presses, the newest engraving equipment, or folding machines to bind the two million books and magazines which spewed from the building each month. They were especially proud of the thirty presses, ranging from the huge cylinder affairs to smaller flat presses which turned out covers and advertising sheets. So fascinating were these that thousands of visitors came each year to watch them in action.

The ground floor of the building held what may have been the largest library in the world. There were four million books stored here—six thousand different titles. If a midwest dealer wanted a thousand Bertha Clays, he only had to telegraph and the books would be en route within twenty-four hours. The plates of out-of-print books were stored in the cellar—twenty-three thousand boxes of them weighing (the *New York World* said, in an article describing the building) 1,725,000 pounds and worth, according to Street & Smith, $4,725,000.

The executive and editorial offices were on the sixth floor. Quartered oak was the motif, and each office held the tall, cumbersome roll-top desks considered to be the last word in office furnishing in 1905. The place was immaculately clean. Ormond Smith insisted upon cleanliness in his plant and in neatness among his employees. Women secretaries and bookkeepers wore dark skirts, modest shirtwaists and starched collars.

When an editor or a department head was summoned to Ormond Smith's office he was sure to put on his coat and straighten his tie. One day Smith passed a coatless, tieless man in the corridor. "See how essential that man is," he muttered to his brother. "If we can spare him, get rid of him. A man whose appearance is that sloppy must do sloppy work."

"He's the new photo-engraver we've been trying to lure away from Munro for two years," George said dryly. "He's the most careful, meticulous worker we ever had in the engraving room."

Ormond Smith just grunted.

The tremendous success of the firm could perhaps best be summed up in a sentence: Street & Smith was publishing books, weeklies, libraries and magazines aimed at families living in homes where the table was covered with a red-checked cloth and where the evening meal was called supper. Since the great majority of all Americans used a red-checked tablecloth and called the evening meal supper, the firm prospered.

If there was such a thing as a composite Street & Smith writer, one would have to nominate Laura Jean Libbey, whose serials, highly successful in the *Weekly*, were now in book form. There were twenty-two of them, and there would be more later. She was so prolific that at one time she kept six publishers busy printing her romances.

She wrote five hours a day, on a typewriter run by the one-finger system, and was never at a loss for a word. She saw herself as a realist aiming at idealism. She had a creed for her art, which doubtless explains her public: "I think a novel should do good and should lift people out of themselves." And standing coyly beside the piled volumes of abductions, dynamitings, marriages compelled from parental deathbeds and heroines whirled on gigantic fly-wheels, she added: "I don't like improbable novels that don't deal with things that happen in everyday life. I like to know the young people round us, their hopes, loves, dreams, sorrows, joys, aspirations, perplexities, ambitions."

They were all there, the hopes and dreams, crammed in with indistinguishable heroines, green-goggled robbers, verses old and new, quoted by characters as well as set at the heads of chapters, and physicians who said gravely, "This has the appearance of a severe case of shock," when they found someone with a head battered in. They were all there, described in a sort of emotional shorthand recognizable to her readers, in such lines as, "Was the white dove he loved so well even now in the clutches of the vulture?" Or of another: "One glance—then a wild, horrified cry—it was Coralie's wedding veil and the wreath of orange blossoms crushed and torn to a shapeless mass." And, darkly: "My love for you has been my curse."

Her titles are in this same shorthand: *Had She Loved Him Less!*, *Lotta, the Cloak Model, Madcap Laddy, the Flirt, The Price of a Kiss,* or *When His Love Grew Cold* (her own favorite, because she wrote it in a time of personal sorrow), or *Miss Middleton's Lover,* or *Parted on Their*

Theodore Dreiser

She overheard her mourners

Bridal Tour, which again was a favorite of hers because it was her first story.

In each book, as chapter titles, were more of these word-signs. "Death Shall Be Your Bridegroom," "The Last Hope Gone," "We Must Never Meet Again," "I Have Found You Out"—all these from one book, *What is Life Without Love* which bears upon its title page: "By Miss Laura Jean Libbey, the greatest living novelist, whose stories no author has ever been able to equal and whose fame as the favorite writer of the people has never been surpassed."

Critics laughed at her; no one liked her books except the people who bought some fifteen million of them. Laura Jean Libbey had more than the satisfaction of fifteen million sales. She tasted immortality, deliberately, with her tombstone. It was a splendid one. She bought it abroad and had her pen name, not her married name, carved on it. And she would sit in the cemetery and listen to the words of passers-by who thought she lay below it. "It's all right for your heirs to put it up," she said, "but then you don't see it." She died in 1924, well off, respected and loved—by everyone except the critics.

For every O. Henry published by the firm there were twenty Laura Jean Libbeys. Men and women who would afterward achieve literary eminence were learning their trade by writing for one or another of the publications, but the standbys were the Mrs. Georgie Sheldons, the Horatio Algers, the Bertha M. Clays and the other practitioners of literary mass production.

Business was booming for the firm during the early years of the new century. Clarence Vernam was now advertising manager for the organization, and a highly successful one. He was a man with a vibrant personality, a forerunner of the modern high-powered, publicity-minded executive. He was one of the organizers of the Calumet Club at 15 East 56th Street; he was a gentleman jockey, a golf enthusiast, and he angeled several Broadway theatrical ventures. Convivial, never adverse to a drink or a good time, Vernam kept the pages of *Ainslee's, Smith's* and *Popular* filled with advertising. A complete antithesis to austere Ormond Smith, the two were nevertheless great friends, with a mutual respect for the particular and unique talents each possessed. Vernam was a great storyteller, and he would delight Ormond and George with his tales of adventure in the high financial, theatrical and society circles he frequented. The firm, in buying the property on Seventh Avenue and 17th Street, had included in the purchase a three-story brownstone home on 16th Street. An alley ran through the street at this point, and by buying the house the firm could use the alley for trucks hauling away the millions of papers, magazines, weeklies, books that were spewing out of the presses every week. The clubs (Salmagundi and the Aldine on top of the Fifth Avenue Building at 23rd Street) where Ormond Smith usually lunched had become very popular, and after having to wait in line a few times for a luncheon table, Ormond decided to convert the 16th Street house into the firm's private luncheon club. He hired a fine cook, a Japanese butler, and he and his brother, George, began to lunch there nearly every day. Here they would entertain visiting writers or important advertisers. Clarence Vernam and Editor Charles MacLean were usually included. It was here that Vernam would enthrall the others with his tales.

Vernam invariably took the month of August off; his annual vacation coincided with the racing season at Saratoga. He was always accompanied by his great friend, Joe Moore, who then owned the *Morning Telegraph* and the *Newark Star-Eagle*. They would leave their wives at home. The two men-about-town would always start the day (Vernam would tell the fascinated if disapproving Ormond Smith) with three brandy milk punches made by the bartender of the old United States Hotel. Then they would spend the afternoons at the track and at night would visit the casinos which were running wide open. Vernam might lose some money at the track and at the roulette tables, but he'd always return to New York with a batch of advertising contracts. So, incidentally, would Joe Moore.

By 1908, William Henry Ralston had been given an office of his own—a sure sign that Ormond Smith had big things in mind for him. He had become a jack-of-all-trades in the firm. He did editorial chores for the various editors, he helped George Smith with circulation problems, and was often given special jobs to do by O. G. His office was next to the one occupied by Thomas Glynn, still editor of *The New York Weekly*. Glynn was a favored person in the firm. He had virtually brought up O. G. and G. C. (as George was now called) in the business, and both had deep affection for the veteran who was now well advanced into his seventies.

Ormond Smith was not an effusive man. There were those who mistook his reserve for coldness. He was a formidable figure, with his piercing eyes and his walrus mustache, and many thought him to be unapproachable. The truth is that he had no time to suffer fools, and incompetence disgusted him. But those who had worked closest to him knew that his stern exterior was a misleading façade. Many of the serial and dime-novel writers who had helped establish the success of the firm fell upon evil days in later years. The voluminous files that survive give eloquent testimony in the form of letters of gratitude to him (and from the widows of those who died penniless) that O. G. had a warmth that his appearance and occasional curtness belied.

It was becoming increasingly evident that the venerable *Weekly* had had its day. It had been the mainstay of the firm, the rock on which the whole Street & Smith structure had been built, but it had served its purpose.

"How long are you going to keep that damn *New York Weekly* alive?" one of his Wall Street friends asked him one day.

"As long as Tom Glynn is alive," he said shortly.

The *Weekly* was Tom Glynn's life. He had no interest at all in the various new and profitable ventures which had sprung from it. He and George Ormond Smith (nominally Glynn's assistant) shared an office. George Ormond Smith was a brother of the original Francis Smith. Now he was eighty-four, but he made the long trip from Halsey Street, Brooklyn, every day to sit with Tom Glynn and chat about the old days. These two cronies were loved by everyone in the firm.

George Ormond Smith made no concession to changing sartorial styles. During the winter he appeared at the office every day in a black stovepipe hat, black Prince Albert, starched shirt and black bow tie. When the warm weather came he changed to a white stovepipe (they were called Ben Harrisons after the President who had popularized them), the same Prince Albert, with a white lawn tie.

The offices had partitions, and now and then Ralston, sitting in his office, would hear Tom Glynn call, "William, come in here for a minute." He would hurry into the next office to greet Glynn and Uncle George. Glynn would invariably give him an all-tobacco little cigar (they were called Between-the-Acts) and say, "Now let's all light up and take it easy for awhile." And young Ralston, in a hurry to get back to work, would sit and listen to the old stories, the old jokes which the two men loved to repeat. On Saturday, Street & Smith closed at one o'clock. About eleven, Ralston would hustle to get the pay envelopes for himself and his two office neighbors. This was a Saturday ritual. He would hand each of them his envelope and invariably Uncle George would arise, reach for his tall hat, turn to Tom Glynn and say gravely, "Well, I have to leave."

"You can't leave, George," Glynn would protest. "Why, it's only eleven-thirty. We don't close shop until one."

George would shrug his shoulders, hand out the pay envelope on which his name appeared and say slyly, "I've got orders to go, Tom. You see the envelope says GO Smith."

Tom Glynn would roar with laughter at the bad pun based on the initials, and Ralston would chime in dutifully. Then he would walk to Brooklyn Bridge with Uncle George, see that he got aboard the Halsey Street trolley car and then return to work. Finally, Tom Glynn became too ill to make the daily trip to the office, and when O. G. realized that this was Tom Glynn's last illness, he sadly discontinued the venerable *Weekly*.

The urge to publish a really successful magazine for boys remained with Ormond Smith. It was one of the few editorial triumphs which had eluded him. He decided to try again. He and his brother discussed the venture at great length. Ralston, for the first time, was brought into these discussions. He did little but listen, but he felt a warm glow at the prospect of being asked about possible circulation, production, or even editorial problems that might arise. The new magazine was still only a crude dummy when Gilbert Patten approached Ralston.

"I hear the firm is coming out with a new adventure magazine for boys," he said. "What are you going to call it?"

"Mr. Smith hasn't named it yet."

"Well, obviously it is going to succeed the *Tip Top* weeklies," Patten said casually. "Why not call it, say, *Top Notch?* Not a bad title. And incidentally, I'd like to be editor of the thing."

"Why not ask O. G.?" Ralston said.

"I could do it easily enough from Maine," Patten said. He had a deep attachment to his place, "Overrocks," near Camden, Maine, and he did most of his work there. "You know how we could work

Bremerton Wash.
September 19, 1912.

My Dear Sir:—

Will you please favor me with your kind attention and a prompt reply? "I hope you will."

Will you see if there is any more of them gun silencers, which where on sale a few years ago about 1910, for sale at the present date; if so please reply promptly, for there is a life at stake.

I will await your reply with anxiety, and please do not forget to write what peice they are sold for.

I enclose a two cent stamp, for your answer, and oblidge

T. H. Black add. above.

P.S. "answer promptly please."

"A life at stake"

Ormond G. Smith's home in Centre Island, New York

it? Every Friday you could come to Overrocks with the manuscripts submitted that week. I'd work on them during the week end and you could bring everything back with you on Monday."

"I don't know," Ralston said doubtfully. "You better see the Boss about that."

Patten did see O. G. about it. "Not a chance," Smith said coldly. "I want my editors where I can step across the hall and speak to them. No man can edit a magazine from six hundred miles away."

Smith did accept Patten's title for the magazine, and he did make "Burt L. Standish" editor in name, but Patten only wrote for the new publication. His name, of course (owned by Street & Smith), was still a potent force, and the cover always displayed in big type, "Edited by Burt L. Standish." The man Smith picked to be editor was a short, stocky, round-faced former *New York World* Sunday-feature editor named Henry Wilton Thomas, who, for years, would be known and loved by his co-workers as "Hank" or "Tommy." Hank Thomas had a gift for dry humor, and when the occasion warranted it, for vigorous and colorful invective.

Thomas never admitted that he was editing a magazine for older boys. "I only want high-class adventure fiction that adults will like," he'd tell prospective writers who wrote in offering manuscripts. He never seemed to sense that the stories they wrote and which he eagerly accepted were, in fact, juveniles of a rather superior class.

The first issue of *Top Notch* appeared March 1, 1910, as a twice-a-month, five-cent publication. It did have a fresh, youthful appeal. Usually Patten had a Frank Merriwell story in *Top Notch*. These were about Frank Merriwell, the businessman. Editor Hank Thomas never did like the Merriwell stories (he thought they were too juvenile for his "adult" magazine). For years he feuded with Gil Patten, which made him just about the only man who found it difficult to get along with amiable, easygoing Patten. Thomas had a passion for alliterative titles. His idea of a great title would be *Buffaloed in Buffalo* or *Whisked to Wisconsin*. One day he became excited about a title, *Landed in Atlanta,* and he asked Patten to spend a couple of weeks in Atlanta absorbing local color.

"I've got a lot of friends in Atlanta," he said. "I'll give you letters to them. They'll help you. My idea is to have a young northerner land in Atlanta—get it?—and he meets the Atlanta people, and although at first he doesn't like them much and naturally they're suspicious of the Yankee, but after awhile . . ."

Patten listened to the outline, drew some expense money and headed for Georgia. He returned and worked a week on his story. Then he sent it to Thomas. He received a call from the editor asking him to drop in. Thomas told him bluntly that he didn't like the story at all.

"But damn it," Patten exploded, "it's your story. You told me what kind of characters you wanted; you told me the plot, you told me . . ."

"There's one thing I didn't tell you," Thomas interrupted icily. "I didn't tell you to write a rotten story."

Top Notch soon reached the 200,000 mark in circulation. It was a solid circulation; returns from newsstands were less than two per cent. Hank Thomas had great pride in the magazine he edited. A staff artist usually did the action covers for the publication. One day a cover had been accepted and sent to him. He didn't like it and he stormed into George Smith's office.

"Did you okay this cover and send it to me?" he asked belligerently.

"Why, sure, Hank," Smith said, surprised. "Pretty good cover, don't you think?"

"It's a horrible cover," Thomas cried. "Why, damn it, G. C., you think that anything is good enough for *Top Notch*. You give me stuff you won't use in any of your other magazines."

"This is a fine drawing; it'll make a good cover," Smith said.

"All right, all right, I'll use it," the editor raged, "but I don't like it. However, you own the magazine. It's your property, and from now on if you want to show the red, palpitating rear end of a hen on the cover, it's all right with me."

George Smith roared with laughter. No one could get angry with Hank Thomas. *Top Notch* was his baby and he was devoted to it. The magazine was a big money-maker for seventeen years. Thomas retired to live in Italy, and with his retirement, the magazine began to decline. Not even Ormond Smith could explain why phenomenally successful magazines would start losing their popularity, but it invariably happened.

"Magazines, like people, grow old," Smith would say, and that became a guiding principle in the firm. When a magazine grew old it was time to retire it.

CHAPTER
EIGHT

SEA STORIES

STREET & SMITH

A cover of *Love Story Magazine*, first published in 1921

CHAPTER

EIGHT

The changing American scene, with its accompanying development in tastes, interests and customs on the part of the public, never escaped the close editorial scrutiny of the owners of Street & Smith. By 1915 an industry still in its infancy gave every evidence of becoming a permanent American institution. The motion picture had already so captured the fancy of the public that it made idols of stars like Pearl White, Kathleen Williams, Beverly Baine and Francis X. Bushman.

It was the heyday of the star, and fan clubs dedicated to their worship were being formed all over the country. *Motion Picture Magazine* was the only publication which devoted itself completely to the new industry. Its success prompted Henry Ralston to suggest to O. G. that the firm get on the bandwagon and publish a weekly devoted exclusively to motion pictures. O. G. approved the idea and suggested that young Gerald Duffy, son of Richard Duffy, first editor of *Ainslee's,* be made editor.

Gerald Duffy had inherited much of the magic with which his father had been touched. He and Ralston worked out a formula, and the result was *Picture-Play Weekly.* The first issue appeared September 4, 1915, and it sold out within hours after it hit the newsstands. It was an overnight success. The first cover showed a picture of Charles Chaplin in a scene from his new picture, *In the Park.*

Young Duffy created a feature for the magazine which to this day has survived in and out of movie magazines. He would select a successful film and assign a writer to translate it into a short story.

Among the departments in the magazine was one called "Hints for Scenario Writers" by Clarence J. Caine.

It is assumed that the majority of those who follow this department have had some experience in preparing scripts for the market, but for the benefit of beginners even the most simple questioning pertaining to photo-play writing will be treated at some time or another in the future. Any scenarioist who is in doubt as to anything which comes under the head of script writing is welcomed to write in and state his trouble. Questions will be promptly answered through this department or personally.

Hundreds of letters from hopeful script writers arrived every week. "Film Flams" by Dean Bowman was the forerunner of today's Louella Parsons type of film gossip column. The first issue presented such items as:

That the picture-play business is growing some is attested by the startling assertion that there are now over five thousand pantomime performers employed in the infant industry in southern California, and, by actual count, some two thousand keep an automobile.

Doctor W. A. Evans, the eminent Chicagoan who was selected as foreman of the Eastland horror jury, says that the movies are fast correcting the early flickering that caused headache and eye troubles, and from experiments suggests that the shining light be thrown from below by lowering the projector, instead of from above, as is now done.

When Billy B. Van, at his studio in New Hampshire, the other day invited all the professionals summering at Lake Sunapee to witness the taking and making of a film, Ruth Chatterton, the leading lady whom Henry Miller exploits, acknowledged that the movies held great possibilities and were destined to preserve the drama as the phonograph will perpetuate the music of today. Can it be possible?

In connection with the high-salary phase of the movies it was revealed recently that contracts have been signed by Miss Kitty Gordon and the World Film Company for fifteen hundred dollars a week for one year, between Robert Warwick and the Peerless Company for a lump sum of one hundred and four thousand dollars for his services for two years, and between Miss Lillian Lorraine and the Balboa for seven hundred dollars a week for one year.

Within a month circulation had risen to 100,000. Ormond Smith immediately increased the price to ten cents. Two years later it rose to fifteen cents. But this did not deter eager movie fans from buying it. During the late twenties, *Picture-Play Weekly* reached the incredible circulation of 400,000 copies.

Cover of *Picture Play* magazine, first published in 1915

J.C. Leyendecker   Edward Penfield

Howard Chandler Christy   James Montgomery Flagg

Covers for *Popular* and *Ainslee's* by famous illustrators of the day

The same year they established *Picture Play Weekly* Ormond and George Smith sensed a fading interest on the part of their readers in the *Tip Top* weeklies. This series was beginning to show its age. Even Nick Carter and Frank Merriwell were losing their deep-rooted appeal. The decision was made to condense the *Tip Top* weeklies and combine and publish them as a semi-monthly. That venture lasted only eight months. Perhaps sentiment suggested that its successor be called *Wide Awake,* the name of the first publication issued by the original Francis Smith in 1850. But, like its predecessor, it too expired as a result of public indifference.

Frederick Tilney had been editor of the *Tip Top* weeklies. He was a versatile, energetic man who spent eight hours a day getting out the weeklies and eight hours a day studying medicine at Long Island University. When he attained his medical degree he decided to concentrate on his chosen profession. As Dr. Frederick Tilney he later became one of New York's best-known neurologists.

O. G. asked Ralston to find another editor. One of the applicants for the job was Frank E. Blackwell, a reporter and feature writer for the *New York Sun*. Ralston had on hand a Frank Merriwell story —one of the rare ones which had been ghosted for Gilbert Patten. The story needed considerable editing and tightening. He gave it to young Blackwell as a test.

Three days later Blackwell returned. Ralston read his fine version of the story and hired him immediately.

Neither Ralston nor Ormond Smith ever regretted the decision. Blackwell's qualifications were well suited to a Street & Smith editorship. His judgment was good, he was well liked and he could always rewrite a yarn quickly and satisfactorily.

Ormond, his brother, George, and Ralston frequently renewed their discussions of how to recapture the young male audience. Finally O. G. approved an idea of Ralston's: the firm would publish a semi-monthly magazine devoted only to detective fiction.

"Youngsters are getting tired of reading about the same characters week after week," Ormond Smith mused. "They're even getting fed up with Nick Carter. Let's discontinue the *Nick Carter Weekly* and start a magazine that will have a dozen different detectives as characters. Perhaps some of them will catch on. We'll call it—oh—let's see . . . What do you think of *Detective Story Magazine,* Will?"

"Sounds good to me," Ralston said. "How about letting Blackwell handle it? I like his work."

"You and George work it out," Ormond Smith said.

The head of the firm usually operated that way. He was the Boss, and no one ever forgot it, but he was a man who delegated authority to those in whom he had confidence. Ralston still had no title, but more and more Ormond and George were depending not only on his judgment but on his capacity for administering and executing the most minute details of a magazine operation. Through the years Ralston had risen to a position which in another firm might be called Assistant to the President. He was completely dedicated to his job and personally devoted to Ormond and George Smith. He expected the same loyalty to the firm from the employees of Street & Smith that he himself gave to the partners. He was a meticulous taskmaster who kept a sharp eye on all personnel as well as on editorial and production problems. He was only thirty-four, but seventeen of those years had been spent with the firm and his loyalty was fierce and uncompromising. Younger members of the staff grumbled at his disciplinarian methods; more mature employees respected him tremendously, and today when you mention the name of Henry Ralston to the people who worked for him over the years, their eyes light up and they'll relate a hundred and one kindnesses they remember.

When O. G. handed Ralston and George Smith the new venture, they sat down in their shirt sleeves and figured out the problem from editorial, production and circulation angles. When they were finished, there were no loose ends dangling. They made up a dummy of the first issue, showed it to O. G., who gave his approval, and on October 5, 1915, *Detective Story Magazine,* a ten-cent semi-monthly was seen on the newsstands of the country for the first time. The editor? Who else but Nicholas Carter?

The first issue contained five short stories, by Nathan Day, Frank Parks, Ross Beeckman, R. Norman Grisewood and Will R. Joyes. There were two serials, *Brits of Headquarters* by Hilary Blake, and *The Yellow Label* (from the archives of Nicholas Carter). There was one novelette by Arnold Duncan, *Through Slatted Blinds.* Ormond Smith wanted this magazine aimed at youngsters as well as adults who enjoyed stories of murder and larceny. This made the job of

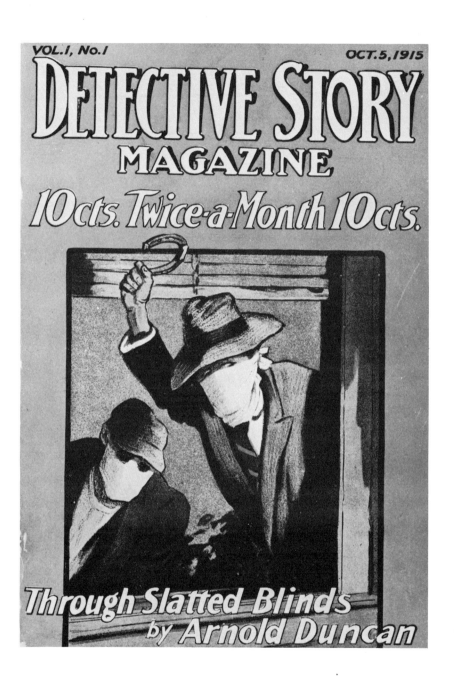

Detective Story was first published in 1915

editing the publication a tricky one. Ralston and Editor Blackwell spent a great deal of time searching for material that would not be too sophisticated for the young reader nor too juvenile for the adult. They effected a compromise that was successful from the beginning.

It was a policy of Ormond Smith's to start a new publication on a semi-monthly basis. If it showed signs of durability he would switch it to a weekly. A magazine had to have a wide appeal to sell fifty-two issues a year, and there had to be an endless flow of editorial matter to feed the insatiable monster.

By 1917 the success of *Detective Story Magazine* was assured. It became a weekly and it was off on one of the most sensational and enduring careers any magazine in the country had ever enjoyed. It would thrive and lead the field of detective fiction for thirty years. Its popularity was no accident; Ralston and Blackwell corralled the best writers of detective fiction here and abroad. By the time it became a weekly the inevitable happened; adults had taken the magazine to their hearts. Ormond Smith realized that the compromise hadn't quite worked. Youngsters read it, all right, but most of the letters which came in (every one of which was carefully studied) made it evident that youngsters just didn't have ten cents each week to spend on a magazine.

In 1918, Ralston, who kept in constant touch with English publishing firms, had read a story by a writer named Edgar Wallace. He liked the man's style and wrote to his publishers in London. He secured the American rights to three stories which Wallace had written for the "penny dreadfuls" so popular in England at that time. They formed a series, *The Lapses of Larry Loman,* and were published in *Popular Magazine* in 1918 under the subtitles, *The Crime Trust, The Affair of the Stokehole* and *The Cure.* Ralston paid $100 for each story. These were the first stories ever printed in the United States by the man who was destined to become perhaps the most widely read crime-story writer of the first half of the twentieth century. Now Ralston, with 128 pages to fill every week, again contacted Wallace.

Wallace had become well known in England. His agent responded that he would be glad to give Ralston a story for $500 and he sent the story along. It was called *Stamped in Gold.* Ralston wrote back, saying that although he would pay $500 and more for originals, this one was, after all, a reprint. By the time it would appear in *Detective Story Magazine* it would have already been printed in an English publication and, for all Ralston knew, might then be pirated by some American publisher. He suggested that $350 would be a fair price. Wallace accepted the offer. This was the first of eighty-nine Wallace stories which would appear in the magazine.

Edgar Wallace was a product of the London slums. Orphaned at the age of ten days, he was adopted by a Billingsgate fishmonger and his wife. His formal education ended at ten when he had to go out and hustle for a few pennies. He sold newspapers, shined shoes, worked in printing offices, worked as a laborer mending roads, and finally went to sea as a deckhand. A long and violent attack of seasickness ended that phase of his career. He became a milkman's helper and then joined the army. He was sent to South Africa, and it was in the service that he discovered the joys of reading. Wallace decided that writing could be a pleasant and not very taxing diversion so he left the army and went to work as a reporter for a South African newspaper. During the Boer War he worked as a correspondent for Reuters. Wallace quickly mastered the skill of turning out fast and colorful copy. Then he discovered the "penny dreadful" and began his career as a crime writer, receiving the standard rate of fifteen dollars per thousand words. He made a fair living, but it was not until Street & Smith introduced him to the American market that he skyrocketed into fame and fortune.

His stories were rich in atmosphere. His childhood in the slums gave his stories an authenticity lacking in the yarns by writers who did not know the Whitechapel or East London patois first hand. He had an extraordinary gift for creating suspense, and this knack of attaching a "cliffhanger" to the end of an installment was a valuable one commercially. He had resource, inventive powers, an eye for character, remarkable memory for the incidents of his youth, and an amazing capacity for work. He seemed to know instinctively what other writers of detective stories had to learn by trial and error. Edgar Allan Poe, the pioneer in the modern detective story, wrote five tales of deductive analysis. Anthony Boucher, perhaps the most knowledgeable of all critics of the medium, has said that in these five stories Poe anticipated all of the standard elements required of the detective story of today—from the Locked Room to the Least Suspected Person. It is hardly likely that Wallace ever read Poe until long after he had established himself as the Laureate of Crime, but he had an instinctive knowledge of these basic ingredients and he exploited them all. A hearty, bluff, amiable man, he was loved by everyone; he had absolutely no pretensions in judging his own work. Once when asked to explain his tremendous popularity, he uttered what well might have been the philosophy which helped make Street & Smith the largest publisher in the world.

"The ordinary man lives a rather restricted life," he said. "He is a creature of circumstance. One day is very much like another. But almost every one of us has dreams. We all want to get away from ourselves. We all crave some sort of excitement, some vicarious experience. It is this that the detective story supplies. It takes people out of themselves and often out of mischief."

Wallace was never at a loss for a plot. The ideas bubbled in his brain and fought for expression. In the midst of the grueling job of writing a crime novel a week, he was known to halt the novel and dash off a play in twenty-four hours—and a play that made good. He once wrote an eighty-thousand-word serial in three days, but his average rate of speed was from sixteen to twenty thousand words a day, about five times what the most industrious novelists were then capable of doing.

In thinking out a plot, he began with the denouement and worked backwards to arrive at the beginning, usually without making notes. Then, when the puzzle was satisfactorily worked out, he began to dictate and found this part of the task remarkably easy. Wallace used a dictaphone, talking into it as the spirit moved, day or night

Yet he had no special system about his work. In addition to his writing he had innumerable other interests, the most engrossing of which was his fondness for horse racing and for betting on the races. That took much of his time. But somehow the work got done—detective novels, plays, magazine articles, movies, newspaper reviews, short stories. It is said that one-fourth of the books sold in England during the 1920's were written by him. Life amused him tremendously and he often said so.

"I love life," he said. "I like horses, I like women for their beauty and charm, and their wisdom, too. As the Scotchman said, or somebody else, 'I've got my troubles, but most of them never happened.' "

Edgar Wallace died in 1932 at the age of fifty-six. By then, *Detective Story Magazine,* partly because of his contributions, was known as the most popular and widely read crime publication in the world.

In 1919, Ormond Smith felt that it was about time that venerable Buffalo Bill was laid to rest. The weekly which featured the old gentleman was beginning to slow down. It was still profitable, but Ormond and George felt that the day of the five-cent weekly was almost over. *Buffalo Bill Stories* was the only one which had survived. It was tying up a precious press that might be more profitably employed.

"Try to sell *Buffalo Bill*," Ormond Smith told Ralston just before Ormond left on a trip to France.

Ralston tried, but no one wanted the old character. The trade naturally felt that if Smith wanted to unload the killer of buffaloes and Indians his course had been run. Unable to sell the property, Ralston suggested to George Smith that they discontinue the weekly and start a new magazine—*Western Story Magazine.* Smith liked the idea and gave Ralston the green light. Frank Blackwell was put in charge, and on July 12, 1919, *Western Story Magazine,* Formerly *New Buffalo Bill Weekly,* appeared on the newsstands of the nation. On the cover was the reminder, "Big Clean Stories of Western Life." The "Formerly *New Buffalo Bill Weekly*" was dropped after eight weeks and for some thirty years thereafter the magazine was known as *Western Story Magazine.* It was one of the most profitable ventures the firm had ever known. It cost ten cents, was published twice a month, and its first issue contained 128 pages. Its policy was declared in its first issue under a heading, "The Round-Up." It read:

Max Brand

Edgar Wallace

179

Greetings, Readers, gentle and otherwise!

In this, the first issue of *Western Story Magazine,* in its vastly enlarged and improved form, we make to you our initial bow, in what practically amounts to a brand-new magazine.... Hunched up over a desk, are you? Well, read about the life you would like to lead, and the life you *will* lead, just as soon as you can throw off the bonds that keep you from making a break for the woods or the rolling plains, with rivers flowing through them, out, out, at the beckoning lure of more adventure, onto the vast Pacific.

... Night has come. The ponies are hobbled, the big horns are grazing along the river bank. Supper is over. The fire burns brightly. Join the circle of recumbent forms round it, and the best writers of western adventure stories will entertain you.

For a time, the magazine continued to publish one Buffalo Bill yarn in each issue. The first number contained two novelettes, two serials, five short stories and eight miscellaneous items. William Slavens McNutt (who became one of Hollywood's most prolific and highest-paid writers), Wilson Mead, Jackson Gregory, Bertrand W. Sinclair, Preston Ward, A. M. Chisholm and William McLeod Raine were all in the first issue. All of them would appear in many succeeding numbers of *Western Story.*

By November, 1920, *Western Story Magazine* had hit the 300,000-mark in circulation. Smith decided that it was strong enough to become a weekly. He was right. But the magazine really began its amazing climb toward the half-million mark in 1921 when a manuscript came into the office with the then unfamiliar name of Max Brand as its author. The story of Max Brand himself is an extraordinary one.

In 1922 a slim volume of poetry called *The Village Street* appeared. Its ninety-eight pages contained twenty-one poems. It was by Frederick Schiller Faust, and it attracted just about as much attention as does the usual slim volume of verse. However, one discerning critic, William Rose Benét, writing in the *Literary Review,* said: "Here is a small book by a new poet. Delicate strength is in this book and vivid description. It is something to discover a modern writer so sensitive to the effectiveness of simplicity and clarity. This book shows evidence of careful workmanship. We ourselves hope for more poetry from this author."

It was not until 1931 that Frederick Faust published another book of poetry. *Dionysus in Hades* appeared in a limited edition of 500 copies in England. Leonard Bacon said: "The stately *Dionysus in*

Hades, though it pleased not the million, is nobly planned, nobly felt, nobly written."

These two thin books of excellent verse and a few other poems are all that survive of Frederick Faust, who was killed in action in Italy, May 11, 1944. They may not have "pleased the millions," but the two hundred books, the dozens of motion pictures, the five hundred serials and the countless short stories he wrote under the name of Max Brand, and seventeen other aliases, did indeed please the millions. Max Brand, to use the name by which he was best known, was called the king of the pulps. He wrote about shipwrecks in the south seas, sinister crime lords of the mysterious Far East, pirates who once roamed the Caribbean, fabulous heroes of sport, welders and bridge workers and pilots, prize fighters and secret-service men and bull fighters, and of life in high and low society. But mostly Max Brand wrote westerns.

Bret Harte and Mark Twain were perhaps the co-parents of the modern western story. Harte's *The Luck of Roaring Camp* appeared soon after the Civil War. The East began to discover the fascination of the frontier country. It was a turbulent period, and echoes of the wild, lawless life of the western towns were heard in Boston and New York and Philadelphia. Mark Twain achieved great success with his *Roughing It,* Francis Parkman kindled more interest with *The Oregon Trail,* and Stewart Edward White wrote *The Westerners.* Max Brand wrote about a different kind of West. Bret Harte wrote under the handicap of actually knowing the West; so did Mark Twain, who had worked as a reporter in Virginia City. Zane Grey, who followed them, also knew the prairies, the mining towns, the vastness, the beauty and the vitality of the West.

Max Brand labored under no such disadvantage. He knew nothing about the early West (any more than he knew about crime in the Far East, Caribbean pirates, bridge workers, pilots or bull fighters), but he created a West as people imagined it to be. He wrote of gamblers and ranchers and pioneers and cowboys and quick-tempered gunmen. He began writing westerns in 1918, and the demand for his synthetic but exciting product was so great that he wrote more than a million words a year for the next twenty-five years. His stories never attempted to demonstrate an awareness of the historical importance of the period they purported to depict. Max Brand was not a historian; he was simply an imaginative storyteller. He himself said that his books, serials and short stories had no more literary merit than his readers had literary perception. But millions loved *The Untamed, Destry Rides Again, Singing Guns, Montana Rides* and the hundreds of stories which appeared in *Western Story Magazine* alone, under the names of George Owen Baxter, George Challis, Peter Dawson, Martin Dexter, Evin Evans, John Frederick, David Manning, Hugh Owen, Nicholas Silver and, of course, Max Brand. He might have three serials and two short stories in an issue of *Western Story Magazine,* and at the same time have stories in *Far West Illustrated, Detective Fiction, Weekly Story Magazine, Blue Book, Black Mask, Argosy* or *Adventure.* While his left hand manufactured tailor-made stories for the pulps, his right hand, moving only a bit more slowly and cautiously, was turning out serials for such respectable slicks as *Collier's, Cosmopolitan* and *The Saturday Evening Post.* At the height of his writing career he went to Hollywood where he turned out the Doctor Kildare series of pictures as easily as he turned out westerns. A Hollywood writer who manages to produce seven or eight pages of copy a day is considered to be a fast workman. There are still writers at Warner Brothers who will recollect with awe that Max Brand wrote as many as fifty pages a day, and that these pages, unchanged, would constitute part of the actual shooting script. He did his first Kildare script in thirteen days.

The man Frederick Faust had no respect at all for the pulp and screen writer, Max Brand. Faust was a highly literate, sensitive, poetic and cultured man. "Junk, sheer junk," he'd laugh when someone at Warner Brothers said he had liked a western or a thriller which he had written. Brand had a great capacity for friendship. He was generous, warm-hearted, and it is likely that he never had an enemy in his life—not even the anonymous German or Italian who fired the mortar that killed him, for this one-man literary factory was almost as popular in Europe as in his native land.

Max Brand regarded the writing of fiction as a house painter or an accountant would look upon his particular job—it was a means of making enough money to live comfortably. He had a zest for living, an appetite for the good things in life, a fabulous capacity for concentration, and a family which he loved. His parents died when he was quite young, and he had known poverty for many years. He worked his way through the University of California and, with his instinctive flair for writing, won practically every literary honor the undergraduate world of the University had to offer. He was editor of the campus humor magazine and the moving spirit in *The Occident,* a student publication which printed the best work done by the undergraduates. With a classmate, Sidney Howard, who later became famous as a dramatist, he wrote a play, *Fiat Lux,* which was produced by the class of 1915. He also wrote a number of poems for the various student publications.

After a hitch with the Canadian army in World War I, he began to write professionally. He read one of Zane Grey's magnificent western novels, and it was possibly this prolific and popular master of western stories who influenced him most. There was one great difference between the two men—Zane Grey breathed life into his tales, Max Brand manufactured his. He reserved the tortuous process of serious writing for the two little volumes of verse and a few poems which later appeared in *Harper's* and *The Literary Digest.* But the Frederick Faust who admired Shakespeare, Chaucer, Homer, Dante and the music of Bach never infringed on the territory which Max Brand had staked out as a path to riches. The classicist and scholar never interfered with the assembly line presided over by Max Brand. He would laugh when colleagues said it was a pity that he couldn't spend more time on poetry. Poetry isn't important, he'd tell them smilingly (and unconvincingly); money is important. And so, to use his own words, he "hacked away."

When he was working and living in Hollywood he often visited the Campbell Book Shop in nearby Westwood. Owner Robert Campbell always had in stock the latest American and English literary magazines. Max Brand (who was called "Heinie" by everyone who knew him) would drop in to peruse the new magazines. As he looked through them, Campbell knew that Frederick Faust and not Max Brand was in his store. It was the poet and serious writer who ordered books on literary criticism, Shakespeare or new translations of the Greek poets. It was Frederick Faust who delighted in the esoteric writing of James Joyce and who, idling through a volume of poems, would declaim with sheer delight the music of a verse he had chanced upon.

Cervantes was a special idol of his, and once he said to Campbell, "Damn it, Bob, Cervantes was fifty-six before he started *Don Quixote.*

STREET & SMITH'S

WESTERN STORY

MAGAZINE
Title Registered U. S. Patent Office.

EVERY WEEK

Yearly Subscription, $6.00   Six Months, $3.00   Single Copies 15 Cents

Vol. CXI   Contents for April 2, 1932   No. 6

Publication issued every week by Street & Smith Publications, Inc., 79-89 Seventh Avenue, New York, N. Y. Ormond G. Smith, President; George C. Smith, Vice President and Treasurer; George C. Smith, Jr., Vice President; Ormond V. Gould, Secretary. Copyright, 1932, by Street & Smith Publications, Inc., New York. Copyright, 1932, by Street & Smith Publications, Inc., Great Britain. Entered as Second-class Matter, September 4, 1917, at the Post Office at New York, N. Y., under Act of Congress of March 3, 1879. Foreign subscription, $8.50.
We do not accept responsibility for the return of unsolicited manuscripts.
To facilitate handling, the author should inclose a self-addressed envelope with the requisite postage attached.
STREET & SMITH PUBLICATIONS, INC., 79 7th AVE., NEW YORK, N. Y.

Max Brand, George Owen Baxter and David Manning were Frederick Faust

He was a broken-down old soldier who had spent his life in poverty, in prison and in hospitals, and yet he had enough spirit left to write something they'll be reading as long as they publish books. There's still time for me to do something worthwhile."

"You're getting $3,000 a week at Warner's," Campbell chided him.

"For writing stuff I won't even read or look at when it comes out as a picture," Faust muttered.

But occasionally he would come on another errand. "I've got an order for a serial about India," he would tell Campbell. "I don't know a damn thing about India, Bob. You got any old books that can fill me in?"

Campbell usually did. Once Max Brand bought three hundred volumes of the Everyman Library with the wry comment that he could find background here for at least three hundred books. He never borrowed plots—he did borrow backgrounds. He was a magician who created illusions with words. Millions read his stories set in India, China or Alaska and felt that they were eye-witnesses at events that had actually taken place.

The writing of stories that will entrance the millions is a highly specialized craft. Plot and action are the two ingredients of the pulp story, and no man ever lived who could invent so many plots (not even Balzac) or so crowd a few thousand words with action as Max Brand. The competition was terrific among pulp writers. "Serious" writers who condescendingly tried the medium in the hope of picking up some quick cash, seldom were able to sell their stories. The pulp trade demanded constant creation, not leisurely characterization or exposition or description. Max Brand had a limitless capacity for creating new plots and new heroes two or three times a week. No man since the days when Walter Scott was turning out his Waverly Novels ever spewed forth so many words. He wrote about thirty million of them during his career, and most of them were words of action. Readers of the pulps wanted their stories unadorned by any stylistic decorations; they wanted no philosophic digressions, scenic descriptions or probing of character. They wanted their heroes to be full-blooded, courageous he-men; they wanted their villains to be black enough to hate from the opening page. And, above all, they wanted continuous action. The fact that more than six million copies of his books were bought by enthusiastic fans is conclusive evidence that he gave them what they wanted.

No one knew this better than Frank E. Blackwell, editor of *Western Story Magazine*. He knew that he had a gold mine in Max Brand, and he never stopped mining. He would always feature the Brand stories and titillate readers with what would appear "next week." A typical blurb of his would be:

> Banner issue next week, folks. The first installment of a great serial by George Owen Baxter. Baxter calls his latest (and many of you will think it his best) *Lucky Larribee*. Dashing title that! and the story does not belie its name. Then there is a complete novel by Max Brand. Brand's handle for the story is *Speedy's Crystal Game,* and it's as fast as its name. Comes along toward the end of the magazine the second installment of *The Golden Spurs* by David Manning. And then, folks, with next week's issue begins a serial by a new man, Evin Evans: *Montana Rides.* Some of the critics on this here editorial ranch have declared this yarn to be something extra. We await your verdict. She sure does move, that's one thing certain.

Corny? Just about as corny as the television cigarette commercials you hear every night; as corny as the ranting of a hysterical revivalist preacher. Shrewd Editor Blackwell, who wrote that blurb in 1932, knew that the country had produced more than three billion bushels of the product in that year and that Americans had consumed most of it. The consumption of corn has always been a peculiarly American enthusiasm, whether it be on the cob or off the typewriter. Editor Blackwell saw no reason to repudiate the honored American tradition.

As a matter of fact, Evin Evans' story had to be postponed until a later issue because late advertising had come in. But it made no difference, for hundreds of letters would come to the desk of Editor Blackwell debating the relative merits of George Owen Baxter, Max Brand, David Manning and the "new" writer Evin Evans. Had anyone ever told the faithful reader that they were all one and the same man, he would have risked getting scalped. Each reader had his favorite.

Later "Peter Henry Morland" appeared as a contributor. He wrote *Beyond the Outpost,* and the flood of enthusiastic fan letters meant that author Morland had to stay alive. So the obliging writer created a few characters with such names as "White-Water Sam," "Flash," "Old North," "Geraldi," "Spot Lester," gave them horses

Edward J. Clode, Inc.
156 Fifth Ave., N. Y. C.
"A Mysterious Disappearance"
By
Louis Tracy
(57,000 words)
Am. Sr. Rts.

~~1500~~

make out
two (2) checks
one to be
Cabled

Frederick Faust
Cut Check to:
Frederick Faust, Guaranty
Trust Co., 50 Pall Mall,
London, England → $2000⁰⁰
Mail check to:
Irving Bank - Columbia
Trust Co., Personal Trust
Dept., Woolworth Bldg.,
N. Y. for → 3000⁰⁰
"Sutton Hall"
(80,000 words)) this was
Am. Sr. Rts. $1000 too
much. We
got $6000 more back by only paying
$2000 for "Pleasant Jim" on July 15

PAID JUL 1 - 1927

5000

Harley P. Lathrop
1037 Eighth St.
East Las Vegas, N. Mex.
"One Way to Pick An
Honest Man"
(7200 words)
Am. Sr. Rts.

PAID JUL 1 - 1927

216

Editor Blackwell thought $5,000 was too much

to ride and outlaws to fight, and soon Pete Morland (as the fans called him) became almost as popular as Max Brand. His heroes were chivalrous and courageous; they lived hard, died quick and always called women "ma'am." They were subject to hair-breadth escapes, they loved their horses and their eyes were inclined to narrow as their hands slid to their six-shooters. Sometimes a horse was just as important to a Max Brand story (we use Brand in the generic sense to cover all of his pseudonyms) as was the man who rode him. Sometimes the two were silent, understanding partners.

He sold his first story to *Western Story* in 1921. It was called *The Voice of La Paloma,* and he received $660 for the fifty-thousand-word novel. More often than not his titles were changed. This one became *Jerry Peyton's Notched Inheritance.* That same year he sold a serial, *Iron Dust,* for $1,900, *The Ghost Wagon* for $500, and he was off. Henceforth no issue of *Western Story* was complete without at least one of his stories. The following year his price went up. *Outlaws All* (which appeared as *Ronickey Doone's Reward*), a six-part serial, brought him $2,000, and *Smiling Charlie,* eighty thousand words of action, brought him $4,000.

When the 350,000 readers of *Western Story* opened their weekly package they would always see something like this:

JERRY PEYTON'S NOTCHED INHERITANCE
by George Owen Baxter

Chapter I
THE BEQUEST

When the doctor told Hank Peyton that he was about to die, Hank took another drink and closed the secret inside his thin lips; but when on the third morning following he fell back on his bed in a swoon after pulling on his boots, Hank lay for a long time looking at the dirty boards on the ceiling until his brain cleared. Then he called for his tall son and said, "Jeremiah, I'm about to kick out."

Or they would read:

THE CURE OF SILVER CANYON
by John Frederick

Chapter I
EIGHT MEN OF MYSTERY

This is a story of how Lew Carney made friends with the law. It must not be understood that Lew was an outcast; there was one law which Lew always held in the highest esteem; he never, as far as possible, allowed anyone near him to violate that law. Unfortunately, that law was the will of Lew Carney.

George Owen Baxter would be back again as soon as his previous serial had run its five weeks' course:

DONNEGAN
by George Owen Baxter

Chapter I
TALE OF DONNEGAN

The fifty empty freights danced and rolled and rattled on the rough road bed and filled Jericho Pass with thunder; the big engine was laboring and grunting at the grade, but five cars back the noise of the locomotive was lost. Yet there is a way to talk above the noise of a freight train, just as there is a way to whistle into the teeth of a stiff wind. This freight-car talk is pitched just above the ordinary tone— it is an overtone of conversation, one might say—and it is distinctly nasal. The Brakie could talk above the racket, and so, of course, could "Lefty" Joe. . . .

"It's like old times to have you here," said the Brakie. "You used to play this line when you jumped from coast to coast."

"Sure," said Lefty Joe, and he scowled at the mountains on either side of the pass.

The old pay-books of Street & Smith tell a story of their own. In 1927 Brand received the fantastic price of $5,000 for *Thunder Moon,* another eighty-thousand-word serial. Editor Blackwell was away on a vacation when payment was made. When he returned he looked over the pay-book and was shocked at the $5,000 figure. In neat red-inked handwriting is his laconic notation: "Paid too much—deduct a thousand." By 1930, however, *A Friend in Need* brought him $5,000, and this time Blackwell himself set the price. *Silvertip, The Silver Stork* and *Brothers of the West* were among his more successful stories. Occasionally the real Frederick Faust broke through, and reading the stories now you come across passages of real beauty. He was never a hack in the sense that he was second-rate or imitative; he was a literary craftsman of high degree. He may have led a literary double life, but he was no unhappy, tormented genius. He usually spent a couple of hours each morning at his poetry; this in itself gave him the satisfaction he never received from his lucrative westerns.

Perhaps Max Brand's magic lay in his ability to make the reader believe that his most wildly melodramatic situations could in fact occur. Sometimes his heroes were supermen, and the reader associated himself with these fabulous creatures just as a youngster to-day identifies himself with a Willie Mays or a Rocky Marciano. Once a reader had accepted the superman quality of the hero, it was easy to believe in the incredible feats he performed.

Max Brand's best work may well become a permanent part of western folklore.

Western Story had a truly fine array of writers. H. Bedford-Jones, Will James, J. Allan Dunn, Frank Richardson Pierce, Courtney Riley Cooper, Alan LeMay and William Colt MacDonald were frequent contributors to the magazine, but none was as prolific as Max Brand. Top-rank fiction writers like James Oliver Curwood, Albert Payson Terhune and even Damon Runyon occasionally tried their hands at westerns.

During the depression of the 1930's, *Western Story Magazine* was hit hard. Faust sold his last story to the magazine in 1937, a 2,200-word short story, "Eagles Over Crooked Creek." Blackwell apologetically sent him a check for $112.

The magazine was growing old. A typical issue of those days would be as follows, with the prices paid to authors reflecting the financial climate of the time.

NOVEL

TITLE	AUTHOR	PRICE PAID
Trigger Law	Ney Geer	$325.00

SERIALS

Wolves of the Chapparall	Paul Lehman	150.00
Jinglebob Jenkins	Wm. MacDonald	134.12

SHORT STORIES

Shell Game	Ken Gilbert	84.00
Shorty's Long Shot	Roy Humphries	90.00
Chief Plays Vigilante	George Corey Franklin	76.00
Deputy for a Day	Cliff Walters	38.00

ARTICLES

Jim White—Cowboy Explorer	Chas. McNichols	40.00

FEATURE

Interesting and True	H. Fred Young	15.00

DEPARTMENTS

Short Contributions		83.00

The total amount paid to authors in this typical 1938 issue was $1,037.12.

The name of Max Brand now began to appear with more frequency in the slicks. To him it was entirely a question of economics. He had bought himself a magnificent villa in Florence. In his study were two desks; one held a typewriter, on the other was a quill pen with which he wrote his poetry. Italy was his adopted home, but he seldom used the country as a setting for any of his fiction. He sat in his villa writing blood-chilling stories of high adventure, and then he'd leave the typewriter and go to a sidewalk bistro to enjoy the things he loved—good conversation and fine cheese and old wine and succulent figs and ripe pears. Brand loved Italy, but he never became an ex-patriot; he remained passionately devoted to his own country.

He was also devoted to his friends, and his generosity became a legend. Writers hurt by the depression only had to send a note saying, "Dear Heinie, things have been tough lately. If you could spare a quick hundred . . ." There would be a check in the next mail. He made enormous sums of money and he lived as lavishly as a Medici. He had a house full of servants, tutors for his three children, and he bought hundreds of books every year. Carl Brandt, his literary agent and best friend, was getting $30,000 for every serial he sold to *Collier's,* and up to $2,000 for short stories in other slick magazines.

Meanwhile, quite unknown to him, a Max Brand cult was forming back home. Darrell C. Richardson of Covington, Kentucky, a Baptist minister, had developed a hobby of collecting Western Americana and it soon became obvious to the eager researcher that Frederick Faust had written more words than any man who had ever lived. For his own amusement Mr. Richardson published a little periodical called *The Fabulous Faust Fanzine.* To his amazement he found that there were hundreds who shared his enthusiasm for the writings of Max Brand. He eventually published a fascinating book, *Max Brand, the Man and His Work.* It contains several articles about Faust and his writings by those who knew him best. The last twenty-five pages are filled with the titles of the stories, articles, films and poems written by Faust. This labor of love is an enduring tribute to the King of the Pulps. The subject never lived to read it.

During World War II Faust managed to wangle a war correspondent's credentials from *Harper's Magazine.* He wasn't satisfied to interview men who had returned from the lines. He wanted to "get the feel" of men in combat. He had been writing about fighting all his life; now he wanted to compare the fantasy with the reality. He joined a platoon whose objective was to take the small town of Santa Maria Infante in southern Italy. He wanted to write his first eye-witness account of men reacting to danger. It might have been a great story, but he never wrote it. A shell fragment in the chest killed him. He was only fifty-two when he died, but he hadn't missed much. He had achieved fame and fortune; he had the love of a fine family and the devotion of many, many friends. He wrote his own epitaph. It had appeared in *Harper's Magazine* in 1933.

> Only the young fear death.
> A god has crossed their path, and they are sure
> Of Happiness, if it would but endure.
> Only the young fear death;
> For when companions vanish on the way
> And leave us one by one,
> Is it not better done
> Than to come lonely to the end of day?
> Only the young fear death.
> The aged speak not of it. At the door
> They stand with cheerful faces to the last,
> Like men who on the homeward way have passed
> The steps of darkness many times before.

CHAPTER

NINE

WESTERN STORIES

STREET & SMITH

A cover of *Western Story Magazine,* first published in 1919

CHAPTER

NINE

Since the great success of the Bertha M. Clay books, Ormond Smith had been considering the idea of a magazine aimed exclusively at the women's market. He had tried it once in 1913, but the ineptly named *Women's Stories* failed to catch on. The conviction persisted, however, that his original idea was sound. There were highly successful magazines for women in the field of the slicks, but he felt that these did not cater to the mass-circulation mind which he was out to capture—the same public which had been loyal for so long to the romances printed in *The New York Weekly*. The *Weekly* was dead, but that huge audience hadn't died with it. He decided to try a quarterly to be called *Love Story*. He put it into the hands of Amita Fairgrieve, a woman of charm and editorial acumen.

The first issue hit the newsstands in May of 1921. Its literary quality, if one may (with misgiving) use the phrase, approximated that of the *Weekly* in its heyday. It opened with a novelette, *A Fatal Temptation*, by Bertha M. Clay, the first installment of a serial, *Love Triumphant* by Ralph Kaye Ashley, three short stories, three poems and two departments. A poem by Dora Greenwall set the tone of the publication.

HOME

Two birds within one nest;
Two hearts within one breast;
Two spirits in one fair
Firm league of love and prayer,
Together bound for aye, together blest.

An ear that waits to catch
A hand upon the latch!

A step that hastens its sweet rest to win,
A world of care without,
A world of strife shut out,
A world of love shut in.

One department which immediately became immensely popular was highly reminiscent of the same kind of feature in the pages of *My Queen* twenty years earlier. It was headed, "Heart Talks with the Troubled" and gave advice to the lovelorn.

· *Love Story* remained a quarterly for only two issues, and then in August, 1921, it became a semi-monthly. A new department, "Over the Editor's Desk," was inaugurated.

> The editors of *Love Story Magazine* take pride in announcing the addition to their staff of Doctor Augusta Winton, whose first article of a series on "How to be Beautiful" will appear in the next issue.
>
> Doctor Winton has made an exhaustive study of the subject of Beauty and its inextricable relationship to Health. She is exceptionally well equipped to give advice and instructions on problems related to this important subject, and will be glad to answer any questions sent to her in care of this magazine.
>
> Girls! Suppose *you* were stenographer to a millionaire and he suddenly asked you to pose as his daughter for a few months or a year? What would you do? Would the thought of all the lovely things you could have—the pretty clothes, the jewels—and all the good times he and his wife could give you, tempt you to agree? Would the thought of the comforts you could buy for your widowed mother and little sister influence you in the same direction for more unselfish reasons?
>
> This is the problem that confronted Dorothy Humphreys. How she met it and what befell her in consequence is told in "An Innocent Pretender," by Georgette MacMillan in the August 25th number.

The public liked the new magazine, but advertisers remained a little shy. In this issue there were only three advertisements, a full page taken by the Wurlitzer Company to extol its musical instruments, a full page devoted to the International Correspondence Schools, and a full-page advertisement headed:

New Secrets in Jujitsu
Makes You Master of Men

It told how a girl equipped with this science would no longer be at the mercy of a ruffian or a bully but would be able to defend herself effectively and "be able to retain her presence of mind." The secrets of jujitsu by Captain C. Smith would answer these questions.

The following issue explained the purpose of the magazine:

LOVE STORY MAGAZINE

has recently made its appearance. Its contents are, as its name implies, based upon the greatest thing in the world: *Love!*

Love Story is *not* just another of those sex-problem magazines, which have done incalculable harm.

Love Story is clean at heart, and its stories are written around the love of the one man for the one woman.

Civilization has been built upon this sort of love—all the great accomplishments of mankind have been inspired by good women who were greatly beloved.

Love Story Magazine will take a place in your life that no other magazine can occupy, because *Love Story* has an irresistibly human appeal.

Within a year the circulation had climbed to 100,000. Strangely enough, less than three per cent of those who bought the magazine were subscribers. Its circulation was ninety-seven per cent newsstand. When Amita Fairgrieve resigned to live in Bucks County, Pennsylvania, where she wanted to raise a family, her place was taken by Ruth Ebeling, an experienced sob sister out of Terre Haute, Indiana. However, it wasn't until 1929 that *Love Story* shifted into high gear with the advent of Daisy Bacon as editor. Within three

Bill Barnes, which was begun in 1928   Daisy Bacon

years this remarkable young woman had raised the circulation of *Love Story* to 600,000.

The 1920's were a time of youthful revolt and a gleeful assault on the old standards. The public lapped up *Flaming Youth*, never realizing that the Warner Fabian who wrote it was really gentle Samuel Hopkins Adams, having a chuckle at the public's expense. *Bad Girl* and *The Beautiful and Damned* were best sellers and conceded by critics to represent the age. James Branch Cabell was lucky enough to have his *Jurgen* banned, with the result that it acquired an audience which otherwise might have ignored it. Young America laughed mockingly at the eternal truths, and Love in general was relegated contemptuously to an old-fashioned past. It was a decade of extravagance in styles, manners and morals. Only a superb ham like Aimee Semple McPherson could bring people into the temples of faith, and a third-rate ham like Texas Guinan could fill the Broadway tabernacles with men and women constantly looking for something new.

Daisy Bacon, with the zeal of a crusader, undertook to defy the customs and tempo of the whirlwind twenties. It was the era of smart and glib writing, and millions were reading the kind of fiction typified by Michael Arlen's *The Green Hat*. New York was flocking to the brittle sophistication of *Charlot's Revue*, starring three newcomers from London—Jack Buchanan, Beatrice Lillie and Gertrude Lawrence. Daisy Bacon believed, contrary to the opinion of critics, that there still was a huge audience which wanted straight old-fashioned romance. She felt that sentiment and femininity were due for a revival.

"Because the girl of today knows that she can earn her own living, she dares to be feminine again," the courageous young editor told a *New York Post* reporter. "She doesn't have to marry to get somebody to support her—she can do that herself—and so she considers other things besides a man's money-making abilities. She looks for charm, companionship and other intangibles in marriage today, where formerly she had to consider whether or not a man was likely to be a good provider. This doesn't mean that romance is out. Quite the contrary. Why, women are just beginning to know what romance is all about, and how to go out after it."

The magazine became so successful that Smith made it a weekly and it became the top newsstand seller in its field. No other publication of its type approached it in sales. Later on the indefatigable

Daisy Bacon would also edit *Real Love* (a first-person magazine which lasted two years), *True Love Stories, Pocket Love* (collections of stories between paper backs) and *Romantic Range,* but none achieved the success of *Love Story.*

Miss Bacon had an infallible instinct for choosing stories that would make the average woman forget either her unhappy financial state, her dreary husband or her aching heart. Daisy's own slim finger was never away from the feminine pulse of the nation; she knew just what the girls of all ages wanted. Romance-hungry girls were able to identify themselves with the beautiful blue-eyed heroines of the stories she published. Neither Ormond nor George Smith ever interfered with Daisy Bacon. She had made *Love Story* the most valuable Street & Smith property (it even prospered during the depression years of the early 1930's) and they felt that she had the touch which would keep it successful. They were right. No editor was ever able to present the game of hearts in such a beguiling manner as Daisy Bacon. And so expert was she in the magazine editing business that she edited the overseas edition of *Detective Story* during World War II.

Daisy Bacon wrote a book called *Love Story Writer* containing advice to those who wished to write romantic stories. Actually, it was a book which a writer of any kind of fiction would find rewarding. She had some interesting comments on her own magazine.

"During the many years that *Love Story* enjoyed its large circulation and weekly status," she wrote, "it was never successfully imitated, as any circulation man can tell you. Authors and literary agents have told me how other editors and their publishers went about trying it. They would take two or three issues of the magazine and classify the stories in the way authors try to pigeonhole them. Then they would call in a number of writers and assign a given topic to each of them. The result was that the magazines they turned out would not hold up under examination and reading, just as the quickly-run-up copies of original dress designs frequently come apart at the seams when worn. One publisher summed it up when he said in his biography that he gave up trying to publish a magazine in the romantic field because each one that he put out was only an imitation of an imitation of *Love Story Magazine.*"

The 1920's were the years of experimentation at Street & Smith. All kinds of new magazines were tried out; some failed, most reached into the circulation stratosphere of one-hundred-thousand-and-up-ward. There were new and youthful faces in the big Seventh Avenue office of the Fiction Factory now. Ormond Gould (son of Cora Smith Gould and nephew of the two owners) came to work after Princeton, the United States Navy and a couple of years studying and working in Paris. George Campbell Smith, Jr., came about the same time. Ormond was made an assistant to Henry Ralston, who was now chiefly concerned with circulation, distribution and the book-publishing branch of the firm. Young George went to work for Editor Frank Blackwell. Both learned fast—publishing was obviously in the blood of any descendants of the original Francis Smith.

The American News Company had been distributing the Street & Smith publications ever since that company had been organized during the 1890's. Now Ormond decided that it was time for a change. He felt that the policy of the American News Company, in charging the firm for handling and transportation of returns, was inequitable. He told Ralston to sound out the independent distributors. Ralston did, and discovered that they were eager to handle the Street & Smith publications. Ormond Smith organized the Chelsea News Company and put Ralston in charge of it. This subsidiary henceforth would distribute the magazines and books to 725 independent wholesalers and to 17,000 additional retail outlets. Expenses were reduced when Ralston requested that only the covers of unsold magazines be returned. Within eight years the firm had saved a tremendous amount of money which formerly was spent on handling and shipping. The independents did a magnificent job of distribution for Street & Smith.

During the early 1920's, Ormond Smith (whose first love was always books) launched the Chelsea House publications to compete with the established book-publishing houses of the day. Chelsea House, under Ralston's management, published cloth-bound books which sold for $1.75 and later were increased to $2.00 a copy. The first novel published was *Free Range Lanning,* a superior western written, of course, by Max Brand under the name of George Owen Baxter. Within three years fifty-two books had been issued. Such popular writers as Chris Booth, W. B. M. Ferguson, Reginald Wright Kauffman, A. M. Chisholm, James Fellom and Ernest M. Poate (a surgeon who wrote fascinating detective novels into which

Anton Otto Fisher cover for the first *Sea Stories*, 1922

medical jurisprudence entered to a fascinating degree) were some of those who made Chelsea House profitable.

Ormond Smith had been studying the successful operations of Grosset & Dunlap, who were publishing reprints of novels at seventy-five cents.

"If people will pay seventy-five cents for a re-issue of a book," he mused aloud to Ralston, "why won't they pay the same for a story that has appeared in a magazine as a serial but which has never appeared in book form?"

They combed old issues of *Popular, Ainslee's, Western, People's* and *Detective Story* and printed the best of the serials as cloth-bound books under the aegis of Chelsea House, at seventy-five cents. During the next ten years three hundred sixty-two of these reprints were published. Lending libraries bought both the two-dollar and the seventy-five-cent editions. In the words of the trade, the name Chelsea House stood for "good reading." The average sale of a Chelsea House book was twenty thousand, far above the average of the standard publishing firms.

As early as the 1920's the pilot was already replacing the detective as the wish-fulfillment lurking in the heart of every youngster. Immediately aware of boys' growing interest in aviation, Ormond Smith launched a magazine in 1928 designed to cater to this interest. *Bill Barnes, Air Adventurer* was the result. The great flight of Charles Lindbergh intensified interest in flying and Bill Barnes was the gainer. He did things with a plane that not even a Lindbergh could do—but he did them only in the fictional pages of the magazine.

If a boy (or a young man) was old-fashioned enough to prefer the sea to the sky, there was a new publication, *Sea Stories,* for him to devour. This was a cut above the ordinary juvenile. It was a happy, salty magazine which rode the circulation waves joyfully for several years.

Sport Story Magazine was another fictional treat offered to the readers of the twenties. This was the golden age of sports, and the interest generated by the colorful champions of the day (Jack Dempsey, Bill Tilden, Babe Ruth, Paavo Nurmi) stimulated an immediate rise in circulation to a figure of 150,000. This was not large by Street & Smith standards, but it was a steady circulation with relatively few newsstand returns. *True Western Story* and *Complete Story*

Magazine were two other successful magazines of the period. *Complete Story Magazine* was merely *People's* with a new name. Its success was chiefly due to the fact that Archie Sessions remained as editor.

In 1929 the firm bought the titles and good will of all the Frank A. Tousey publications. One of Tousey's most popular five-cent weeklies had been *Wild West Weekly*. It had been Ormond Smith's experience that he could take almost any successful weekly and transform it into a magazine. The weeklies on the whole were little more than pamphlets. A magazine was usually printed on better paper, was four times as large, had a slick cover and depended largely upon advertising income. *Wild West* was an immediate hit and remained so for sixteen years. *Live Girl Stories* was a mediocre bit of flotsam which lasted less than a year, but *Best Detective Magazine* immediately made its mark. Since it contained the best detective stories from all of the other Street & Smith magazines it could not have done otherwise.

In 1931 the firm ignored the depression and brought out a new publication, *The Shadow*. This magazine was really born by the accident of a radio announcer's voice. A year previously, Street & Smith had taken to the radio to increase the circulation of *Detective Story Magazine*. The radio material was culled chiefly from *Detective Story*, and for some reason the impact of the broadcast narrations was more exciting than the printed versions. The announcer who led into the half-hour weekly dramatized program called himself "The Shadow." When this mysterious character with the ominous voice asked, "What evil lurks in the hearts of men? The Shadow knows," chills ran down the spines of four or five million listeners. The name of "The Shadow" was Orson Welles.

The firm was quick to exploit the popularity of the radio character. These scripts, incidentally, were written by Harry E. Charlot, who died of poison under highly mysterious circumstances four years later. John Nanovic was made editor of *The Shadow*, and he immediately contracted with Maxwell Grant to write twenty-four book-length stories in twelve months featuring a character who fought the underworld with benefit of police help. The prolific Grant obliged, and *The Shadow* met with instantaneous favor.

The first issue of the quarterly magazine known as *The Shadow* appeared in April, 1931. It contained a book-length detective novel by Grant called *The Living Shadow*, and three articles on crime. The inside cover of the magazine contained just one paragraph, which read:

The Shadow magazine was begun in 1931

This is to certify that I have made careful examination of the manuscript known as *The Living Shadow,* as set down by Mr. Maxwell Grant, my raconteur, and do find it a true account of my activities upon that occasion. I have therefore arranged that Mr. Grant shall have exclusive privilege to such further of my exploits as may be considered of interest to the American Public.

It was signed "The Shadow."

The Eyes of the Shadow, The Shadow Laughs and *Gangdom's Doom* were highlighted in succeeding issues. Readers had once believed that Nick Carter actually existed, that Frank Merriwell was a living person and now in 1931 the sons of those early worshippers of Carter and Merriwell were sure that The Shadow was the greatest master of crime detection the world had ever known. The first three issues of *The Shadow* were completely sold out and The Shadow Club had some 50,000 members.

Before he was through Maxwell Grant would write 178 book-length stories about The Shadow, a total of 7,500,000 words. The Shadow would baffle police as much as the criminal world and curdle the blood of readers for twenty highly profitable years. Inevitably The Shadow became a radio show and for years was one of the most popular mystery shows on the air.

The *Doc Savage* magazine was another which made its mark in the early 1930's. Dr. Clark Savage was a scientific criminologist far removed from the Nick Carter type. He could (and did) quote Lombrosso, Kant and other European authorities on crime at the bang of Author Lester Dent's typewriter. Dent, a veteran of *Popular Magazine,* was a master of plot, and the circulation of *Doc Savage Magazine* reached 200,000 shortly after its first number hit the stands.

The cost of pulp had risen to an alarming degree; advertisers had pulled in their horns, but romance and adventure were still marketable commodities—if the price was right. Ormond Smith saw to it that the price of their publications remained right, and if the depression years landed many blows on the venerable firm, none hit a vital spot.

Not only some of the publications were showing their years—the big building on Seventh Avenue so proudly extolled in the booklet issued in 1905 was also beginning to creak in every joint. For more than thirty years the presses had been roaring day and night, and the building was in a permanent state of jitters. It vibrated from top to bottom. The roll-top desks and the heavy-paneled quartered oak were still there, but time had not been kind to them. The corridors were stacked with heavy rolls of paper and bales of returns. There were back numbers and old books all over the building. Ormond Smith hated to throw anything away.

Smith seldom delegated complete authority to anyone, but by now he had made Frank Blackwell Editor-in-Chief, and Blackwell did a great deal of the editorial buying. William "Pop" Hines was Art Director, and he was authorized to buy covers and illustrations. A short man with a thick blond brush mustache, Pop Hines was completely bald. When chided about his billiard-like dome he would say mildly, "It's good to be bald. Do you know that no bald man ever went insane?" After thirty years of the eye-straining work involved in photo-engraving, lettering and art work, Pop Hines was almost completely blind, but this was a secret he kept from even his closest co-workers. He wore thick-lensed glasses, but most people thought that these were part of the equipment of a man who had to study the fine screens used in the Ben Day engraving process. One of his most valued assistants was Millard Hopper, one of the fastest lettering men in the trade. Hopper was the only man on the staff who was allowed an hour and a half for lunch. Every day at 11:45 he'd put his pens and pencils aside and hurry to the Flea Circus on West 42nd Street. He was a big man on 42nd Street, for Hopper was the world's checker champion. Each day during the lunch hour he would take on as many as thirty aspiring checker players at once. It was seldom that he ever lost a game. Then he would hurry back to the office to bend over the drawing board until five o'clock.

Bill Lawlor was an assistant art director who spent much of his time handling the art work of *The Shadow*. A heavy black cape, a wide-brimmed black hat and a black mask always hung on a coat rack in the corner of the office. When a cover was needed for *The Shadow*, Lawlor would yell for an artist, don the black regalia which was the trademark of the famous character, and act as the model. The thought of paying for the services of a professional model would have horrified Pop Hines. Just as years before *Popular Magazine* had been the incubator which hatched writers for *The Saturday Evening*

An early cover of *Doc Savage* magazine, first published in 1933

A view of the art department in the twenties

Post, so now the firm had become an incubator where the greatest illustrators in the country were professionally born.

Harvey Dunn, later President of the Society of Illustrators and acknowledged dean in the field of action painting, was one of those who gladly accepted the standard twenty dollars for an illustration or a hundred dollars for a *Western* cover. Joseph Leyendecker, who later received top prices for *Post* covers, illustrated stories and painted covers for Pop Hines. Dean Cornwell, today one of the best mural painters, was a steady contributor, as were Walter Baumhofer and Winfield Scott. Nick Eggenhofer came from Germany, and along with many other young artists hurried to Street & Smith to find rent money. Pop Hines gave him some assignments for *Western.* Eggenhofer had never seen a cowboy, never painted a horse, and of course had never been west of Seventh Avenue, Manhattan. But he needed the work and he hurried to his friend Harold von Schmidt, even then considered to be one of the truly fine exponents of authentic western art. Von Schmidt was glad to fill in his fellow artist with the facts of western life as expounded in the pulp magazines. Tom Lovell, Charles La Salle and Anton Otto Fisher were others who labored for the Fiction Factory and who afterward achieved important artistic stature. Fisher was unsurpassed as a marine artist, and his covers were perhaps the one reason for remembering *Sea Stories.* N. C. Wyeth could paint anything, his fellow artists said. Hines usually gave him farm scenes to do. When the Nick Carter stories were revived, Hines was smart enough to get Amos Sewell to illustrate them. Today Sewell gets as much for one *Saturday Evening Post* cover as he then received for a year's work on *Nick Carter.*

"We all worked for Street & Smith," he now says, "because the established artists were getting the good assignments. Perhaps the experience was good for us—it was certainly a humbling experience. Pop Hines always had a wet palette in his office. We'd bring in our illustrations, and if he didn't like them he'd tell us to get busy and change them then and there."

Howard Munce, the current President of the Society of Illustrators and art director of a large advertising firm, began his career as a youngster in the art department at Street & Smith, and he still pales a bit when he recalls the days when you had to please Pop Hines or borrow money to pay your rent.

"I suppose Pop was awfully good at his job," Munce admits. "He ran an artistic assembly line and he looked upon paintings and drawings submitted to him much as a shop foreman looks upon the products of his machine shop. They had to conform exactly to his specifications. Hines would get illustrations to be used in any given issue and paste them onto a board. If one was too large he'd merely take a sharp knife and cut it down to size. They used to say that Pop would crop off the head of Whistler's "Mother" if he thought it would fit the page better. But he was a pretty nice guy anyhow."

CHAPTER

TEN

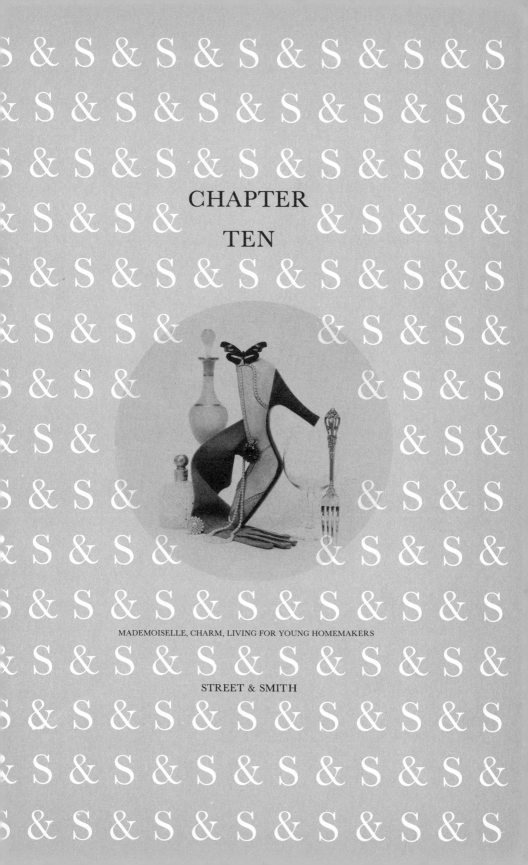

MADEMOISELLE, CHARM, LIVING FOR YOUNG HOMEMAKERS

STREET & SMITH

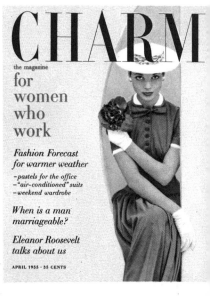

Typical covers of *Mademoiselle, Charm* and *Living for Young Homemakers*

CHAPTER

TEN

In April, 1933, the world appeared to come to an end for the Old
Guard at Street & Smith. Ormond Smith died at the age of seventy-
three, and eleven days later seventy-five-year-old George Campbell
Smith followed his brother. The old-timers—Ralston, Frank Hatton
in charge of the presses, Alec Anderson, cashier for twenty years,
Emil Dellavalle, shipping head, Clarence Vernam and Frank Blackwell were saddened and shocked. The members of the family—
Ormond Gould, George Campbell Smith, Jr., and Gerald Smith
(Ormond Smith's son), an undergraduate at Princeton, Mrs. Artemas Holmes and Mrs. Wilmurt O. Swain, the two married daughters
of George Campbell Smith—all were stunned and grief-stricken by
the two deaths that followed one upon the other in the span of a few
days.

Editorial tributes to both brothers were impressive, but the real
tributes came in the form of letters from old Street & Smith writers
and from the widows of men who had once contributed to the Fiction
Factory. Only Ralston and George Campbell Smith had known of
Ormond's generosity to those who had been members of the Street
& Smith family. Typical of the letters which came to Ralston after
the deaths of the two heads of the firm was one from the widow of
Frederic Dey. It revealed the true nature of Ormond Smith who
wasn't known to many. It read:

April 25/33

My dear Mr. Ralston:-

May I send you a word of tender sympathy on the passing of your
dear friend, Mr. Ormond Smith? His kindness to Fred in many epi-
sodes, and his generous provision for me—all—all through the years—

gave him a special place in my thoughts, known only to me. So, I write you, and through you to the firm—not that it matters to you, but as an expression of myself.

Faithfully Yours,
Haryot Holt Dey

The two brothers had seemed indestructible. They had weathered depressions, cut-throat competition and changes in reading and publishing styles. The void left by these wizards of publishing seemed too large ever to be filled. But the Smith sons and daughters had a strong sense of duty to the family tradition. The responsibility of carrying on was theirs, and they tried to forget their grief by presenting a strong united front to the trade, which, sympathetic personally, would seize on any sign of weakness now to make inroads on the company which had been seventy-eight years in the making. George Campbell Smith, Jr., was made president of the firm, Ormond Gould executive vice-president, and Clarence Vernam and Artemas Holmes vice-presidents.

They faced an almost impossible task. The depression had taken the country by the throat and was shaking it into a limp, bewildered, chastened mood. Magazines and publishing firms were among the first to suffer from the horrible economic drought. People had to buy bread; magazines and books were luxuries they didn't need. True enough, they did seek some inexpensive escape from their worries, so they continued to buy *Detective Story* and *Love Story*. These two magazines suffered less than did the slick magazines which depended heavily upon advertising revenue. The one book that did sell in this gloomy period was Hervey Allen's *Anthony Adverse*. It was nicely spiced with sex, but it was neither strident nor impudent. It was definitely not the kind of book which would have had a runaway sale in the 1920's, but in 1933 it sold nearly 300,000 copies. Most book publishers were having a very difficult time. Street & Smith's book publishing subsidiary, Chelsea House, quietly passed out of existence. The public was apparently in no mood for the eternally optimistic but false happy ending. This was not the best of all possible worlds, and the virtuous young lady did not always marry the wealthy son of the boss. The 1930's were sobering years when the main problem was existence, not entertainment. And 1933 was the year during which even such sacrosanct institutions as banks were proved vulnerable. In retrospect it is difficult to understand how and why it was that Street & Smith survived, but survive the old firm did. Some of the old publications were shelved, but the structure of the firm remained unshakable. Obviously the day of Laura Jean Libbey, Mrs. Georgie Sheldon and Horatio Alger was done. The firm had to adjust itself to a new type of reader.

The new management soon showed that it had the same courage to begin enterprises, the same sense of anticipating trends which had characterized the remarkable team of Ormond and George Smith.

It was Henry Ralston's daughter, Helen, then a senior at Emma Willard School at Troy, New York, who made a casual suggestion to her father one day. She and her schoolmates were dissatisfied with the prevailing magazines for women which specialized in fashions. *Vogue* and *Harper's Bazaar* were wonderful publications, she said, but they featured fashions and a price range way out of reach of the ordinary young woman. Why wasn't there a single fashion magazine for the average smart young woman?

Ralston submitted the idea to George Smith and Ormond Gould. A magazine devoted exclusively to women's fashions was out of their field. It was a revolutionary proposal and they had grave doubts about its possibilities. However, in the tradition of their predecessors,

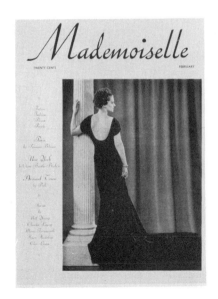

Mademoiselle's first issue, February 1935   Twentieth anniversary, February 1955

215

they decided it was worth a try. Fiction was to be emphasized in the editorial content. Two of the pulp editors, Orlin Tremaine and Desmond Hall, were assigned the task of executing the idea.

When the men were baffled in their hunt for a title, it was Desmond Hall's wife who suggested the name *Mademoiselle*. No one was completely sold on it, but no one could come up with anything better. Tremaine and Hall proceeded to assemble an initial issue without even bothering to make up a dummy.

George Smith was so dubious about the venture (as was everyone else connected with the firm) that he decided not to publish it under the Street & Smith imprint. If it made its way, he would eventually announce that it was a Street & Smith publication. The Mademoiselle Corporation was formed to carry out the disguise and Henry Ralston set out to find an office for the *Mademoiselle* staff far from the parent building. He finally rented a suite in the Columbia Broadcasting Building on Madison Avenue and 52nd Street.

Not since Fanny Fern had left the first baby on the church steps in one of her early serials had there ever been a more unwanted child. It is, of course, a basic tenet of fiction that the child born out of wedlock is brilliant, beautiful and destined for high position. Little *Mademoiselle* was not in the tradition. In February, 1935, it certainly was not the magazine smart young women were looking for. It was a slim, twenty-cent, ninety-six page slick-paper monthly (the first 100-percent slick-paper publication the firm had issued). The lead article was by Clare Boothe Brokaw (Luce), and it was an attempt to convey the sophisticated atmosphere of New York, which other magazines were doing just as well. There were several short stories, and a "Beauty for Mademoiselle" department edited by the Princess Bibesco. Smart young ladies were advised that:

> Eyelashes are made like fish hooks for trout, curved, and as sharp as a needle. No more butterfly kisses—they scratch the lover's cheek and make it bleed.

> In the Paris jungle all furs are dyed.
> Moles turned green, foxes turned blue—but a real blue, not the dull sandy color generally known as blue fox.
> My own are deep sapphire.

It went on like that. Surprisingly, only one page was devoted to fashion—shoes. Toward the back of the book, *l'envoie:*

And So Mademoiselle Has Called——
She has called once. If you have enjoyed her personality—her bubbly,
youthful interest—won't you ask her to call again? She has been for-
mally introduced to you.

Mademoiselle was popular with no one. Angry news dealers phoned
in to ask what kind of a magazine this thing was. A great many men,
they said, had grabbed for it eagerly, somehow associating it with the
naughty Mademoiselle from Armentières of World War I days. It had
been presumably planned for girls in the eighteen-to-thirty age group
of limited means. They were puzzled by the hodge-podge of naïveté,
attempts at sophistication and third-rate fiction.

President George Smith reacted more strongly than the news
dealers. He turned to Ormond Gould and said, "What in heaven's
name is this thing? It doesn't look like a Street & Smith magazine.
In fact, it doesn't look like any magazine I ever saw."

The first impulse of the firm was to kill it. Hasty judgments were
overruled, however, and it was decided to revamp and change its
style. Orlin Tremaine was sent back to edit the pulps, and Desmond
Hall was kept at the unhappy assignment of making something out
of *Mademoiselle*. Betsy Talbot Blackwell, who had been an editor of
the successful *Charm* magazine published by Bamberger's Department Store of Newark, was persuaded to join the staff. She was
asked to become managing editor, but she preferred the job of
fashion editor.

There was no issue of *Mademoiselle* in March of 1935. Desmond
Hall and Betsy Blackwell were trying desperately to gather enough
material to bring out an issue of which they need not be ashamed.
The April number was a great improvement. There were five stories,
four general articles, five articles on fashion, and six departments.
The articles and art work on fashion reflected the superb taste and
editorial skill of Betsy Blackwell. *Mademoiselle* had groped its way out
of ignominy. Betsy Blackwell was appointed Editor-in-Chief. Circulation in its early days was around 37,000, not very encouraging in
view of the time, money and effort which had been expended on the
magazine. It was not helped by the basic reorganization which took
place in the company at that time.

George Campbell Smith survived his father by only four years.
Artemas H. Holmes (always called the Judge), who was married to

one of the daughters of George Campbell Smith, became president of the firm. Henry Ralston became vice-president.

"Judge" Holmes, plagued by a bad heart, resigned after a year and the Board of Directors called in the firm of McKinsey, Wellington and Company (business consultants) to survey the property and recommend executive changes. Pending the investigation, an Operating Committee was formed composed of Henry Ralston, Franklin E. Forsberg and Chief Accountant Archer Church. The business consultants advised going outside the firm for a chief executive. Gerald Smith, son of the late Ormond, was considered too young and inexperienced to take over. He was learning the trade, but it was too big and complex an operation to entrust to him yet. A quiet, shy, friendly and able young man, Gerald Smith was serving under Ralston, learning the intricacies of circulation.

The man suggested by the consultants and approved by the Board of Directors was Allen Grammer. He was made president of Street & Smith in 1938, the first time in eighty-three years that the firm was headed by someone not a member of the family. Stock control, however, remained with the heirs of Ormond Smith, who had bought out most of the interest held by George Campbell Smith's heirs.

None of these fundamental changes in the management of the

Editor-in-Chief Betsy Talbot Blackwell, Bradbury Thompson,
Bernice Peck, Cyrilly Abels, and Kay Silver

company affected the growth of *Mademoiselle* or the position of Betsy Blackwell. Calmly, serenely and confidently she led her magazine (affectionately called *Millie* by the staff) into the forefront of fashion publications.

Mademoiselle's modest 37,000 circulation had stirred hardly a ripple in publishing circles and had not yet caused the publishers of *Harper's Bazaar* or *Vogue* any sleepless nights. But Betsy Blackwell, under her frivolous Sally Victor hats and behind her vivacity and charm, was a gal who knew where she was going. She knew that there was a place for a magazine which would dedicate itself to women readers in the eighteen-to-thirty age group. In addition to being a writer and an editor, Betsy Blackwell had learned the esoteric trade of merchandising during her years on Bamberger's *Charm*. She had a chance to put some of her theories into practice on the magazine. She began working with manufacturers and retailers who, hearing her talk of her desire to carry her readers from the urge to buy to completed sale, were understandably cooperative. There were three groups of readers who wanted good fashions at moderate prices: (a) career girls, (b) college girls, (c) young married women. The common denominators of these young women were better-than-average education and the concomitant better-than-average taste. Editorially and fashion-wise she had to satisfy these groups.

High-fashion magazines heretofore had operated on the same basis as do manufacturers of automobiles who seem reluctant to allow readers of their advertisements into the sordid secret of what the product costs. Editor Blackwell inaugurated a policy which made *Mademoiselle* the first fashion magazine in the country to state in its editorial pages the retail price of the dress, hat, coat or accessory displayed and, in addition, told the readers where in their community the products could be purchased. What was done was so simple that one is puzzled why it hadn't been done before. She merely established direct communication between the fashion industry and its biggest customer—the smart young woman educated to enjoy quality but without a champagne purse.

Betsy Blackwell's interests, however, went beyond the right fashions at the right prices for her readers. She cared about the whole person—her education, her job, her mind, her health, her future, and on occasion even her soul. In July, 1938, an entire issue was devoted to the subject of careers for women. One of the features of the issue was a job chart—perhaps the first of its kind ever published. Extensive research went into the project. The chart listed nearly every career open to women; it discussed the possibilities of employment in each field, the qualifications necessary to succeed and the potential earning power of the job. The comments which accompanied the various aspects of each job were serious in intent but were presented in a lively fashion. If, for instance, a girl wanted to be a dress designer, she could expect to start at $40 a week with a chance of eventually rising to $20,000 a year.

> Start when you are very young and claw your way up. Don't expect a responsible job until you've had experience; a designer who fails to click can throw a firm into bankruptcy in one season.
>
> Nothing is too good for a designer who produces. Seventh Avenue, the funniest, most hysterical spot in the world, runs entirely on nerves and promise. All designers enjoy bad tempers and hair-trigger nerves.
>
> There's an old saying on Seventh Avenue, "If you've got a good designer, hang onto her even if you have to marry her." There it is.

The amazing response to this one issue convinced Editor Blackwell that she was right about the interest girls had in careers. It was a negation of polls taken on college campuses which stated flatly that 80 per cent of all college girls were only interested in matrimony. Henceforth *Mademoiselle* would have monthly career articles reflecting the job market and the interests of young women, and two special career issues a year directed to the girl with a job or the girl looking for one. Young Betsy Blackwell had brought into being a women's magazine, which, while entirely original and modern in concept, nevertheless was not too far removed from the old *New York Weekly* —it not only entertained but it was "a journal of useful knowledge."

Year-round contact with college undergraduates was maintained and at least two articles each month were run discussing education and college activities. She made the College Board a regular department of the magazine. Now, each June, *Mademoiselle* brings twenty college girls to New York to work on the annual college issue published in August. The girls are paid for their work and, through the guest editors and campus reporters who travel to colleges all over the country, Editor Blackwell and her staff have been able to anticipate the needs and interests of the college girl. It wasn't long before *Mademoiselle* became known as "The College Girls' *Bible*."

Mademoiselle never lost sight of its early readers—the college undergraduates and young career women who were the magazine's first devotees. As they married and became young mothers, *Mademoiselle* began to recognize their new interests and special problems: child-birth and infant care; children's reading, sleeping and play habits; family relationships; working mothers; where and how to live—every phase in the lives of these busy young wives and mothers became *Mademoiselle's* immediate concern. If you were a girl between eighteen and thirty, you couldn't miss finding things of interest in the magazine.

Ever mindful of the mass move to Suburbia, *Mademoiselle* published, in June, 1952, a "Suburbia issue," which has now grown into a semi-annual affair. These issues are devoted to young marrieds and suburban life, and other issues throughout the year include what suburbanites are thinking, doing, wearing.

For most of her twenty years with *Mademoiselle*, Mrs. Blackwell has enjoyed a close association with two key members of her staff. One is Bernice Peck, the magazine's present Health and Beauty Editor, who wrote copy, sparked ideas, handled the payroll, modeled, and answered phones as the first issues were appearing. Since the days when she was contributing to every department of *Mademoiselle*, she has become one of the best-known women in her own particular field. A quiet humor has endeared her to her colleagues; a sharp business sense has endeared her to the trade, and her monthly articles on health and beauty are rated the best of their kind. The other staff member is Kay Silver, *Mademoiselle's* first Merchandise Editor, who became Fashion Editor when Mrs. Blackwell moved to Editor-in-Chief. Kay Silver has done more to originate and influence the fashion tastes and preferences of smart young women than anyone in the business.

Bradbury Thompson, Art Director since 1945, has been lavishly decorated with medals, awards and honors from the American Institute of Graphic Arts, the Art Directors Club and the National Society of Art Directors.

Polly Weaver, who joined *Mademoiselle* in 1943, is College and Career Director. Her standing with college deans and vocational officials all over the country is unique in the magazine field. Contributing Editor Leo Lerman, who covers the entertainment and art worlds, enjoys a kind of celebrity of his own with celebrated figures in the ballet, opera, theatre and literary worlds whom he writes about in his monthly feature, "Something to Talk About."

Mademoiselle's literary standing is a story all of its own. In its early years the magazine simply couldn't compete with already established magazines in the prices they were paying Fannie Hurst, Faith Baldwin, Adela Rogers St. John. Furthermore, these were "slick" writers, and Editor Blackwell felt that newer, younger writers might be her readers' dish of tea. At this period—the thirties—there was practically no outlet for young writers. In any event, prompted by economic factors, young, unknown writers were cultivated by the magazine's first Fiction Editor, Marian Ives, and was continued by her successor, George Davis. Some of the fiction published was decidedly *avant-garde*, and Betsy anticipated rightly that not all of it would be acceptable to her readers. To these she explained that they could skip the stories, that there was enough else in the magazine—of fashion, beauty, features—to justify the price on the cover. In the meantime, a cult of *Mademoiselle* fiction fans was growing, especially among college undergraduates, and when anthologies of best short stories began to include the magazine's fiction, necessity turned into policy. It became increasingly clear that the more literate reader, far from missing the banal, formula story, welcomed the change and was eager to read the best new authors.

Since then, in keeping with its economic upswing, *Mademoiselle* has published such distinguished contemporary writers as Katherine Anne Porter, Elizabeth Bowen, William Faulkner, Tennessee Williams, Jessamyn West, Carson McCullers, Jean Stafford, Wystan H. Auden, Colette, Moravia, Marcel Ayme, Robert Penn Warren. The policy of nurturing new writers has continued, and a conspicuous example is the discovery of Truman Capote by Fiction Editor Margarita G. Smith. *Mademoiselle's* fiction policy has had divided loyalty not only from its readers, but with Street & Smith's management. Characteristically, however, they have always maintained a hands-off policy.

It is impossible to discuss *Mademoiselle's* fiction and features, or, for that matter, any part of its editorial operation, without mentioning the literary and organizational genius of its Managing Editor for the past twelve years, Cyrilly Abels. *Mademoiselle's* success—in sifting and defining the modern woman's attitude toward development in the arts and sciences, education and sociology, politics and marriage—is in good part a reflection of Miss Abels' own ceaseless curiosity and her genuine interest in every phase of modern-day living. Her idealism is matched by her practical ability to keep track of and to capture for *Mademoiselle* a gifted writer or artist. She is responsible for one of the most notable literary scoops of our time—the publication in *Mademoiselle* of the late Dylan Thomas' verse play, *Under Milk Wood,* hailed by press and public as "unprecedented in publishing history." Another of her publishing scoops was bagging T. S. Eliot for the only interview he granted on his recent visit to the States.

For some reason unfathomable to the pleased but puzzled staff, a great many men read the magazine. A few years ago a request came in from the Harvard Club asking if there was a binder available—the club's copies of *Mademoiselle* were so thumbed that they had become virtually unreadable. It is a matter of record that there are practically no members of the Harvard Club who would qualify as "intelligent young women between the ages of eighteen and thirty," the audience the magazine constantly keeps in mind, but a great many members do read *Mademoiselle.*

Betsy Blackwell has an apparent disregard for money that verges on the sacrilegious to the uninitiated. During the lean years of the magazine she sent staff members all over the country; she thought nothing of spending some enormous sum for a new promotion stunt. Thomas H. Kaiser, treasurer of the firm, would shudder every time he received a request from Betsy Blackwell for additional money,

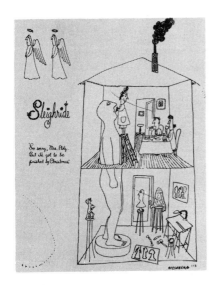

Mademoiselle introduces Steinberg, 1941

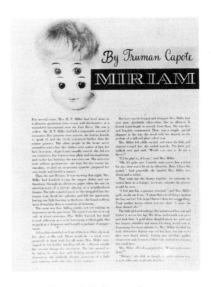

A *Mademoiselle* literary first, 1945

but because her apparently wild schemes invariably paid off he would merely sigh and sign the necessary voucher. He objected only once. Once he was about to sign a request from Betsy for $250,000. He noted that Editor Blackwell had written that she wanted to buy a four-engined plane painted in what by now was known as "Mademoiselle Pink." He hesitated and decided to ask Grammer, then president of the firm, about it.

"I'm sure Betsy really needs the plane or she wouldn't ask for it," he said almost apologetically. "But in view of the amount asked for, I thought you had better also okay her request."

Grammer nearly fainted until he realized this hoax had been cooked up by Betsy and Gerald Smith who thoroughly enjoyed practical jokes on each other as well as on their fellow-executives. The business relationship between Gerald Smith and the various editors was always a very cordial one, enlivened at all times by his sense of humor. One day Betsy was delighted to receive a present from him. It was an enormous Dutch wooden shoe (naturally, painted pink). It was filled with fine black earth, and attached to the shoe was a note: "Please water carefully day and night for six weeks." For six weeks the embryo plant was carefully watered. Every morning the staff would rush in to see what had sprouted. But not even the semblance of green appeared until the six weeks were up. Then one morning Betsy found her staff popeyed with amazement. Overnight the earth in the shoe had blossomed. Dozens of green sprouts, at least eight inches long, completely hid the earth and the shoe itself. It appeared as though the horticultural miracle of all time had taken place until a more knowledgeable member of the staff took a sharp look at the sprouts, pulled one of them up and said simply, "Onions." Early that morning Gerald Smith had placed the fully grown onions in the shoe.

Mademoiselle has been responsible for many firsts in its field— some of these prompted by sheer economic necessity. During its early years the magazine could not afford to maintain a Paris office, so Betsy decided to report extensively on young American designers who up to then had been completely neglected by publishers. The magazine was first to cover fashions in regional markets— clothes from St. Louis, Los Angeles, San Francisco, Miami, Chicago, Kansas City, Boston and Dallas were featured to the everlasting

St. Paul's Lutheran Church
Church Street and Beaumont Avenue
Teaneck, New Jersey

Pastor
THE REV. ALBERT P. STAUDERMAN
61 Church Street
Phone: Teaneck 7-5189

To the Editors and Publishers   Aug.28, 1950
  of "Mademoiselle"
Elizabeth, New Jersey

Kind Friends:

On this dull August day it is intriguing, not to say flattering,
to receive your unexpected invitation to accept reservation number 137
which you have set aside in my name for an anniversary subscription to
"Mademoiselle." You say of this unusual offer, "Mademoiselle fits your
needs so closely." Perhaps it does, although up to this point I have
been ignorant of it!

Joining a "select audience of smart young women" could be a pleasure at any time, I am sure. Especially so since Mademoiselle has an
intense and active interest in me and my world. For instance . . . .

"Clothes to fit every mood...as you will wear them yourself."
That's what I need! Heretofore my horizon has been lowered by an affinity for drab blacks and oxford greys, with only the slightest dash of
color occasionally on my vestments. A "practical, versatile office
dress" could easily be something sensational in my life. Especially
the practical part. And "evening wear for those special dates" would
also bring about a wholly new life for me. No wonder you add something about "stirring feminine hearts all the way from Fifth Avenue to
Wilshire Boulevard." Lead me to it!

Even the advice about my career could help, especially about "the
problems you'll face...the salary you'll earn." Indeed they do answer
my most important question, as you state, before I have time to ask it!

Best of all is this business about "creating a prettier, more
enchanting you." This is a situation that has cried for a remedy for
many years, now. I would happily settle either for the prettier part,
or the more enchanting part. Either one will do. After all, I can't
have everything!

Immediately catching my eye is the fact that you propose to give
me "clever tricks of eye make-up, skin care, hair styling, etc." The
hair styling is especially what I need. Honestly, I had just about
given up hope. Most people in my condition have only one trick left.
They let it grow long on one side and then carefully plaster it over
the bald top of their dome.

There's so much else. Shopping for perfumed pencils for my desk
ought to do wonders for my morale, and learning how to behave as a
bride will be fun.

It was surely nice of you to think of me. As you say, this is a
tempting bargain. My trouble, I guess, is really inhibition. I've
been spending too much of my time learning how to keep out of temptation.

I appreciate your interest in me. I like you very much, too.
You're so different!

Yours delightedly,

Albert P. Stauderman

Rev. Albert P. Stauderman

A polite refusal to subscribe to *Mademoiselle*

gratitude of the local manufacturers. The magazine was the first in
its field to register the growing trend from New York City to the
suburbs. Branch stores of all the leading New York establishments
were gradually being opened in Westchester and Long Island, as
well as in the suburbs of other big cities, and these were listed in
the magazine as a reader shopping service. One merchandising coup
which Editor Blackwell pulled—and which later proved a boon to
an entire industry—was to persuade the luxury-priced milliners to
add to their custom-made line an inexpensive junior or "debutante"
line. Her theory was that the customers for expensive millinery
would inevitably grow older and ultimately die off and, in the meantime, their daughters should begin to know and enjoy hats with the
stamp of their famous creators. It is a fact that no expensive milliner
could exist today without its subsidiary, a lower-priced, ready-made
line. She applied the same merchandising principles to ready-to-
wear carried by otherwise exclusive specialty shops.

Fashion designers and manufacturers admit that the magazine has
had a great influence on all publications read by women. In the
world of publishing you can quarrel with everything except success
—as *Mademoiselle's* innovations became established and successful,
other magazines had to shake admiring if envious heads and follow
along.

Picture Play, Charm's predecessor   First issue of *Charm*

Betsy Blackwell supervises her complex operation from the most unfunctional office ever seen on Madison Avenue. It looks at first glance more like an elegant drawing room than a command post from which is directed a huge, enormously profitable business. But on Betsy Blackwell it looks good.

The color scheme is basically dark green walls and deep-piled rug —the better to show off the furniture in antique light green. Generally referred to as "the bower," the office combines eighteenth- and nineteenth-century furniture from France and England which seems to point up the contrast between the past and today's "smart young woman." Because of an aversion to desk drawers, Mrs. Blackwell has a nineteenth-century, elaborately-carved English desk which, for all intents and purposes, is practically drawerless and is eternally snowed under with art work, stories and advertising copy. By some abracadabra, however, seldom is anything lost, and almost everything gets off the desk the day of arrival. On the desk there is always a single red rose in a slender silver vase, and a handsome Georgian silver inkstand, a gift from the firm to Mrs. Blackwell on the occasion of her twentieth anniversary with the organization. Beside the desk is an ancient lacquered gaming table used as a prop for two telephones.

On the wall opposite is a mural by John Burton Brimer. There is some question as to whether Mrs. Blackwell's mural is a portrait of her or of *Mademoiselle;* in any case its main elements are what most interest them both, to wit: fashion (especially fabulous hats and shoes), and writing (depicted is the first typewriter ever to be patented).

Mrs. Blackwell's hobbies are collecting antique slippers, dolls and fans. All are well represented in her office. In one corner of the room there is a Chinese red lacquer vitrine holding two hundred pairs of miniature shoes collected over the years from all corners of the globe. It is surmounted by two huge glass bells, each of which houses a fully costumed antique doll. Dominating the room is a crystal chandelier shaped in a series of six graceful plumes. Less conspicuous, but easily the most valuable piece in the room, is an early eighteenth-century English wine cooler. Spread along the L-shaped window ledge fronting Madison Avenue and Fifty-seventh Street are mementoes reflecting the impact Mrs. Blackwell and *Mademoiselle* have had on the world at large. These include the

Nieman-Marcus Award "for distinguished service in the field of fashion," a scroll officially declaring Mrs. Blackwell "Ami de Paris," a photograph of her with young Queen Elizabeth, a certification as "Ambassador Extraordinary" from the San Francisco Chamber of Commerce, an "Award for Inspiration to Youth" from Junior Achievement, an ASTA Travel Journalism Award "in recognition of outstanding public service in the furtherance of foreign and domestic travel" and letters from the heads of the Armed Services testifying to the work done by *Mademoiselle* during the war for the WACS, WAVES and SPARS.

When she took over *Mademoiselle*, Betsy Blackwell said, "We are going to try to be a completely rounded guide, philosopher and friend to intelligent young women. We are going to try to bring good taste—good taste in fashion, in cosmetics, in decorating, in every aspect of living—to smart young women everywhere."

In 1955 *Mademoiselle* celebrated her twentieth birthday. She has become a beautiful, smart and independent young woman who in a very real sense is a counterpart of the beautiful, smart and independent young woman of America.

A hundred years ago Francis Smith could run the whole editorial

Eleanore Hillebrand Bruce, Editor-in-Chief Helen Valentine, Ralph R. Whittaker, Jr., Estelle Ellis, and Cipe Pineles at new *Charm's* Fifth Anniversary luncheon

content of *The New York Weekly* alone; fifty years ago Charles Agnew MacLean could edit *Ainslee's* with very little help. Today readers are discriminating. Each department of a magazine must be headed by an expert in the particular field or knowledgeable readers will be heard from. Over the years Betsy Blackwell has attracted a brilliant staff to the magazine who work in splendid harmony to produce what the publishing trade calls a "beautiful package."

With a circulation in excess of 500,000, *Mademoiselle's* advertising would have delighted old Clarence Vernam. The 1955 August issue ran to an amazing total of 388 pages over-all—the largest consumer book of the year published in the United States. *Mademoiselle* had justified *Time's* description of her some years before as "an awkward girl in pigtails . . . grown into a publishing miracle."

In 1941 the magazine *Picture Play* was twenty-six years old. It was showing its age too, creaking in every limb. Like so many magazines before it, the venerable publication had outlasted its audience. It was laid gently to rest and its place was taken by *Your Charm.* Muriel Babcock, who had been editor of *Picture Play,* was made editor. Fashions played an important part in the new publication, but it became increasingly evident that people wanted something more for their money.

The magazine was only a year old when a lawyer for Bamberger's Department Store came to call on Henry Ralston. He informed Ralston that his client, who for many years had been publishing a highly successful house organ called *Charm,* was a bit annoyed with Street & Smith for using a title which so closely resembled that of its own publication. Ralston acknowledged that the lawyer had a point. Legal arrangements were concluded amicably, and the firm acquired the right to use the title *Charm.*

Charm was put into the editorial hands of Elizabeth Adams, later succeeded by Frances Harrington. Under its new title it achieved a respectable circulation of 200,000. The audience at which it was directed was the girl to whom a job was a stopgap between school and marriage. In 1950 Helen Valentine was brought in from the amazingly successful *Seventeen,* to which she had given birth and which she had nursed to strong maturity.

Street & Smith has always been fortunate in having truly fine editors. The tradition began with the original Francis Smith, one of the best of his day, and continued with Charles Agnew MacLean, Edward Stratemeyer, Archie Sessions, Henry Wilton Thomas, Richard Duffy, Daisy Bacon—just to name a few—and Helen Valentine belongs in that select company.

During his lifetime Ormond Smith had read and approved nearly everything that went into the various publications. There were times when he overruled the judgment of even his best editors. After the deaths of O. G. and his brother, the management changed this policy to a great extent. In line with the custom of the magazine trade, an editor was given a relatively free hand. He or she would stand or fall as the magazine prospered or failed. In 1949 Gerald Smith became president of the firm, the next year Henry Ralston retired, Ralph Whittaker was made executive vice-president and Arthur Lawler was brought up from the legal profession and made vice-president and secretary. Smith, only thirty-five, realized that no one man could supervise the details of producing a number of magazines as diverse in their appeal as fashion, sports, science-fiction, dozens of comic books (highly popular in the wartime 1940's) and various annuals. He was a strong believer in the modern business practice of decentralization. The sensible thing to do was to hire an editor who was a specialist in the field covered by the magazine and give him (or her) complete responsibility. The Street & Smith editors today are without exception such specialists, and they operate with a minimum of interference from what every editorial staff calls the "front office."

Helen Valentine was a fortuitous choice to head *Charm*. As a youngster she had been a part-time copy writer for the advertising firm of Lord & Thomas at $8,500 a year, a top salary for such a job. When the depression of the early 1930's hit the business world, she was one of the first to be fired—she was making too much money. She went to *Vogue,* where she handled promotion during those desperate depression days. One gloomy day she was fired and her assistant was given the job.

It was then that she joined the Street & Smith family. Frank Forsberg hired her to do promotion for *Mademoiselle.* She found the congenial atmosphere and the challenge of a difficult job fascinating. Mrs. Valentine was with *Mademoiselle* for six years when Walter Annenberg tried to persuade her to join his organization to edit a fan magazine he was publishing. It was called *Stardom*—the mere title made her shudder. "There is nothing in the world I'm less interested in than a movie magazine," she told Annenberg frankly.

Annenberg was persistent and asked what kind of a magazine she would be interested in running.

"There's room today for a publication aimed at teen-agers," she told him. "They've been neglected by the established fashion publications. Everyone treats them as though they were silly, swooning bobby soxers. "I think they're young adults and should be treated accordingly."

She proceeded to develop her idea while Annenberg listened carefully. The more he heard the more he was impressed. Paper was scarce but it was permissible to transfer tonnage from one book to another and *Stardom* was expendable.

And so over a luncheon table the fabulous *Seventeen* was born. Helen Valentine felt sick about leaving Street & Smith because of her affection and respect for Gerald Smith and the whole organization, but no one with the instinct of an editor can resist the challenge of starting a new magazine. Without even submitting a dummy of the first issue to Walter Annenberg, Mrs. Valentine launched *Seventeen* which, within eighteen months, had achieved a circulation of a million. This

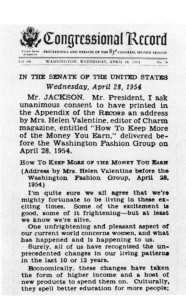

Helen Valentine in *Congressional Record*

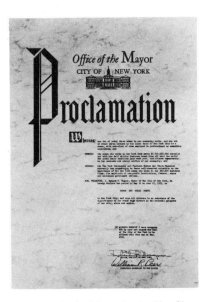

Proclamation by Mayor inspired by *Charm*

was one of the greatest publishing coups of the day. *Seventeen* became so successful that it ceased being a challenge to the energetic Helen Valentine. It was a *fait accompli.*

In 1950 Gerald Smith asked her to return to the fold to run *Charm.* Somehow *Charm* had gone off the beam; this good-looking magazine was not getting the wide reader acceptance it deserved. It was important that *Charm* make good. In 1949 the surviving pulp magazines had all been put to rest. *Detective Story, The Shadow, Doc Savage* and *Western Story* all followed *Love Story* into oblivion. Each had been a money-maker, but each was weighted down with years. They could not compete with the entertainment offered by radio, movies and something new called television. Only *The Shadow* and *Nick Carter* had been adaptable for use in these new media. It was increasingly evident to Gerald Smith and his associates that the public wanted a lot for its twenty-five or thirty-five cents. It wanted a good-looking package, fine art work, interesting articles, entertainment and service.

Helen Valentine was interested.

"We've gone astray somewhere," quiet Gerald Smith said. "Perhaps the public we're aiming at is too limited. What do you think?"

"*Charm* still seems to be aiming at young women who are working temporarily until they can find themselves husbands," Mrs. Valentine said. "The recent census figures show that there are more married women than single women working. So, of course, their spending potential includes not only their own salaries but their husbands'. Remember, it's the wife who selects the new car, the new refrigerator, the new furniture, and of course her own and often her family's clothes. What these women—not women of one age group but of all ages—really need is a fashion-service magazine."

Gerald Smith urged her to continue.

"The woman who works needs help in fitting her job into her life," she said. "Do you know that the average woman who works—I hate the expression 'career woman'—has 120 days off each year? This includes Saturdays, Sundays, legal holidays and two weeks of vacation. How is she going to spend these 120 days? The right magazine could help her. The woman who is married and has a job really leads a three-way life. She works from nine to five; she has to maintain a home and be a wife and mother after five, and then she lives a different life during those 120 days I mentioned."

Gerald Smith admitted that the magazine hadn't been aiming at the girl or woman who was permanently employed.

"During the war there were millions of girls working, but for the most part they were temporary workers. Today," Helen Valentine went on, "we have a class of permanent working women—married and unmarried. A magazine should cater to their hopes and problems and dreams."

Gerald Smith was quick to sense the soundness of her conclusions and turned over to Helen Valentine complete charge of *Charm*. From the very beginning Editor Valentine concentrated on women who were doing two things at once: running a home and running a job. The two activities were not incompatible, she believed. She felt that *Charm* could make things easier for the woman who felt that a job was an important part of her life. The first issue of *Charm* under Helen Valentine's direction came out August, 1950. In her first issue she presented her credo:

WE WORK TOO

When a magazine acquires a new editor, its readers have a right to know her plans. So, after a warm hello, come have a look at our ideas for *Charm*—and for you. It has long seemed to me that we women who work (whether we be teachers or typists, nurses or saleswomen or editors) have needed a magazine. We have found good fashions in one, good beauty advice in another, good food in a third—an article here and there that recognized our problems, but no single magazine meant only for us. There are 18,000,000 of us and, for the first time in the history of this country, more are married than single.

The significant common denominator between all of us is not age, not money, not type of job, but rather it is the fact that we are in business. We must run two shows, our jobs and our homes, and we must expend time and energies wisely if we wish to succeed in doing both well. And that is precisely what *Charm* hopes to help you do.

We'll be personal shoppers for you in clothes and cosmetics and things for your home—in books and music and movies and ideas—we'll be guinea pigs for everything we tell you to wear or cook or do. Unless it's right for us, we won't pass it on to you. We will spend your money carefully because we know what it means to work for a salary. We will show only those fashions which seem to us particularly good both in style and value, fashions we want to wear ourselves. If we show you some things which seem a bit high in price, it will be because they represent some *extra* measure of quality, some promise of superior style or stamina.

The five articles which followed were personal stories about members of the staff. If Helen Valentine were ever asked at whom she aimed her publication, she could in good conscience say that she was publishing the magazine for the members of her own staff. In capsule form they represented the huge audience of women who held two jobs. The old cliché (born perhaps in the arrogant mind of some neolithic man) to the effect that a woman who was a success at her job could not at the same time be a success as a wife and mother was laughed out of existence by *Charm*. Helen Valentine herself is a living refutation of the absurd beliefs about women that were for so long accepted as dogma by many in our land.

Says Mrs. Valentine, "We envision the magazine's readers as the millions of women who are contributing to the nation's welfare through their jobs in hospitals, schools, government, industry, banks and stores. These women are working sometimes because they have to, often because they want to—because they find in their jobs personal stimulation as well as the financial means to a fuller life for themselves and their families. Today there are more than twenty million of us working in this country, and our more than thirty-two billion-dollar paycheck has helped set new standards for higher education, more comfortable homes, better vacations."

One of *Charm's* most successful series has been "She Works In. . . ." —articles which concentrate on one city and show what it means to live and work there. Each article is a profile of a particular woman done against a profile of the city itself. The woman is selected with the greatest care and only after considerable research and discussion. In each case she must be a successful human being doing a good job in a field which is significant to the city. And because *Charm* wants to find out what the city itself considers important in terms of its own commercial and social life, several members of the staff visit the city and interview officials in the government, members of the Chamber of Commerce, top business executives, heads of agencies, and key members of women's business and professional clubs.

In Philadelphia, for example, it was found that the Woman's Medical College was the only such college in America and that the city was justly proud of it. So here a woman doctor was selected as the subject of "She Works in Philadelphia." In Houston, the citizens were pleased that *Charm* did not do the obvious and select the daughter of some oil tycoon who was condescending to work for a living. Rather, *Charm* recognized the enormous emphasis that Houston was placing on its cultural activities and the gratifying strides they had made, and chose the woman who was the director of the Alley Theatre. In Cleveland, where the idea of the Community Chest was born, and where there is a high degree of social conscience, an executive welfare worker was the subject of the piece.

In addition to spotlighting the life and career of one woman, each article also outlines the over-all employment picture for women in the area. The series thus has double impact: the appeal of an outstanding personality plus an interesting and important definition of a city's economic and cultural conditions.

An all-important part of *Charm's* service to women who work is its Housekeeping Department, headed by Charlotte Adams. Knowing that for her readers housekeeping is an after-hours job, Mrs. Adams is always in close touch with every industry in her field to find the newest simple-to-prepare, quick-to-serve food products, time- and work-saving appliances that will help busy working women manage their homes with ease and efficiency. And reader response to this department is proof of the confidence it has earned from the women it serves. Of the approximately four thousand letters that come to *Charm* each month from readers, often more than half concern homemaking problems.

Because reader mail is one gauge of audience-reaction to the magazine, every letter is given careful attention and answered in-

First *Mademoiselle's Living*, Autumn 1947

First monthly *Living for Young Homemakers*

dividually. Questions to the Jobs Department (there were 777 during May, 1955) on job opportunities are meticulously researched to give the best possible information to the inquiring reader. Altogether, 3,909 letters came to *Charm* during May—and less than one per cent were complaints. And while Mrs. Valentine is not overly upset by such complaints as the one objecting to "flat-chested models," her great concern for reader satisfaction demands close examination of any criticism of an article, feature or advertisement.

Helen Valentine firmly believes that in this fast-changing age no magazine can retain a static position and stay in front of the parade. She knows that to hold her audience—and enlarge it—she must anticipate new problems which may confront her readers, new enthusiasms which may catch their attention and interest. The magazine of 1950 is just not good enough to be the magazine of 1955. She has studied the complex problems of attracting and keeping readers, and the fact that *Charm* has the highest circulation in the fashion publishing field would indicate that she has mastered them.

Helen Valentine, like any successful editor today, is an excellent co-ordinator, and her wholehearted enthusiasms for her chosen pro-

William E. Hague, *Editor-in-Chief Edith Brazwell Evans, Guy Monypenny,* and Cecile Hayward at *Living* conference

fession and her own particular magazine has infected her whole staff. Her experienced associates Cipe Pineles (art director); Mary Roche (managing editor); Eleanor Hillebrand Bruce (fashion and merchandise) and her ten bright assistants; Estelle Ellis (promotion director) and a fine, competent and enthusiastic staff make life pleasant for the Editor-in-Chief. And Mrs. Valentine's personnel policies make life pleasant indeed for her associates. Giving her editors free rein within their own departments is a part of her policy; full recognition of achievement is another very important part. Mrs. Valentine knows well the work of every member of her staff, and an unusually fine job never goes unnoticed. And, more than that, she makes sure good work is brought to the attention of the Street & Smith management, too.

All of the statistics and theories which Helen Valentine discussed with Gerald Smith in 1950 have proven to be valid. Since then her position has been strengthened by national surveys on the subject of the woman who works. One research organization, for instance, issued a report that ten million families in the country received two paychecks (in most cases because of working wives)—a statement which amazed everyone in the trade except Helen Valentine. These statistics have brought about remarkable policy changes in retailing. Once stores became aware of the purchasing power of the working woman market, they decided to stay open at least one night a week to serve the married (and single) woman who was occupied with a full-time job. For years the stores catering to the lower-income bracket families had kept their lights on long after the conventional closing time, but it is only during the past four years that the best Madison Avenue, Fifty-seventh Street and Fifth Avenue stores (and their counterparts throughout the country) have realized that one of their most important customers—the woman who works—is so vital to their trade that it is a matter of good business to remain open at night. Today, 85 per cent of the first-class retail stores in the country remain open at least one night a week to take advantage of the huge buying of working women.

And there has been an important change in daytime policies, too. It had been customary to keep skeleton staffs in the stores during the lunch hour. *Charm* contended that full staffs should be maintained to help the working customer who wanted to shop during this period. *Charm* went even further and suggested thirty-minute fashion shows, box lunches, and clothes displayed ready to be purchased. To the amazement of many skeptics the lunch-hour business under this scheme boomed.

Neither Editor Valentine nor any member of her staff will take credit for these innovations, but the fact remains that increasingly the trade watches the publication presided over by Helen Valentine and often takes cues from it.

Helen Valentine works about ten hours a day in a pleasant office overlooking Madison Avenue. Its décor is as modern as the magazine she runs. She has a strange allergy to her handsome desk; it is always remarkably uncluttered. There is a low coffee table in front of a comfortable couch, and this is her workbench. This table is covered with all the impedimenta of the editor's trade. It is the focal point of her otherwise serene-looking, air-cooled office, whose motif is a cool olive green. To the left of her desk is a small table holding a tea service of white Limoges china. The fact that their editor's name is Valentine has spurred her staff to celebrate Valentine's Day and each year they present her with a few additional pieces of Limoges.

In addition to her impressive executive ability, Helen Valentine's sense of humor and capacity for warmth and friendship have earned her a deservedly high position not only in her own editorial family, but in the entire trade.

Mrs. Valentine has become one of the leading authorities on the Woman Who Works, and she is in great demand around the coun-

Dorothy Dawe Trophies to *Living*

Visitors at a *Living* model home

try as a speaker. At a session of the 83rd Congress, the Honorable Henry M. Jackson, United States Senator from the State of Washington, arose to ask for unanimous consent for the publication in the Congressional Record of an address made by Mrs. Valentine in Washington, D. C. The talk, "How to Keep More of the Money You Earn," was a brilliant plea for legislation which would give tax relief to married women workers—and it was incorporated in the Congressional Record.

Under Mrs. Valentine's editorship, *Charm* has not only attained the largest circulation of any woman's fashion book, but has made gratifying commercial progress. The faith that advertisers put in her judgment is attested to by the fact that *Charm,* in the first six months of 1955, stood second in number of advertising pages gained among all the consumer magazines, both weeklies and monthlies, published in the United States.

In the days after World War II, Gerald Smith realized that one of the chief problems confronting young married people was the desperate housing shortage. Newly married couples were living wherever they could find space, and the space they found was—as often as not —highly unattractive, very expensive and badly furnished. His perceptive editorial mind noted that these youngsters needed advice on home building, home decorating, on the various aspects of making a livable place out of the poor raw material they were forced to utilize. Sensing their needs and the importance of this young market, he brought out a quarterly in 1947 rather awkwardly named *Mademoiselle's Living* (the Magazine for Smart Young Homemakers). Betsy Blackwell was Editor-in-Chief. It was a beautiful, 192-page, profusely illustrated publication. Its policy was announced in the first issue:

> Our generation knows what home means! We've traveled, we've seen other countries. We've seen our own country, too. We've lived in dingy rooms near Army camps in small towns from coast to coast. We've packed and crated and shipped and moved on. We've tried to make impossible quarters livable with a few yards of chintz, a few treasured belongings. . . . Now we've come home! Home means a lot to us. . . . We want beauty and color and comfort in our homes, and they mustn't wear fabulous price tags or we can't afford them. We want to build homes of our own, and we don't want to mortgage our children to do it. We want the benefits of modern science, of modern efficiency, now, in our everyday lives.

This is your magazine. It does not speak to the affluent middle-aged. It does not cater to the settled and the stodgy. Its main purpose is to help you integrate your home, your family and your life. It is devoted to your problems, your budgets, your ideas, your lives. Its best wish is to show you how to live today, as you want to live, and how to tailor tomorrow to your dreams.

Betsy Blackwell had her hands full running her own *Mademoiselle* and this new and attractive stepchild. The pace she set for herself was a killing one and it was not long before she decided to give up the dual editorship.

Edith Brazwell Evans, who had been Coordinating Director of *Mademoiselle* in charge of markets and market developments, was made editor, and in 1949 the word *Mademoiselle* was dropped from the front cover; the lusty, rapidly growing youngster no longer needed to be tied to its mother's apron strings. It was now called *Living for Young Homemakers,* but in the trade it was known simply as *Living.* Edith Evans resolved to keep the magazine keyed directly to the housing requirements of young families in the middle-income class, in line with the announced editorial policy in the first issue. When Edith Evans discussed housing, architecture and decoration she knew what she was talking about. Long before she became a member of the Street & Smith family, this remarkable young woman out of Johnson City, Tennessee, had studied design, art and architecture. She had also been associated in various merchandising capacities with A. H. Harris in Dallas and with Macy's and Saks Fifth Avenue in New York. Edith Evans is a thorough professional in her field. Slim, chic, witty, she can talk design with Raymond Loewy, architecture with Frank Lloyd Wright, discuss the stress a two-by-four will take and then argue about the proper way to mix concrete with any foreman in the field. (If pressed, she could probably mix the damn stuff herself.) An insatiable collector of antiques, she has nursed a grudging admiration for contemporary design to the point where she is so knowledgeable on the subject that quite often her opinion of a new line of modern furniture will make or break it. Violently allergic to air travel, she spends hundreds of hours a year in airplanes, racing across the country to deliver her trenchant speeches, to cajole builders into undertaking what often seems to them an alarming departure from the safe old routine, to descend in helicopters at grand openings of new housing developments, to be charming, amusing and authoritative while wishing with a vengeance that the brothers Wright had turned their talents elsewhere.

In 1948, both the home decorating and building industries needed guidance and needed it badly. The attitude persisted that furniture was purchased only once in a lifetime—when one had sufficient cash in hand—and until that halcyon day came along, makeshift was the word, furniture-wise, for the average young home. Most well-designed pieces, at that time, were expensive. They were manufactured with an eye on the chairman of the board rather than on the rising young executive (or the young plumber or the young dentist). Taste was associated with money; if one had no money (or not much of it) one presumably had no taste. There was little choice for the purchaser, little consideration of the fact that a steam fitter might possibly have as much taste as a bank president. To use a symbol, it was Louis Seize (and the money to buy it) or nothing else. Horatio Alger was expected to work like a dog until he could *afford* Louis Seize, and how he lived in the interim didn't much matter. This particular Horatio, however, was married and had a family. He needed help, and that help *Living* was determined to give him.

Times had changed, however, from the old days when Francis or Ormond Smith could bring out a new magazine and drop it if

Arthur P. Lawler,
Vice-President and Secretary

Ralph R. Whittaker, Jr.,
Executive Vice-President

it was not immediately successful. Despite the acceptance accorded *Living for Young Homemakers*, it had cost Street & Smith more than two million dollars. With that outlay behind him, Gerald Smith had to face the possibility of spending considerably more or folding the magazine. Only because he was a publisher with conviction and imagination did he continue with it. It was sheer determination that kept the ball in the air until the magazine became a success. Within a year and a half after it became a monthly the circulation had climbed to the 350,000 mark. It wasn't easy. Editor Evans set out to create an honest, understandable magazine with no nonsense about it, no chi chi, no *avante-garde* frippery, no pronouncing from an ivory tower. Since youth, ostensibly, is best served by youth, she chose a staff that could be molded to its audience, rather than a group of arbiters who might be too well established in the traditional editorial pattern to be sympathetic to a departure from it. Young, as bright as she could find them, they were chosen for their background, their ability to create and their propensity for dedication.

Then, from eight in the morning until well into the night, Mrs. Evans (when she wasn't in an airplane) sat at her desk, outwardly cool and *soignée*, inwardly determined to be as infallible an editor as it is permitted a human being to be. The staff worked almost as hard, and since, at the beginning, it was a very small staff (there were as many George Spelvins on the masthead as in the cast of a summer

Thomas H. Kaiser, Treasurer   Walter Hudson, with S & S since 1902

theatre program), their duties were manifold and occasionally unorthodox. Editors doubled in brass, meals were taken on the run, publicity releases were collated by hand at midnight, and backgrounds for room settings were assembled in a loft by hook or by crook (they still are, but with less frenzy and more finesse). *Living,* in short, was a tiger had by the tail, and since neither Mrs. Evans nor her staff had any intention of letting go, out of the pandemonium the snowball was started on its way—a prodigy that was to become (and in not too long a time) the dominating influence in its field.

A campaign was begun—and it is still being waged—to develop a new design concept for manufacturers that would be geared to the pocketbook of the young market. The "young living approach" revolutionized moderately priced furniture design, and in turn influenced all phases of the home-furnishings industry. Trends, today, *begin* in the young market and then seep on up into the higher brackets. "Borax" (the trade's name for undistinguished furniture) still exists, but no one has to buy it if he doesn't want to. There are too many well-designed pieces on the market for the same price.

The field of interior decoration was shaken loose from its elegant moorings and revealed for what it is: a highly complicated craft that is half good taste, half trickery. The reader's taste (hopefully) was taken for granted, but the tricks were taught—carefully, step by step —with the same patience one would use in teaching a child to read. This tutelage continues, and since fashions in decoration change constantly, so do the lessons. They are always, however, guides to visual pleasure without monetary tears.

In the building field, Mrs. Evans became a powerhouse, pioneering tirelessly to bring about acceptance of prefabricated homes, working in the field with builders and architects to achieve better home design in the moderate price bracket. An Evans "first" was the recognition of the builder, rather than the architect, as the key contributor to "more house for the dollar." As the voice of authority on the tastes and needs of the young married market, the magazine's housing philosophy, its "say" on home design, found widespread recognition: up to three thousand *Living* homes may be built in a single year from coast to coast. The prefabricated house is no longer a pariah; instead, it has been not only recognized but embraced by certain glossier publications that, a few years ago, wouldn't have been caught dead with it. During the past few years *Living* has presented a series of homes designed by its own staff architects (or outside men with whom the staff cooperated). Readers could purchase the complete plans and specifications for five dollars, and Editor Evans wisely advised such purchasers to consult a local architect when they began to build. Any of these homes could be built in the neighborhood of $15,000.

Not long ago in a discussion of housing problems, President Eisenhower said, "Millions of families with modest incomes are able for the first time to buy new or used homes." Members of *Living's* staff felt pretty good about that statement, but neither Edith Evans nor her staff had to indulge in any mutual back-patting—others did it for them. In 1954, the National Association of Home Builders presented the magazine with the association's first—and only—publishing award for "distinguished reporting of housing achievements by home builders." Twice, Edith Evans has received the home furnishings industry's highest tribute, the Dorothy Dawe Award for "distinguished reporting on home furnishings." This is comparable to being a two-time Pulitzer Prize winner or Oscar recipient, and although Mrs. Evans is the sparkplug of the magazine, she is the first to speak with pride of the contribution of her brilliant young staff.

One would think that Edith Evans might now be content to rest a bit on her laurels, but to that lady the surface has barely been scratched. To her, the best design in the world is meaningless until it has penetrated to the farthest reaches of young homemaking, and she plans to see that it gets there. She accepts the pleasantly spurious theory that two can live as cheaply as one with more than a grain of salt. She knows they cannot, but she is convinced that life can be made pleasanter when not too much money is bolstered with knowledge and an awakened imagination. That is her credo, and *Living* is the medium which spreads it.

Now boasting a circulation of 550,000, *Living* has been accepted as a valuable medium by advertising agencies. *Living for Young Homemakers,* along with *Mademoiselle* and *Charm,* made the list of the top ten magazines with the greatest advertising page gains during the first six months of 1955. *Mademoiselle, Charm, Living for Young Homemakers*—these are a far cry from *The New York Weekly, The Bowery Boys, Western Story* and *Top Notch,* but they are successful proof of the Street & Smith century-old, incredible publishing genius.

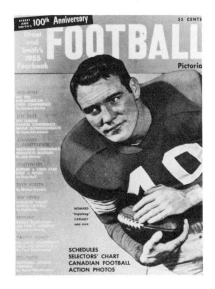

Air Progress

Football Yearbook

Air Trails Model Annual

Baseball Yearbook

Woman's Modern Home Almanac

Street & Smith yearbooks

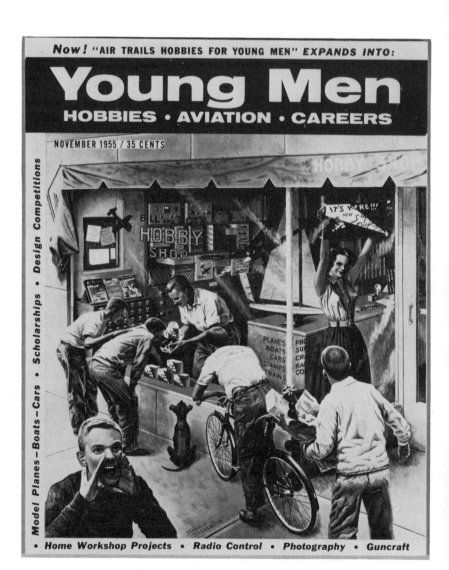

Young Men, most recent Street & Smith publication, 1955

One publication which has survived the erosion of time is the one originally known as *Bill Barnes, Air Adventurer*. In its early years it was devoted to fiction concerning the aerial exploits of its hero. As flying became more commonplace, however, the interest of boys shifted from reading about planes to making models of the more famous types. The names of great aircraft designers were appearing in the news regularly and boys learned that many had been makers of model planes themselves when they were young. The editorial content kept pace with the new trend and the title was changed to *Air Trails*, under Editor William Winter. Alexis Dawydoff, a veteran of experimental flying in thunderstorms for the Air Force, was named technical editor. The magazine soon became the authority in this field and covered all aspects from the simple balsa-wood kit to radio-controlled designs. Gerald Smith, a flying enthusiast who flew his own aircraft, ran a column for a while on light planes. Many of the articles on planes are far too technical for the average adult to understand, but air-minded youngsters find articles explaining the "stability characteristics of the Swedish SAAB 210 Draken double-delta" research plane, or paragraphs about the new "Convair turboprop flying boat R3Y-2 Tradewind 2" not only understandable but fascinating.

In 1947 Albert Lewis, who had been with the National Aeronautics Association for many years, was named editor. Model activity had expanded to boats, cars, guns and numerous other subjects. Also, cable and radio control of models became even more important as youngsters were not satisfied with static models. Whether it was plane, boat or car it must move, and Lewis felt all these new fields needed coverage. Once again the magazine was changed and renamed *Hobbies for Young Men*. During 1954 a series of articles on careers for youth was inaugurated. These proved so popular that additional articles outside the model field became an integral part of the magazine and it was retitled *Young Men*, to describe more aptly its universal appeal. Currently the circulation is about 100,000, and this magazine graphically portrays the ability of Street & Smith to adapt its publication to the ever-shifting tastes of the reading public.

Two hardy perennials bearing the Street & Smith label are the highly successful *Baseball* and *Football* annuals. The first editor was Charles Moran, who also handled *Sport Story, Athlete, Wizard, True Sport* and various other publications in his spare time. The annuals were a success from the start, and after Charles Moran left to write movie scenarios, Sam Andre became the editor. He had come to the firm in 1937 from the *New York American,* for which he had been doing a full page of sports pictures and captions. He helped edit the ten-cent monthly, *Pic,* which had a spectacular life for eight years. In the beginning *Pic* was dedicated to Hollywood (Russell Crouse wrote that department), Broadway (Heywood Broun handled that until his death), and sports (presided over by Joe Williams, sports columnist for the *New York World-Telegram*). When *Pic* was discontinued, Gerald Smith decided to put Sam Andre in charge of the two annuals.

Gerald Smith was always an ardent sports fan; during the late 1940's he was one of the pioneers who, with Arch Ward of the *Chicago Tribune,* formed the All-American Football Conference. For several years he ran the Brooklyn Football Club. As the time approached when it appeared that the All America Conference and the National Football League would merge, Gerald Smith sold the club to Branch Rickey—"a frustrated football coach."

The firm has had great success with the two sports annuals, which sell for thirty-five cents a copy. Gerald Smith gave Sam Andre free rein, and the well-liked former newspaper photographer had no trouble persuading the best baseball and football writers in the land to contribute to his two publications. Today each sells well over 300,-000 copies. Andre knows what sports fans want to read and he gives it to them in two highly attractive packages.

Two specialized annuals are edited by the staff of *Young Men.* One continues the old "Air Trails" title and is labeled *Air Trails Model Annual;* it contains the latest word on model building as well as plans for constructing both new type planes and the more famous older ones. Because of increasing interest in recent years model boat and car activities have been included in this publication. The companion collection called *Air Progress* is devoted exclusively to the large plane field. It traces pictorially the most recent developments in aviation, as well as providing an authoritative reference book for those interested in the history of aviation.

The most recent addition to Street & Smith's annuals is the 1956 *Woman's Modern Home Almanac.* This book is a handy compendium of information on menus, household "how-to's," gardening and other problems of modern living.

CHAPTER

ELEVEN

ASTOUNDING SCIENCE FICTION

STREET & SMITH

December 1954 · 35 Cents

Astounding SCIENCE FICTION

Mars seen from Phobos

An *Astounding Science Fiction* cover by Chesley Bonestell; the magazine was
first published in 1933 as *Astounding Stories*

CHAPTER

ELEVEN

Any reader of science-fiction knows that Arcturus IV (the fourth nearest planet to the sun) is thirty-three light years away from little Mother Earth. A day lasts 159 hours on Arcturus IV and the atmosphere is composed largely of Methane; the inhabitants of the planet are called Methanians. What are they like?

> The Methanians weigh very little compared to us. One of the largest we met was weighed on a Terranian spring scale at one hundred eighty-seven pounds. (They are relatively strong, however, being able to lift twice their own weight.) Their bones are hollow and apparently filled with hydrogen and helium. There is no question but these people have evolved from a race of birds, their appearance seems to indicate it, their history seems to prove it. Their long arms and clawlike hands —three-fingered—are vestiges of once great wings. The only anomaly is their single-toed feet like that of a horse. This adaptation to ground living evolved very rapidly once the power of flight was lost.
>
> The young are born in eggs and the eggs are carried around in skin pockets or pouches similar to those of the now extinct Terranian Penguin until the egg hatches. Both male and female take turns in the hatching process. The young grow rapidly at first and are ready to take care of themselves in about twenty Terranian years.

Does this sound as though it came right out of one of the more fantastic science-fiction tales? It is an excerpt from a report by Dr. J. S. Wick, Director of the Physiological Bureau of the Massachusetts Institute of Technology! It is, of course, an imaginative and fictionized version of the planet told with tongue in cheek.

For the past three years the great seat of scientific learning known as M. I. T. has given its students a course in creative engineering and the above excerpt is a sampling of the delightful course. Professor

John Arnold, in charge of this special department, explains it by saying:

> Our aim is to provide an ever-increasing number of young men trained not only in the basic concepts of science and engineering, but also in the use of their creative imaginations. A great many of the students taking the course are already science-fiction fans, or else take to it very readily. There may be some theory that education must be solemn and serious, but the Creative Engineering Group at M.I.T. does not subscribe to this.

When an institution such as M.I.T. not only encourages its students to read science-fiction but actually formulates engineering problems for them to solve based on hypothetical conditions existing upon planets thirty-three light years away, this new branch of storytelling can hardly be dismissed as sheer unadulterated fantasy.

There is, of course, nothing new in science-fiction. It is as old as the dreams, the fears, the superstitions, the curiosity of man. In the second century A.D., Lucian of Samosata wrote two long stories on voyages to the moon. Writers like Edgar Allan Poe, Jules Verne, Robert Louis Stevenson, H. G. Wells (the master of them all), A. Conan Doyle and Gilbert Chesterton are a few of the writers who based fictional stories on scientific principles (the scientific principles were not always correctly stated, but there was invariably a note of authenticity to them). Today writers in this field can go farther afield than could their predecessors. The era of atomic energy, of rocket ships, of space suits (test pilots actually wear them), of planes that attain speeds that not even the most imaginative science-fiction writer of thirty years ago would have dared to use, has given the writer virtually unlimited scope. No matter how fantastic the tale, the reader cannot dismiss it. In his own time equally fantastic events have occurred and scientific achievements have surpassed the imagination of a Jules Verne or an H. G. Wells. One writer in the field has said, "Until we reach Mars we can write about Mars as we wish." The inspired guess of the writer may actually be the scientific discovery of a decade from now. Twenty years ago there were men writing fiction based on nuclear fission; today school children accept it as fact. Scientists tell us that within a few years the present state of development in that field will seem primitive and almost infantile to the man in the street.

The most important factor in offering a new publication to the masses is timing. Ormond Smith's uncanny ability to sense what the public wanted before other publishers (and the public itself) realized it was incredible. In 1918 he "had a feeling" that the public, excited about the success of the airplane and other new weapons (notably poison gas) in World War I was ready for a magazine dealing with those subjects. He got under way a publication called *Thrill Book* (the forerunner of today's science-fiction magazines), but it was a dismal financial flop. Perhaps the reality of the war was too close to admit of any scientific romanticizing about it.

"I guess I was wrong on this one, Will," Ormond said to Ralston. "We'll just kill it and take our loss." This was one of the many times when O. G. was ahead of the public. Readers refused to take the science-fiction in the little publication seriously. It was not until fifteen years later that Smith, still believing that the public was interested in fiction based on fantasy and science (or pseudo-science), issued *Astounding Stories* under the auspices of Street & Smith. This was a 144-page monthly published the third Wednesday of every month.

Astounding Stories was well named. The first issue contained eight

Astounding Science Fiction predicts the atomic bomb

short stories and three novelettes, each more astounding than the other. "The Orange God" by Walter Glamis led off the new venture. It was a tale of a strange cult in the remote vastness of Tibet (where else?).

Its tempo was set by "A Race Against Time" by Donald Wandrei. Webster Conning, a scientist, has built a slender torpedo-shaped craft which he shows to his girl Ellen.

> "Why, it's a thing of beauty in every detail!" cried Ellen as she took it all in; and then added, in a more puzzled tone: "But what's it for?"
>
> "Time traveling," Web answered succinctly.
>
> "Time traveling?" she echoed. "Why, you must be mad!"
>
> "It's really quite simple," he commenced. "What I've done is to build a time-space traveler, working by atomic energy. Even as long ago as 1913, you know, Rutherford succeeded in partly breaking down the hydrogen atom. By 1933, others succeeded in partially breaking down atoms with high voltages of electricity. But they used up far more energy than they got back, or released. I've simply perfected the method to a point where, with an initial bombardment of fifty volts, I can break down one atom and get back thousands of times the energy I put in.

This was in October, 1933. Not one person in perhaps ten million had ever heard the phrase "atomic energy." The idea of "liberating energy that already exists" was something that a Fermi or an Oppenheimer might discuss, but here was a writer of fiction prophetically advancing scientific possibilities that would within a few short years be proven to be sound. Then the story really slid into the astounding classification. Webster kidnapped the girl and took her on a little trip in his flying machine to the year 995,851, by which time our sad planet had been denuded of all life and the scientist and the girl found themselves to be the only living inhabitants of the sphere.

> "It is up to us, Ellen," the scientist said, "to—to preserve the human race. You see that, don't you?"

That is about as far as imaginative fiction ever gets to the basic facts of life. Fiction-scientists are much like heroes of western movies; romance is usually either played down or presented against a backdrop of strange planets or esoteric mathematical equations.

At the conclusion of many of the stories, "fillers" were used to complete the page. These were invariably items concerning inexplicable or unexplained events which had in fact occurred. Readers were fascinated by these paragraphs:

> In a Los Angeles suburb recently, police found a deserted automobile. In the car was a dead Chinese and a live rattlesnake. The snake's mouth had been sewed up; its poison fangs rendered innocuous. The police are still wondering.

> A farmer's baby disappeared in Finland two years ago, and a long but fruitless search was made for the kidnapers. Recently, woodcutters, felling a tree, found the infant's skeleton in the topmost branches. An eagle had been responsible for the snatch.

> Scotland Yard has the photograph of a room in which a man was shot. Prominent on one of the walls is the picture of a girl. The bullet which killed the man passed through the girl's head in the picture. The girl was the one who shot him.

> A dying priest in Ceylon cursed a jewel, the famous Eye of Buddha, which a French soldier stole from a temple. The jewel left a trail of death and treachery behind it, came into the hands of a Jewish diamond merchant, and was confiscated by Frederick the Great of Germany. The merchant, dying, repeated the curse, and predicted that a future emperor would rule only twelve weeks and that his son would live in exile. The Kaiser's father ruled twelve weeks. At the close of the World War, the Kaiser was exiled.

A department called "Let's Get Down to Brass Tacks"—An Open Forum of Controversial Opinion—defined the policy of the magazine.

> Brass Tacks are handy. They drive right to the heart of any problem or controversy. *Astounding Stories* is back again with a new policy. It is a carefully planned and slowly unfolding policy which will please you more and more as time passes because, first and foremost, you—our readers—are a thinking group.
>
> Our purpose is to bring to you each month one story carrying a new and unexplored "thought-variant" in the field of scientific fiction.
>
> *Astounding Stories* is, perforce, a medium of logical fantasy. It must not become "habit-ridden"—or "grooved"—into a single line of thought. We shall continue to explore the interplanetary airways, the aeons past and future; the interexisting worlds of the present; the shadowy realms which are suggested by vibratory force. You will find no "hack" stories in our pages, nor the dull, windy, lifeless variety. But always you will find real, convincing people; and profound, serious thought animating the structure of the stories. And you will find the best-known authors; and you will find their best work.

The Street & Smith offices are at 575 Madison Avenue

There are no religious or racial lines drawn in outer space as portrayed by imaginative fiction of this type. Science-fiction has wide popularity among Negro readers (newsstand sales in Harlem, Chicago's South Side and in many Negro communities in the South show this to be a fact). It may be because the conflict is usually earthmen against the outer world or against the machine.

It was in 1938 that the name of the now successful magazine was changed to *Astounding Science-Fiction*. John W. Campbell, Jr., was made editor, and to this day he rues the fact that Street & Smith never copyrighted the phrase "Science-Fiction." Instead of being the exclusive property of the firm, the phrase has become generic, to embrace virtually all forms of imaginative literature. Under Campbell (an M. I. T. graduate and writer of fiction himself) the magazine made enormous strides.

During the war scientists caught up with the writers of science-fiction. Radar, the V-2 rocket, the atom bomb and a dozen other offensive and defensive weapons may have been startlingly new to the public; they were old stuff to readers of *Astounding Science-Fiction*. The post-war years have seen even greater scientific strides but when President Eisenhower dramatically announced the planning of a man-made satellite orbiting about our Earth he was on ground long familiar to the readers. Not even the serious critics could laugh at the fantastic when science itself was developing along increasingly fantastic lines. Science-fiction writing has improved immeasurably; it had to improve to compete with front-page news and feature articles. Under the direction of Campbell, circulation of the magazine trebled.

Today many of the best writers in this field are scientists themselves, or at least men who have had scientific training. Typical of these is "J. J. Coupling," invariably included in the annual collections of the best science-fiction. Even his *nom de plume* is in the tradition of the craft. A "JJ coupling" is a type of inter-atomic binding force in crystals. There are many types of couplings (HJ, EJ, EE, HH). John R. Pierce, one of the country's leading communications engineers, editor of a technical journal and author of two weighty tomes on electronics, is actually the man who writes under the name of "J. J. Coupling." At a recent convention of the Institute of Radio Engineers, Dr. Pierce gave a highly technical talk on "Traveling Wave Amplifiers." That afternoon, a talk on science-fiction by "J. J. Coupling" was announced. Many of the learned scientist's associates were amazed when Dr. Pierce strode to the platform to deliver "J. J. Coupling's" address. Later the Institute received a number of protests from scientists who had not been present, to the effect that it was an insult to a man of Dr. Pierce's standing to have a writer of fantasy like "J. J. Coupling" appear on the same program. When J. J. Coupling writes on article for *Astounding Science-Fiction* presenting the thesis that even with our present radio-telephonic equipment we could (by using a radar beam) maintain radio-telephone communication with Mars at less expense than the same kind of communication can be maintained to England, he isn't kidding. He wrote an article for a technical journal putting forth the same argument, and because it was written by Dr. Pierce it was accepted in scientific circles. Even a layman can follow his argument. Radar cannot go through the earth, for the curve of the planet we live on prevents radar from being used to communicate with any ship or land beyond the horizon—Mars is in a direct line with the earth, and there is nothing between the two planets but plenty of space.

Another popular author is "C. Rudmore." He too is a distinguished scientist, but Editor John Campbell is careful to preserve his anonymity. In radar, "crud" is the term for interference that confuses the radar screen. "Crudmore," of course, is an ingenious way of saying "more interference" or "more confusion."

Writers of imaginative literature are usually men who are long on humor. Isaac Asimov (Professor of Biochemistry at the Boston University School of Medicine) is one of the finest of them all. He wrote nine startling stories about robots before the science of cybernetics came into being with the development of a mechanical brain at M.I.T., the theoretical basis for the now not-so-remote possibility of some kind of robot which will do all of our thinking for us. Asimov wrote a charming and hilarious story, "Robot AL 76 Goes Astray." He says of his story:

> I am very pleased with the current furore over what Professor Norbert Weiner of M.I.T. calls "cybernetics." It is the science of "thinking" machines and is, undoubtedly, the theoretical basis for the eventual positronic robot. I have written nine robot stories, and I wrote all nine before I heard of the science, so anything about my robotic conceptions that doesn't fit the rigorous math of Professor Weiner must be forgiven

me. (Another reason for forgiveness—but one I am not anxious to publicize—is that I don't understand the mathematics even after having looked at his book.)

"Robot AL 76 Goes Astray" is a light-hearted story. In a sense, it's a self-satire. Of course, it's a great day for an author when he becomes important enough to be satirized, and if I waited for a spontaneous gesture on the part of others, I could wait decades—centuries, if I lived long enough. So I took care of the satire myself and did it gently.

Incidentally, all my robots have been nice guys. None of them has ever been Frankensteinian products. This is not because of reluctance on my part to utilize plot-clichés in order to turn an honest penny. It's just that I can't believe that a world run in the way we are running this one could possibly be harmed by being taken over by intelligent machines.

In writing about robots, brilliant Isaac Asimov is conforming to a highly respected literary tradition. The first robot (although the word itself was not invented until decades later) to achieve international notice was the celebrated monster created by Mary Shelley. Ever since 1818, the monster has been known erroneously as Frankenstein. Actually, it was the young medical student who put together the odds and ends of corpses he snatched from graveyards and dissecting rooms who was named Frankenstein. Mrs. Shelley never named the monster itself. Yet at least once a week we hear some distinguished (if illiterate) statesman arise to talk of the atom bomb in such terms as, "It will be impossible for us to control the Frankenstein we have created." (This is a minor and perhaps needless observation, but the constant reiteration of the mistake has annoyed me considerably for some twenty years, and I would like to put my annoyance on record.) Anyhow, the monster created by medical student Frankenstein was actually an android and not a proper robot. An android is a synthetic man made in a laboratory out of protoplasm, and once the magic of life is given him, he is able to move about and think independently. But this monster did unquestionably sire the thousands of fictional robots who have stalked the pages of imaginative fiction ever since. Mary Shelley was really trying to preach a sermon; the monster became the instrument of dreadful retribution on the student who had so arrogantly usurped the prerogative of the Creator.

The word "robot" was coined by the Czech playwright Karl Capek (it derives from the Czech verb "to work") and was used in his tremendously successful play *R. U. R.*, produced in New York in 1923. The letters stood for "Rossum's Universal Robots," and the play dealt with an imaginary future state in which mechanical men enslaved to do the work of the world for man revolted against their masters. "Rossum's" was the commercial firm which produced the robots. Perhaps the author, like Mrs. Shelley, intended to give the world a message not to fool around with machines or one of them might rear back and toss a punch which would annihilate the whole human race. The play ends with a dash of sex that intrigued audiences no end. Except for one old carpenter who had helped manufacture the robots, the human race is indeed wiped out. But now the robots start wearing out and they are concerned that their mechanical race will soon rust into extinction. But the old carpenter knows something that they don't know; he knows that the doctor who created them had given them the capacity to love and procreate. He finally tells a boy and a girl robot who are mooning bewilderedly at each other, "Go Adam, go Eve: the world is yours."

To return to Isaac Asimov (always a pleasure, because his stories are more delightful than horrendous), he created a pleasant type of robot complete with built-in controls which prevented him from harboring the slightest enmity for the human beings who created him. His robots on the whole are pleasant characters who would be received not only in the best homes but in the sacred precincts of Harvard or M.I.T.

There are critics who decry science-fiction as a waste of time, but these are men who have not read the best of it. One very respected and learned critic, Gilbert Highet of Columbia University, presided over a delightful radio program called "Persons, Places and Things." In one of his talks he sneered at science-fiction and regretted that this kind of trash was the one new type of literature our own age had produced. In a rather wonderful little book, *Inquiry into Science-Fiction* by Basil Davenport the author relates that Dr. Highet was flooded with protests not only from the ordinary newsstand customer but from professional colleagues. He was asked if he had read Asimov, Coupling, John Campbell, John Collier, or a dozen other literate and skilled practitioners of the art. To the everlasting credit of the erudite Dr. Highet, he immediately plunged into the realm of science-fiction and then devoted a second program to the subject, apologizing for his previous snap judgment and discussing the positive values of im-

New York City in 1955

aginative fiction. His endorsement of this type of literature gave it a cachet it had never enjoyed before.

Basil Davenport, who is a Greek scholar, a translator of French plays and a member of the editorial board of the Book-of-the-Month Club, defines science-fiction as "fiction based upon some imagined development of science or upon the extrapolation of a tendency in society." The word "extrapolation," dear to the hearts of imaginative writers, means "the extension of variables beyond their known ranges." This is about as good a definition as one can find.

John Campbell himself says in the introduction to a volume of his own collected stories, *Who Goes There?*: "Basically science-fiction is an effort to predict the future on the basis of known facts, culled largely from present-day science laboratories." His pre-eminence as a writer and an editor in the field of imaginative writing is due to the fact that he always keeps his own definition in mind, especially when considering stories for *Astounding Science-Fiction*.

Mark Clifton and Alex Apostolides have long been recognized as a skillful team in the field of what some call psience fiction—fiction that deals with the Psi element of telepathy or its allied field. Their "What Thin Partition?" was hailed as one of the finest of all stories in this field, and their "Crazy Joey" published by John Campbell in 1953 is a fine short story by any standard. Again it fits Mr. Davenport's definition. A youngster has the gift of reading minds, which makes him a nonconformist and an object of ridicule among the boys on his block, just because he is "different." Dr. Rhine, in his experiments in the field of extra-sensory perception at Duke University, established the fact beyond question that there are many who have the ability to call the denominations of unseen cards with a significantly greater degree of accuracy than the laws of probability would allow. If the scientific springboard is firm, such authors (both of whom are industrial engineers) leap with assurance into the probable future of the particular science involved.

Sometimes science-fiction comes so close to reality that security officers take sharp notice. This happened in 1944, when only a handful of scientists, government officials and military bigwigs knew anything about the Manhattan Project, then well on its way to final development of the atomic bomb which was to end the war so decisively. Cleve Cartmill, one of Campbell's writers, was working on a story which involved the disarming of an enemy atomic bomb. He wrote Editor Campbell asking just how you would disarm an atomic bomb. Campbell, who was as ignorant of the Manhattan Project as any of us, considered the problem and gave Cartmill his advice. In March, 1944, the story "Deadline" appeared in *Astounding Science-Fiction*. It was hardly on the stands before F.B.I. men swooped down on the astonished John Campbell. They discovered that Author Cartmill lived in Hollywood. Several atomic scientists lived in Southern California. They were sure that scientists working on the project had met Cartmill and had leaked information to him.

Campbell explained the facts of science-fiction to the F.B.I. men.

ADJUSTMENT REQUEST

Name of
Magazine ___ASTOUNDING SCIENCE FICTION___

Date of Agent's Order ___10/25/51___

Date Subscriber Complained ___3/1/52___

"Please CANCEL IMMEDIATELY the subscription and
forward refund for the nine copies still due the
subscriber to the agent listed below. Mr. Overton
was killed while trying an experiment in the magazine".

Agent's Name ___Anna J. Tongren___

Agent's Address ___416 East Main Street___

Agent's City & State ___Ridgeway, Penna.___

A cancellation request with good reason

He showed them an article written as early as 1940 in *The Physical Review,* in which the writer had discussed nuclear fission and, for that matter, the way to disarm an atomic bomb. The article contained the basic concepts necessary to formulate the bomb.

"Any scientist," Campbell assured the F.B.I. men, "knows that such things as atomic bombs can be predicted. You can't force secrecy on nature."

He had a copy of the letter he had sent to Cartmill. The sweating F.B.I. men relaxed. It was obvious that this was just one of those coincidences that can only happen when fiction starts anticipating reality. They didn't exactly tell Campbell why they were concerned; they didn't have to tell him. But to make them feel better, Campbell said that he wouldn't print any more stories dealing with atomic bombs until the war was over. Rather casually he showed them a story, "Solution Unsatisfactory," written by Robert Heinlein and published in *Astounding Science-Fiction* in 1940. This predicted that the war would be ended by the use of nuclear weapons, but the weapon used in that story was not a bomb but a fission product which would be dropped as dust and which would kill everyone in the area infected. This "fall-out" in the form of a lethal dust hasn't yet been announced as an actual weapon in our arsenal, but if it were, it would not surprise writers of imaginative fiction. In any case, the F.B.I. men finally realized that no security had been violated, and they retreated gracefully. Campbell went back to his desk, worried about when a real atomic bomb would be dropped on the enemy.

The future of science-fiction? It seems as assured as the fact that men will always dream and will always want to know what is around the next bend in the road. Let us give Basil Davenport the last word, the words with which he ends his book:

> That Man is a creature with awesome potentialities for achievement and for self-destruction, and that the inhabitants of Earth are not the only powers in the Universe—these are truths that men have never been able to forget for more than a generation or two. It is science-fiction which is telling them to us now.

EPILOGUE

STREET & SMITH

Gerald Hewitt Smith

1912–1955

EPILOGUE

Going over Niagara Falls in a barrel, betting your last cent that you can make a ten the hard way with the dice, and attempting to cross the Atlantic in a canoe are admittedly hazardous undertakings, but the chance of success in each case is no more remote than the chance a publisher takes every time he brings out a new magazine. No one has ever been able to concoct the magic formula which will insure the success of a new book or magazine. The study of magazines which have mass appeal is interesting enough, but it will not guarantee an easy way to produce a sure-fire success.

Art directors say that covers sell magazines; fiction editors insist that people buy magazines for the quality of the short stories and serials; articles editors assert confidently that people today are mainly interested in nonfiction, and the technicians say that typography, make-up and design are important factors in the public's response to a publication. Experienced editors and publishers who have the responsibility of supervising the over-all publication realize that no one feature can be given credit for the sustained success of any given magazine. The risk is naturally minimized by the experience and ability of a good editor and publisher.

The tremendous increase in the cost of publishing a magazine today has made the publishing business a far more hazardous undertaking than it was sixty years ago. In those days Ormond Smith could start a ten-cent weekly, sell it to dealers at six and a half cents and within a few weeks be almost certain that it would hit the hundred thousand mark. If the newsstand returns were under fifty per cent he didn't have to worry much about the publication. Today, if newsstand returns rise above twenty per cent the publisher starts to worry and the editor looks around for a new job.

Experts have held autopsies on the corpse of the dime novel and the ten-cent weeklies. The truth is that they have not become obsolete; it is the dime which has virtually ceased to be a coin of value. The stories themselves survive in the paper-backed twenty-five- and thirty-five-cent books. They're on view at every railroad station, airport, drug store and bookstore. Had Mickey Spillane been writing sixty years ago he would have been a highly successful dime-novel author (he would have had to tone down his overdone sex angles because this aspect of his dubious art would have bored readers of that age). Serious critics say that the reading public will no longer accept a story that is devoid of literary style. The success of Mickey Spillane, the tremendous sale of *Forever Amber,* not too long ago, and so many other "historical novels" featuring the most lurid prose and an absence of any discernible style is a negation of this comfortable theory. *Western Story* and *Detective Story* are dead, but the fiction one found in those pulps now appears between the glossy covers of slick twenty-five- and thirty-five-cent magazines. Writers no longer receive a cent a word. Fiction for which *Western Story* once paid $500 now brings $2,500, and in serial form ten times that much.

Street & Smith has managed to become one of the few centenarian publishing houses in the country because it never continued publications which had begun to show signs of age. The firm's

Arthur Z. Gray, President

basic principles of diversity and cutting away old limbs are still the guiding rule among the executives and editors of the firm.

Gerald Smith died in June, 1955, at the tragically young age of forty-two, but the continuity of editorial policy remains unbroken. At the hoary age of one hundred, Street & Smith is as young as the latest copy of *Mademoiselle,* as far-seeing as the new architectural designs in *Living* and as susceptible to revolutionary editorial ideas as the material in *Astounding Science-Fiction.*

The majority of our citizens no longer sit down to red-checked tablecloths, nor do they call the evening meal supper, but those millions are there just the same and Street & Smith is still giving them what they want in the way of publications.

BIBLIOGRAPHY

No one can write a book embracing one hundred years in the life of a publishing firm without incurring huge debts. I owe something to each of the books listed here. Many of these, long out of print, were somehow resurrected by the indefatigable staff of the Larchmont Public Library. I obtained others through the good offices of Abner Sideman, *Look Magazine* executive who allowed me access to the magnificent library maintained by that magazine.

Bacon, Daisy, *Love Story Writer*
Hermitage House, 1954

Beer, Thomas, *The Mauve Decade*
Alfred A. Knopf, 1926

Bleiler, Everett F. and Dikty, T. E., eds., *The Best Science-Fiction Stories: 1950*
Frederick Fell, Inc., 1950

Boucher, Anthony, ed., *Four-&-Twenty Bloodhounds*
Simon and Schuster, 1950

Branch, E. Douglas, *The Sentimental Years, 1836–1860*
D. Appleton Century, 1934

Butterfield, Roger, *The American Past*
Simon and Schuster, 1947

Campbell, John W., Jr., ed., *The Astounding Science Fiction Anthology*
Simon and Schuster, 1952

Canby, Henry Seidel, *Age of Confidence*
Farrar & Rinehart, 1934

Cater, Harold Dean, ed., *Henry Adams and His Friends*
Houghton Mifflin Company, 1947

Cohn, David L., *The Good Old Days*. Introduction by Sinclair Lewis
Simon and Schuster, 1940

Davenport, Basil, *Inquiry Into Science Fiction*
Longmans, Green & Co., 1955

Ford, Worthington Chauncey, ed., *Letters of Henry Adams (1892–1918)*
Houghton Mifflin Company, 1938

BIBLIOGRAPHY

Holbrook, Stewart H., *Lost Men of American History*
The Macmillan Company, 1948

Johannsen, Albert, *The House of Beadle and Adams and Its Dime & Nickel Novels, Volumes I and II*
The University of Oklahoma Press, Norman, Oklahoma, 1950

Lehmann-Haupt, Hellmut, in collaboration with Lawrence C. Wroth and Rollo G. Silver,
The Book in America, A History of the Magazine and Selling of Books in the United States
R. R. Bowker Company, 1951

Lewisohn, Ludwig, *The Story of American Literature*
The Modern Library, Random House, 1939

Margulies, Leo and Friend, Oscar J., eds., *My Best Science Fiction Story*
Merlin Press, Inc., 1949

Mayes, Herbert R., *Biography Without a Hero*

Merril, Judith, ed., *Beyond the Barriers of Space and Time*
Introduction by Theodore Sturgeon
Random House, 1947

Morris, Lloyd, *Incredible New York*
Random House, 1951

Morris, Lloyd, *Postscript to Yesterdays (America: The Last Fifty Years)*
Random House, 1947

Mott, Frank Luther, *Golden Multitudes*
The Macmillan Company, 1947

Mott, Frank Luther, *A History of American Magazines*
D. Appleton & Company, 1930, Harvard University Press, 1938

Pearson, Edmund, *Dime Novels*
Little, Brown, 1929

Queen, Ellery, ed., *101 Years' Entertainment—The Great Detective Stories 1841–1941*
The Modern Library, Random House, 1946

Richardson, Darrell C., *Max Brand, The Man and His Work*
Fantasy Publishing Co., Los Angeles, 1952

271

STREET & SMITH
PUBLICATIONS

With dates of first publication

WEEKLY PUBLICATIONS

NEW YORK WEEKLY
1855

STREET & SMITH'S LITERARY ALBUM
1865

BOYS OF THE WORLD
1875

LOG CABIN LIBRARY
1889

NUGGET LIBRARY
1889

GOOD NEWS
1890

NICK CARTER DETECTIVE LIBRARY
1891

NEW YORK FIVE CENT WEEKLY
1892

DIAMOND DICK LIBRARY
1895

DIAMOND DICK JR. LIBRARY
1896

RED, WHITE & BLUE LIBRARY
1896

TIP TOP WEEKLY
1896

THE YELLOW KID
1897

ARMY & NAVY WEEKLY
1897

ADVENTURE LIBRARY
1897

HALF-HOLIDAY
1898

TRUE BLUE
1898

KLONDIKE KIT LIBRARY
1898

STARRY FLAG WEEKLY
1898

DO AND DARE WEEKLY
1900

MY QUEEN
1900

SHIELD WEEKLY
1900

COMRADES
1900

BOYS OF AMERICA
1900

BUFFALO BILL STORIES
1901

JESSE JAMES STORIES
1901

BRAVE AND BOLD
1902

OLD BROADBRIM
1902

YOUNG ROVER
1904

ROUGH RIDERS
1904

RED RAVEN
1905

PAUL JONES (formerly Red Raven)
1905

ALL-SPORTS
1905

BOWERY BOY
1905

MIGHT AND MAIN
1906

MOTOR STORIES
1909

PAPER-BACK BOOKS

SPORT STORIES (Jack Lightfoot)
1896

THE EAGLE SERIES
1897

THE DAISY LIBRARY
1897

THE ARROW LIBRARY
1897

STREET & SMITH PUBLICATIONS

MAGNET LIBRARY
1897

HISTORICAL SERIES
1898

THE COLUMBIA LIBRARY
1898

THE MEDAL LIBRARY
1898

THE PRINCESS SERIES
1898

THE DIAMOND HANDBOOKS
1899

THE ROMANCE SERIES
1899

THE ALLIANCE LIBRARY
1899

THE ALFORD SERIES
1899

DER DEUTSCHE-AMERIKANISCHE BIBLIOTHEK
1900

THE BERTHA M. CLAY LIBRARY
1900

THE UNDINE LIBRARY
1900

THE GOLD LIBRARY
1900

THE PERFECTION SERIES
1900

THE EDEN SERIES
1901

THE NEW SECRET SERVICE SERIES
1902

BOUND TO WIN LIBRARY
1903

DR. JACK SERIES
1903

THE BOYS OF LIBERTY SERIES
1904

THE COBB LIBRARY
1904

THE HARKAWAY LIBRARY
1904

THE STAR LIBRARY
1904

THE FAR WEST LIBRARY
1907

THE POPULAR FICTION LIBRARY
1909

THE NEW ROMANCE LIBRARY
1909

NEW SURPRISE LIBRARY
1910

ALGER SERIES
1915

THE SOUTHWORTH LIBRARY
1915

THE PICTURE PLAY LIBRARY
1916

THE DETECTIVE LIBRARY
1917

THE MERRIWELL SERIES
1921

ADVENTURE LIBRARY
1925

LOVE STORY LIBRARY
1926

GREAT WESTERN LIBRARY
1927

WESTERN STORY LIBRARY
1927

MAGAZINES

AINSLEE'S MAGAZINE
1898

POPULAR MAGAZINE
1903

SMITH'S MAGAZINE
1905

GUNTHER'S MAGAZINE
1905

PEOPLES MAGAZINE
1906

NEW STORY & ALL-AROUND
1910

TOP NOTCH MAGAZINE
1910

WOMEN STORIES & LIVE STORIES
1913

TIP TOP MAGAZINE & WIDE AWAKE
1915

DETECTIVE STORY MAGAZINE
1915

PICTURE PLAY
1915

WESTERN STORY MAGAZINE
1919

THRILL BOOK
1919

LOVE STORY MAGAZINE
1921

FILM STORIES
1921

SEA STORIES, EXCITEMENT & COLLEGE STORIES
1922

STREET & SMITH PUBLICATIONS

SPORT STORY
1923

COMPLETE STORIES
1924

TRUE WESTERN & FAR WEST
1925

WILD WEST
1927

OUTDOOR STORIES
1927

FAME & FORTUNE MAGAZINE
1928

OVER THE TOP & HIGH SPOT
1928

AIR TRAILS MAGAZINE
1928

LIVE GIRL, MODERN GIRL, GIRL STORIES, TRUE
LOVE & REAL LOVE
1928

BEST DETECTIVE
1929

THE SHADOW MAGAZINE
1931

PROGRESS
1932

PETE RICE MAGAZINE
1933

NICK CARTER MAGAZINE
1933

ASTOUNDING STORIES
1933

CLUES-DETECTIVE
1933

COWBOY STORIES
1933

DOC SAVAGE MAGAZINE
1933

BILL BARNES AIR TRAILS
1934

AINSLEE'S SMART LOVE
1934

WESTERN WINNERS
1935

MOVIE ACTION
1935

DYNAMIC ADVENTURES
1935

MADEMOISELLE
1935

ROMANTIC RANGE
1935

THE WHISPERER (old)
1936

THE FEDS
1936

THE SKIPPER
1936

POCKET DETECTIVE
1936

HARDBOILED & THE POPULAR
1936

SPORT PICTORIAL
1936

POCKET LOVE
1937

POCKET WESTERN
1937

PIC
1937

CRIME BUSTERS & MYSTERY
1937

UNKNOWN
1939

THE AVENGER
1939

ATHLETE
1939

AIR PROGRESS
1939

THE WIZARD & CASH GORMAN
1940

THE WHISPERER (new)
1940

WESTERN ADVENTURES
1940

NATIONAL MAGAZINE
1941

CHARM (originally Your Charm)
1941

LIVING FOR YOUNG HOMEMAKERS
(originally Mademoiselle's Living)
1947

CLOTH-BOUND BOOKS

LITTLE CLASSICS
1902

LATTER DAY CLASSICS
1902

STANDARD GILT TOP SERIES
1903

BOYS OWN LIBRARY
1903

STREET & SMITH PUBLICATIONS

GIRLS POPULAR LIBRARY
1908

CHELSEA HOUSE BOOKS
1921

MADEMOISELLE'S HANDBOOK FOR BRIDAL
CONSULTANTS
1946

MADEMOISELLE'S HOME PLANNING SCRAPBOOK
1946

THE MADEMOISELLE HANDBOOK FOR THE GIRL
WITH A JOB AND A FUTURE
1946

COMICS

SHADOW COMICS
1940

DOC SAVAGE COMICS
1940

TRUE SPORT PICTURE STORIES
1940

BILL BARNES AMERICA'S AIR ACE
1940

PIONEER PICTURE STORIES
1941

TRAIL BLAZERS & RED DRAGON
1941

ARMY & NAVY & SUPERSNIPE COMICS
1941

SUPER MAGICIAN COMICS
1941

TOP SECRETS
1947

RED DRAGON
1947

GHOST BREAKERS
1948

KID ZOO
1948

BUFFALO BILL
1949

YEAR BOOKS AND ANNUALS

FOOTBALL YEAR BOOK
1940

BASEBALL YEAR BOOK
1941

DETECTIVE STORY ANNUAL
1941

LOVE STORY ANNUAL
1941

WESTERN STORY ANNUAL
1941

ALL FICTION LOVE STORY ANNUAL
1942

SPORT STORY ANNUAL
1942

ALL FICTION DETECTIVE STORIES
1942

SHADOW ANNUAL
1942

SEA STORIES ANNUAL
1943

AIR TRAILS MODEL ANNUAL
1943

ALL FICTION STORIES
1944

SCIENCE IS IN THE AIR
1947

WESTERN ROMANCE ANTHOLOGY
1948

FROM UNKNOWN WORLDS
1948

AIR PROGRESS
1950

WOMAN'S MODERN HOME ALMANAC
1955

INDEX

INDEX

INDEX

PICTURE CREDITS

© University of Oklahoma Press, 37, 47, 61, 81, 117;
Time, 37; Sarony, 47;
Children's Aid Society, 81; Brandt & Brandt, 179;
Gene Smith, 197;
Wide World, 127, 130, 133, 138, 141, 142, 149, 158, 179;
Emery Roth & Sons, 256;
Fairchild Aerial Surveys, 261

S & S

THE FICTION FACTORY
was composed in Baskerville types
on the Intertype Fotosetter
by Westcott and Thomson, Inc., of Philadelphia
who furnished complete films
of typographic and black and white illustrative material to the
Murray Printing Company of Wakefield, Massachusetts
The text was printed by photo lithography

The four-color process illustrations
were reproduced by photo lithography by the
American Colortype Company
of Clifton, New Jersey

The paper used was Oxford Offset
manufactured by the Oxford Miami Paper Company
of New York City

The four-color process jacket
was reproduced by photo lithography by the
Reehl Litho Company, Inc., of New York

The book was bound by the
Colonial Press of Clinton, Massachusetts

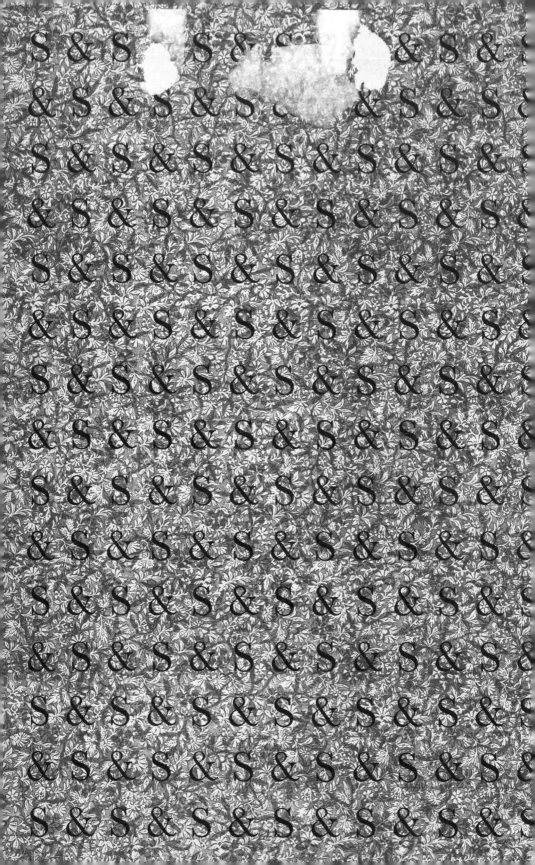